Marcus Aurelius.

Fluid Simulation for Computer Graphics

Fluid Simulation for Computer Graphics

Robert Bridson

A K Peters, Ltd.
Wellesley, Massachusetts

Editorial, Sales, and Customer Service Office

A K Peters, Ltd.
888 Worcester Street, Suite 230
Wellesley, MA 02482
www.akpeters.com

Library of Congress Cataloging-in-Publication Data

Bridson, Robert, 1976--
    Fluid simulation for computer graphics / Robert Bridson.
        p. cm.
    Includes bibliographical references and index.
    ISBN 978-1-56881-326-4 (alk. paper)
    1. Computer graphics--Mathematics. 2. Computer animation. 3. Three-dimensional display systems. I. Title.

T385.B744 2008
006.6'96--dc22

                                                            2008021768

Front cover: "The Foamy Brine" (ink on paper), Robert Bridson, 2006.

Printed in India
12 11 10 09 08   10 9 8 7 6 5 4 3 2 1

For my wife, Rowena,
and children Jonathan, Elliot, Arthur and Eleanor
and Marcus :) ...

Contents

Preface

This book is designed to give the reader a practical introduction to fluid simulation for graphics. The field of fluid dynamics, even just in animation, is vast and so not every topic will be covered, and many wonderful papers will sadly be passed over in the hope of distilling the essentials; this is far from a thorough survey. The focus of this book is animating fully three-dimensional incompressible flow—from understanding the math and the algorithms to actual implementation. However, there is also a small amount of material on height field simplifications which are important for efficiently modeling large bodies of water.

In general I try to follow Einstein's dictum, "everything should be made as simple as possible, but not simpler." Constructing a fluid solver for computer animation is not the easiest thing in the world—there end up being a lot of little details that need attention—but is perhaps easier than it may appear from surveying the literature. I will also provide pointers to some more advanced topics here and there.

I would especially like to thank my former Ph.D. supervisor, Ron Fedkiw, who got me started in graphics and taught me so much; my coauthors and students, many of whom also read and commented on draft versions of this book; Marcus Nordenstam and Double Negative for many productive visits spent developing much of this book for feature film production; Jim Hourihan and Tweak Films for a fantastic visit and continuing conversations; Matthias Müller-Fischer and Eran Guendelman who co-taught the SIGGRAPH course from which this book grew; and Alice Peters and A K Peters for making this a reality.

Robert Bridson
May 2008

–1–
The Basics

− 1 −

The Equations of Fluids

Fluids surround us, from the air we breathe to the oceans covering two thirds of the Earth, and are at the heart of some of the most beautiful and impressive phenomena we know. From water splashing to fire and smoke swirling, fluids have become an important part of computer graphics. This book aims to cover the basics of simulating these effects for animation. So let's jump right in with the fundamental equations governing their motion.

Most fluid flow of interest in animation is governed by the famous *incompressible Navier-Stokes equations*, a set of partial different equations that are supposed to hold throughout the fluid. The equations are usually written as

$$\frac{\partial \vec{u}}{\partial t} + \vec{u} \cdot \nabla \vec{u} + \frac{1}{\rho}\nabla p = \vec{g} + \nu\nabla \cdot \nabla \vec{u}, \qquad (1.1)$$

$$\nabla \cdot \vec{u} = 0. \qquad (1.2)$$

These may appear pretty complicated at first glance! We'll soon break them down into easy-to-understand parts (and in Appendix B provide a more rigorous explanation), but first let's begin by defining what each symbol means.

1.1   Symbols

The letter $\vec{u}$ is traditionally used in fluid mechanics for the velocity of the fluid. Why not $\vec{v}$? It's hard to say, but it fits another useful convention to call the three components of 3D velocity (u, v, w), just as the three components of position $\vec{x}$ are often taken to be (x, y, z).

The Greek letter ρ stands for the density of the fluid. For water, this is roughly 1000 kg/m^3, and for air this is roughly 1.3 kg/m^3, a ratio of about $700 : 1$.

The letter p stands for *pressure*, the force per unit area that the fluid exerts on anything.

The letter $\vec{g}$ is the familiar acceleration due to gravity, usually $(0, -9.81, 0)$ m/s^2. Now is a good time to mention that in this book we'll take as a convention that the y-axis is pointing vertically upwards, and the x- and z-axes are horizontal. We should add that in animation, additional control accelerations (to make the fluid behave in some desired way) might be added on top of gravity—we'll lump all of these into the one symbol $\vec{g}$. More generally, people call these *body forces*, because they are applied throughout the whole body of fluid, not just on the surfaces.

The Greek letter ν is technically called the *kinematic viscosity*. It measures how viscous the fluid is. Fluids like molasses have high viscosity, and fluids like mercury have low viscosity: it measures how much the fluid resists deforming while it flows (or more intuitively, how difficult it is to stir).

1.2   The Momentum Equation

The first differential equation (1.1), which is actually three in one wrapped up as a vector equation, is called the *momentum equation*. This really is good old Newton's equation $\vec{F} = m\vec{a}$ in disguise. It tells us how the fluid accelerates due to the forces acting on it. We'll try to break this down before moving onto the second differential equation (1.2), which is called the *incompressibility condition*.

Let's first imagine we are simulating a fluid using a particle system (later in the book we will actually use this as a practical method, but for now let's just use it as a thought experiment). Each particle would represent a little blob of fluid. It would have a mass m, a volume V, and a velocity $\vec{u}$. To integrate the system forward in time all we would need is to figure out what the forces acting on each particle are: $\vec{F} = m\vec{a}$ then tells us how the particle accelerates, from which we get its motion. We'll write the acceleration of the particle in slightly odd notation (which we'll later relate to the momentum equation above):

$$\vec{a} \equiv \frac{D\vec{u}}{Dt}.$$

The big D derivative notation is called the *material derivative* (more on this later). Newton's law is now

$$m\frac{D\vec{u}}{Dt} = \vec{F}.$$

So what are the forces acting on the particle? The simplest is of course gravity: $m\vec{g}$. However, it gets interesting when we consider how the rest of the fluid also exerts force: how the particle interacts with other particles nearby.

The first of the fluid forces is pressure. High-pressure regions push on lower-pressure regions. Note that what we really care about is the net force on the particle: for example, if the pressure is equal in every direction there's going to be a net force of zero and no acceleration due to pressure. We only see an effect on the fluid particle when there is an imbalance, i.e. higher pressure on one side of the particle than on the other side, resulting in a force pointing away from the high pressure and towards the low pressure. In the appendices we show how to rigorously derive this, but for now let's just point out that the simplest way to measure the imbalance in pressure at the position of the particle is simply to take the negative gradient of pressure: $-\nabla p$. (Recall from calculus that the gradient is in the direction of "steepest ascent," thus the negative gradient points away from high-pressure regions towards low-pressure regions.) We'll need to integrate this over the volume of our blob of fluid to get the pressure force. As a simple approximation, we'll just multiply by the volume V. You might be asking yourself, but what is the pressure? We'll skip over this until later, when we talk about incompressibility, but for now you can think of it being whatever it takes to keep the fluid at constant volume.

The other fluid force is due to viscosity. A viscous fluid tries to resist deforming. Later we will derive this in more depth, but for now let's intuitively develop this as a force that tries to make our particle move at the average velocity of the nearby particles, i.e., that tries to minimize differences in velocity between nearby bits of fluid. You may remember from image processing, digital geometry processing, the physics of diffusion or heat dissipation, or many other domains, that the differential operator that measures how far a quantity is from the average around it is the *Laplacian* $\nabla \cdot \nabla$. (Now is a good time to mention that there is a quick review of vector calculus in the appendices, including differential operators like the Laplacian.) This will provide our viscous force then, once we've integrated it over the volume of the blob. We'll use the *dynamic viscosity coefficient*, which is denoted with the Greek letter η (dynamic means we're getting a *force* out of it; the kinematic viscosity from before is used to get an *acceleration* instead). I'll note here that for fluids with variable viscosity, this term ends up being a little more complicated; see Chapter 8 for more details.

Putting it all together, here's how a blob of fluid moves:

$$m\frac{D\vec{u}}{Dt} = m\vec{g} - V\nabla p + V\eta\nabla \cdot \nabla\vec{u}.$$

Obviously we're making errors when we approximate a fluid with a small finite number of particles. We will take the limit then as our number of particles goes to infinity and the size of each blob goes to zero. This poses a problem in our particle equation, because the mass m and volume V of the particle are then going to zero. We can fix this by dividing the equation by the volume and then taking the limit. Remembering m/V is just the fluid density ρ, we get

$$\rho\frac{D\vec{u}}{Dt} = \rho\vec{g} - \nabla p + \eta\nabla \cdot \nabla\vec{u}.$$

Looking familiar? We'll divide by the density and rearrange the terms a bit to get

$$\frac{D\vec{u}}{Dt} + \frac{1}{\rho}\nabla p = \vec{g} + \frac{\eta}{\rho}\nabla \cdot \nabla\vec{u}.$$

To simplify things even a little more, we'll define the kinematic viscosity as $\nu = \eta/\rho$ to get

$$\frac{D\vec{u}}{Dt} + \frac{1}{\rho}\nabla p = \vec{g} + \nu\nabla \cdot \nabla\vec{u}.$$

We've almost made it back to the momentum equation! In fact this form, using the material derivative D/Dt, is actually more important to us in computer graphics and will guide us in solving the equation numerically. But we still will want to understand what the material derivative is and how it relates back to the traditional form of the momentum equation. For that, we'll need to understand the difference between the *Lagrangian* and *Eulerian* viewpoints.

1.3   Lagrangian and Eulerian Viewpoints

When we think about a continuum (like a fluid or a deformable solid) moving, there are two approaches to tracking this motion: the Lagrangian viewpoint and the Eulerian viewpoint.

The Lagrangian approach, named after the French mathematician Lagrange, is what you're probably most familiar with. It treats the continuum just like a particle system. Each point in the fluid or solid is labeled as a separate particle, with a position $\vec{x}$ and a velocity $\vec{u}$. You could even think of each particle as being one molecule of the fluid. Nothing too special here! Solids are almost always simulated in a Lagrangian way, with a discrete set of particles usually connected up in a mesh.

The Eulerian approach, named after the Swiss mathematician Euler, takes a different tactic that's usually used for fluids. Instead of tracking each particle, we instead look at fixed points in space and see how measurements of fluid quantities, such as density, velocity, temperature, etc., at those points change in time. The fluid is probably flowing past those points, contributing one sort of change: for example, as a warm fluid moves past followed by a cold fluid, the temperature at the fixed point in space will decrease—even though the temperature of any individual particle in the fluid is not changing! In addition the fluid variables can be changing in the fluid, contributing the other sort of change that might be measured at a fixed point: for example, the temperature measured at a fixed point in space will decrease as the fluid everywhere cools off.

One way to think of the two viewpoints is in doing a weather report. In the Lagrangian viewpoint you're in a balloon floating along with the wind, measuring the pressure and temperature and humidity, etc., of the air that's flowing alongside you. In the Eulerian viewpoint you're stuck on the ground, measuring the pressure and temperature and humidity, etc., of the air that's flowing past. Both measurements can create a graph of how conditions are changing, but the graphs can be completely different as they are measuring the rate of change in fundamentally different ways.

Numerically, the Lagrangian viewpoint corresponds to a particle system, with or without a mesh connecting up the particles, and the Eulerian viewpoint corresponds to using a fixed grid that doesn't change in space even as the fluid flows through it.

It might seem the Eulerian approach is unnecessarily complicated: why not just stick with Lagrangian particle systems? Indeed, there are schemes, such as vortex methods (see, e.g., [Yaeger et al. 86, Gamito et al. 95, Angelidis and Neyret 05, Park and Kim 05]) and smoothed particle hydrodynamics (SPH) (see, e.g., [Desbrun and Cani 96, Müller et al. 03, Premoze et al. 03]) that do this. However, the rest of this book will stick mostly to the Eulerian approach for a few reasons:

- It's easier to analytically work with the spatial derivatives like the pressure gradient and viscosity term in the Eulerian viewpoint.

- It's much easier to numerically approximate those spatial derivatives on a fixed Eulerian mesh than on a cloud of arbitrarily moving particles.

The key to connecting the two viewpoints is the material derivative. We'll start with a Lagrangian description: there are particles with positions $\vec{x}$ and velocities $\vec{u}$. Let's look at a generic quantity we'll call q: each particle has a value for q. (Quantity q might be density, or velocity, or temperature, or many other things.) In particular, the function $q(t, \vec{x})$ tells us the value of q at time t for the particle that happens to be at position $\vec{x}$: this is an Eulerian variable since it's a function of space, not of particles. So how fast is q changing for the particle that happens to currently be at $\vec{x}$, i.e., the Lagrangian question? Just take the total derivative (a.k.a. the Chain Rule):

$$\frac{d}{dt} q(t, \vec{x}) = \frac{\partial q}{\partial t} + \nabla q \cdot \frac{d\vec{x}}{dt}$$

$$= \frac{\partial q}{\partial t} + \nabla q \cdot \vec{u}$$

$$\equiv \frac{Dq}{Dt}.$$

This is the material derivative!

Let's review the two terms that go into the material derivative. The first is $\partial q / \partial t$, which is just how fast q is changing at that fixed point in space, an Eulerian measurement. The second term, $\nabla q \cdot \vec{u}$, is correcting for how much of that change is due just to differences in the fluid flowing past (e.g., the temperature changing because hot air is being replaced by cold air, not because the temperature of any molecule is changing).

Just for completeness, let's write out the material derivative in full, with all the partial derivatives:

$$\frac{Dq}{Dt} = \frac{\partial q}{\partial t} + u \frac{\partial q}{\partial x} + v \frac{\partial q}{\partial y} + w \frac{\partial q}{\partial z}.$$

Obviously in 2D, we can just get rid of the w- and z-term.

Note that I keep talking about how the quantity, or molecules, or particles, move with the velocity field $\vec{u}$. This is called *advection* (or sometimes *convection* or *transport*; they all mean the same thing). An *advection equation* is just one that uses the material derivative, at its simplest setting it to zero:

$$\frac{Dq}{Dt} = 0,$$

$$\text{i.e.,} \quad \frac{\partial q}{\partial t} + \vec{u} \cdot \nabla q = 0.$$

This just means the quantity is moving around but isn't changing in the Lagrangian viewpoint.

1.3.1 An Example

Hopefully to lay the issue to rest, let's work through an example in one dimension. Instead of q we'll use T for temperature. We'll say that at one instant in time, the temperature profile is

$$T(x) = 10x;$$

that is, it's freezing at the origin and gets warmer as we look further to the right, to a temperature of 100 at $x = 10$. Now let's say there's a steady wind of speed c blowing, i.e., the fluid velocity is c everywhere:

$$\vec{u} = c.$$

We'll assume that the temperature of each particle of air isn't changing—they're just moving. So the material derivative, measuring things in the Lagrangian viewpoint says the change is zero:

$$\frac{DT}{Dt} = 0.$$

If we expand this out, we have

$$\frac{\partial T}{\partial t} + \nabla T \cdot \vec{u} = 0,$$

$$\frac{\partial T}{\partial t} + 10 \cdot c = 0$$

$$\Rightarrow \quad \frac{\partial T}{\partial t} = -10c;$$

that is, at a fixed point in space, the temperature is changing at a rate of $-10c$. If the wind has stopped, $c = 0$, nothing changes. If the wind is blowing to the right at speed $c = 1$, the temperature at a fixed point will drop at a rate of -10. If the wind is blowing faster to the left at speed $c = -2$, the temperature at a fixed point will increase at a rate of 20. So even though the Lagrangian derivative is zero, in this case the Eulerian derivative can be anything depending on how fast and in what direction the flow is moving.

1.3.2 Advecting Vector Quantities

One point of common confusion is what the material derivative means when applied to vector quantities, like RGB colors, or most confusing of all, the velocity field $\vec{u}$ itself. The simple answer is: treat each component

separately. Let's write out the material derivative for the color vector
$\vec{C} = (R, G, B)$:

$$\frac{D\vec{C}}{Dt} = \begin{bmatrix} DR/Dt \\ DG/Dt \\ DB/Dt \end{bmatrix} = \begin{bmatrix} \partial R/\partial t + \vec{u} \cdot \nabla R \\ \partial G/\partial t + \vec{u} \cdot \nabla G \\ \partial B/\partial t + \vec{u} \cdot \nabla B \end{bmatrix} = \frac{\partial \vec{C}}{\partial t} + \vec{u} \cdot \nabla \vec{C}.$$

So although the notation $\vec{u} \cdot \nabla \vec{C}$ might not strictly make sense (is the gradient of a vector a matrix? what is the dot-product of a vector with a matrix?[1]) it's not hard to figure out if we split up the vector into scalar components.

Let's do the same thing for velocity itself, which really is no different except $\vec{u}$ appears in two places, as the velocity field in which the fluid is moving and as the fluid quantity that is getting advected. People sometimes call this *self-advection* to highlight that velocity is appearing in two different roles, but the formulas work exactly the same as for color. So just by copying and pasting, here is the advection of velocity $\vec{u} = (u, v, w)$ spelled out:

$$\frac{D\vec{u}}{Dt} = \begin{bmatrix} Du/Dt \\ Dv/Dt \\ Dw/Dt \end{bmatrix} = \begin{bmatrix} \partial u/\partial t + \vec{u} \cdot \nabla u \\ \partial v/\partial t + \vec{u} \cdot \nabla v \\ \partial w/\partial t + \vec{u} \cdot \nabla w \end{bmatrix} = \frac{\partial \vec{u}}{\partial t} + \vec{u} \cdot \nabla \vec{u},$$

or if you want to get right down to the nuts and bolts of partial derivatives,

$$\frac{D\vec{u}}{Dt} = \begin{bmatrix} \dfrac{\partial u}{\partial t} + u\dfrac{\partial u}{\partial x} + v\dfrac{\partial u}{\partial y} + w\dfrac{\partial u}{\partial z} \\ \dfrac{\partial v}{\partial t} + u\dfrac{\partial v}{\partial x} + v\dfrac{\partial v}{\partial y} + w\dfrac{\partial v}{\partial z} \\ \dfrac{\partial w}{\partial t} + u\dfrac{\partial w}{\partial x} + v\dfrac{\partial w}{\partial y} + w\dfrac{\partial w}{\partial z} \end{bmatrix}.$$

If you want to go even further, advecting matrix quantities around, it's no different: just treat each component separately.

1.4 Incompressibility

Real fluids, even liquids like water, change their volume. In fact, that's just what sound waves are: perturbations in the volume, and thus density and pressure, of the fluid. You may once have been taught that the difference between liquids and gases is that gases change their volume but liquids

---

[1] With slightly more sophisticated tensor notation, this can be put on a firm footing, but traditionally people stick with the dot-product.

don't, but that's not really true: otherwise you wouldn't be able to hear underwater!

However, the crucial thing is that usually fluids don't change their volume very much. It's next to impossible, even with an incredibly powerful pump, to change the volume of water much at all. Even air won't change its volume much unless you stick it in a pump, or are dealing with really extreme situations like sonic booms and blast waves. The study of how fluids behave in these situations is generally called *compressible flow*. It's complicated and expensive to simulate, and apart from acoustics doesn't enter that visibly into everyday life—and even sound waves are such tiny perturbations in the volume and have so small of an effect on how fluids move at a macroscopic level (water sloshing, smoke billowing, etc.) that they're practically irrelevant for animation.

What this means is that in animation we can generally treat all fluids, both liquids and gases, as *incompressible*, which means their volume doesn't change.[2] What does this mean mathematically? There's a more rigorous explanation in Appendix B again, but we can sketch out a quick argument now.

Pick an arbitrary chunk of fluid to look at for some instant in time. We'll call this volume Ω and its boundary surface $\partial\Omega$ (these are the traditional symbols). We can measure how fast the volume of this chunk of fluid is changing by integrating the normal component of its velocity around the boundary:

$$\frac{d}{dt}\text{volume}(\Omega) = \iint_{\partial\Omega} \vec{u} \cdot \hat{n}.$$

For an incompressible fluid, the volume had better stay constant, i.e., this rate of change is zero:

$$\iint_{\partial\Omega} \vec{u} \cdot \hat{n} = 0.$$

Now we can use the divergence theorem to change this to a volume integral. Basically, this is a multi-dimensional version of the Fundamental Theorem of Calculus: if you integrate the derivative of a function, you get the original function evaluated at the bounds of your integration (see Appendix A for a review if you need to brush up on your vector calculus). In this case, we

---

[2]Even if we need to somehow animate sonic booms and blast waves, they're basically invisible and extremely fast moving, thus most audiences have no idea really how they behave. It's probably a much better idea, from an artistic/perceptual/economic viewpoint, to hack together something that looks cool than try to simulate them accurately.

get

$$\iiint_\Omega \nabla \cdot \vec{u} = 0.$$

Now, here's the magical part: this equation should be true for any choice of Ω (any region of fluid). The only continuous function that integrates to zero independent of the volume of integration is zero itself. Thus the integrand has to be zero everywhere:

$$\nabla \cdot \vec{u} = 0.$$

This is the *incompressibility condition*, the other part of the incompressible Navier-Stokes equations.

A vector field that satisfies the incompressibility condition is called *divergence-free* for obvious reasons. One of the tricky parts of simulating incompressible fluids is making sure that the velocity field stays divergence-free. This is where the pressure comes in.

One way to think about pressure is that it's whatever it takes to keep the velocity divergence-free. If you're familiar with constrained dynamics, you can think of the incompressibility condition as a constraint and the pressure field as the Lagrange multiplier needed to satisfy that constraint subject to the principle of zero virtual work. If you're not, don't worry. Let's derive exactly what the pressure has to be.

The pressure only shows up in the momentum equation, and we want to somehow relate it to the divergence of the velocity. Therefore, let's take the divergence of both sides of the momentum equation:

$$\nabla \cdot \frac{\partial \vec{u}}{\partial t} + \nabla \cdot (\vec{u} \cdot \nabla \vec{u}) + \nabla \cdot \frac{1}{\rho} \nabla p = \nabla \cdot (\vec{g} + \nu \nabla \cdot \nabla \vec{u}). \quad (1.3)$$

We can change the order of differentiation in the first term to the time derivative of divergence:

$$\frac{\partial}{\partial t} \nabla \cdot \vec{u}.$$

If the incompressibility condition always holds, this had better be zero. Subsequently, rearranging Equation (1.3) gives us an equation for pressure:

$$\nabla \cdot \frac{1}{\rho} \nabla p = \nabla \cdot (-\vec{u} \cdot \nabla \vec{u} + \vec{g} + \nu \nabla \cdot \nabla \vec{u})$$

This isn't exactly relevant for our numerical simulation, but it's worth seeing because we'll go through almost exactly the same steps, from looking at how fast a volume is changing to an equation for pressure, when we discretize.

1.5 Dropping Viscosity

In some situations, viscosity forces are extremely important: e.g., simulating honey or very small-scale fluid flows. But in most other cases that we wish to animate, viscosity plays a minor role, and thus we often drop it: the simpler the equations are, the better. In fact, most numerical methods for simulating fluids unavoidably introduce errors that can be physically reinterpreted as viscosity (more on this later)—so even if we drop viscosity in the equations, we will still get something that looks like it. In fact, one of the big challenges in computational fluid dynamics is avoiding this viscous error as much as possible. Thus for the rest of this book, apart from Chapter 8 that focuses on high or even varying viscosity fluids, we will assume viscosity has been dropped.

The Navier-Stokes equations without viscosity are called the *Euler equations* and such an ideal fluid with no viscosity is called *inviscid*. Just to make it clear what has been dropped, here are the incompressible Euler equations using the material derivative to emphasize the simplicity:

$$\frac{D\vec{u}}{Dt} + \frac{1}{\rho}\nabla p = \vec{g},$$

$$\nabla \cdot \vec{u} = 0.$$

It is these equations that we'll mostly be using.

1.6 Boundary Conditions

Most of the, ahem, "fun" in numerically simulating fluids is in getting the boundary conditions correct. So far, we've only talked about what's happening in the interior of the fluid: so what goes on at the boundary?

In this book we will only focus on two boundary conditions, *solid walls* and *free surfaces*. One important case we won't cover is the boundary between two different fluids: most often this isn't needed in animation, but if you are interested, see papers such as that by Hong and Kim [Hong and Kim 05].

A solid wall boundary is where the fluid is in contact with a solid. It's simplest to phrase this in terms of velocity: the fluid had better not be flowing into the solid or out of it, thus the normal component of velocity has to be zero:

$$\vec{u} \cdot \hat{n} = 0.$$

Things are a little more complicated if the solid itself is moving too. In general, we need the normal component of the fluid velocity to match the normal component of the solid's velocity, so that the *relative* velocity has zero normal component:

$$\vec{u} \cdot \hat{n} = \vec{u}_{\text{solid}} \cdot \hat{n}.$$

In both these equations, $\hat{n}$ is of course the normal to the solid boundary. This is sometimes called the *no-stick* condition, since we're only restricting the normal component of velocity, allowing the fluid to freely slip past in the tangential direction. This is an important point to remember: the tangential velocity of the fluid might have no relation at all to the tangential velocity of the solid.

So that's what the velocity does: how about the pressure at a solid wall? We again go back to the idea that pressure is "whatever it takes to make the fluid incompressible." We'll add to that, "and enforce the solid wall boundary conditions." The $\nabla p / \rho$ term in the momentum equation applies even on the boundary, so for the pressure to control $\vec{u} \cdot \hat{n}$ at a solid wall, obviously that's saying something about $\nabla p \cdot \hat{n}$, otherwise known as the normal derivative of pressure: $\partial p / \partial \hat{n}$. We'll wait until we get into numerically handling the boundary conditions before we get more precise.

That's all there is to a solid wall boundary for an *inviscid* fluid. If we do have viscosity, life gets a little more complicated. In that case, the stickiness of the solid might have an influence on the tangential component of the fluid's velocity. The simplest case is the *no-slip* boundary condition, where we simply say

$$\vec{u} = 0,$$

or if the solid is moving,

$$\vec{u} = \vec{u}_{\text{solid}}.$$

Again, we'll avoid a discussion of exact details until we get into numerical implementation.

As a side note, sometimes the solid wall actually is a vent or a drain that fluid *can* move through: in that case, we obviously want $\vec{u} \cdot \hat{n}$ to be different from the wall velocity–rather to be the velocity at which fluid is being pumped in or out of the simulation at that point.

The other boundary condition that we're interested in is at a free surface. This is where we stop modeling the fluid. For example, if we simulate water splashing around, then the water surfaces that are *not* in contact with a solid wall are free surfaces. In this case there really is another fluid, air, but we may not want the hassle of simulating the air as well. And since air is 700 times lighter than water, it's not able to have that big of an effect on the water anyhow. So instead we make the modeling simplification that the air can be represented as a region with constant atmospheric pressure. In actual fact, since only *differences* in pressure matter (in incompressible flow), we can set the air pressure to be any arbitrary constant: zero is the most convenient. Thus a free surface is one where $p = 0$, and we don't control the velocity in any particular way.

The other case in which free surfaces arise is where we are trying to simulate a bit of fluid that is part of a much larger domain: for example, simulating smoke in the open air. We obviously can't afford to simulate the entire atmosphere of the Earth, so we will just make a grid that covers the region we expect to be "interesting." (I'll preemptively point out here that to simulate smoke, you *need* to simulate the smoke-free air nearby as well, not just the smoky region itself—however, we can get away with not simulating the air distant enough from all the action.) Past the boundaries of the simulated region the fluid continues on, but we're not tracking it; we allow fluid to enter and exit the region as it wants, so it's natural to consider this a free surface, $p = 0$, even though there's not actually a visible surface.[3]

One final note on free surfaces: for smaller-scale liquids, surface tension can be very important. At the underlying molecular level, surface tension exists because of varying strengths of attraction between molecules of different types. For example, water molecules are more strongly attracted to other water molecules than they are to air molecules: therefore, the water molecules at the surface separating water and air try to move to be as surrounded by water as much as possible. From a geometric perspective, physical chemists have modeled this as a force that tries to minimize the surface area or, equivalently, tries to reduce the mean curvature of the surface. You can interpret the first idea (minimizing surface area) as a tension that constantly tries to shrink the surface, hence the name surface tension; it can be a little more convenient to work with the second approach using mean curvature. (Later, in Chapter 6 we'll talk about how to actually measure mean curvature and exactly what it means.) In short, the model is that there is actually a jump in pressure between the two fluids,

---

[3]Technically this assumes there is no gravitational acceleration $\vec{g}$ included in the equations. If there is, we would take the hydrostatic pressure $p = \rho \vec{g} \cdot \vec{x}$ as the open boundary condition. To avoid having to do this, we can write the momentum equation in terms of the pressure perturbation from hydrostatic rest: $p = \rho \vec{g} \cdot \vec{x} + p'$. Substituting this into the pressure gradient cancels out $\vec{g}$ on the other side, and we can use the simpler open boundary condition $p' = 0$.

proportional to the mean curvature:

$$[p] = \gamma\kappa.$$

The $[p]$ notation means the jump in pressure, i.e., the difference in pressure measured on the water side and measured on the air side, γ is the surface tension coefficient that you can look up (for water and air at room temperature it is approximately $\gamma \approx 0.073N/\text{m}$), and κ is the mean curvature, measured in $1/\text{m}$. What this means for a free surface with surface tension is that the pressure at the surface of the water is the air pressure (which we assume to be zero) plus the pressure jump:

$$p = \gamma\kappa. \tag{1.4}$$

Free surfaces do have one major problem: air bubbles immediately collapse (there's no pressure inside to stop them losing their volume). While air is much lighter than water, and so usually might not be able to transfer much momentum to water, it still has the incompressibility constraint: an air bubble inside water largely keeps its volume. Modeling the air bubble with a free surface will let the bubble collapse and vanish. To handle this kind of situation, you need either hacks based on adding bubble particles to a free surface flow, or more generally a simulation of both air and water (called *two-phase* flow, because there are two phases or types of fluid involved). Again, we won't get into that in this book.

- 2 -
Overview of
Numerical Simulation

Now that we know and understand the basic equations, how do we discretize them to numerically simulate fluids using the computer? There are an awful lot of choices for how to do this, and people are continuing to invent new ways; we won't be able to cover even a fraction of them but will instead focus on one high-quality approach that works very well for graphics.

2.1   Splitting

The approach works on the basis of something called *splitting*: we split up a complicated equation into its component parts and solve each one separately in turn. If we say that the rate of change of one quantity is the sum of several terms, we can numerically update it by computing each term and adding them in one by one.

Let's make that clearer with an incredibly simple "toy" example, a single ordinary differential equation:

$$\frac{dq}{dt} = 1 + 2.$$

You of course already know that the answer is $q(t) = 3t + q(0)$, but let's work out a numerical method based on splitting. We'll split it into two steps, each one of which looks like a simple forward Euler update (if you want to remind yourself what forward Euler is, refer to Appendix A):

$$\tilde{q} = q^n + 1\Delta t, \tag{2.1}$$

$$q^{n+1} = \tilde{q} + 2\Delta t. \tag{2.2}$$

The notation used here is that q^n is the value of q computed at time step n, and Δt is the amount of time between consecutive time steps.[1] What we have done is split the equation up into two steps: after the first step (2.1), we get an intermediate quantity $\tilde{q}$ that includes the contribution of the first term (= 1) but not the second (= 2), and then the second step (2.2) goes from the intermediate value to the end by adding in the missing term's contribution. In this example, obviously, we get exactly the right answer, and splitting didn't buy us anything.

Let's upgrade our example to something more interesting:

$$\frac{dq}{dt} = f(q) + g(q). \tag{2.3}$$

Here $f()$ and $g()$ are some black box functions representing separate software modules. We could do splitting with forward Euler again:

$$\tilde{q} = q^n + \Delta t f(q^n), \tag{2.4}$$
$$q^{n+1} = \tilde{q} + \Delta t g(\tilde{q}). \tag{2.5}$$

A simple Taylor series analysis shows that this is still a first-order–accurate algorithm if you're worried (if you're not, ignore this):

$$\begin{aligned}
q^{n+1} &= (q^n + \Delta t f(q^n)) + \Delta t g(q^n + \Delta t f(q^n)) \\
&= q^n + \Delta t f(q^n) + \Delta t\left(g(q^n) + O(\Delta t)\right) \\
&= q^n + \Delta t(f(q^n) + g(q^n)) + O(\Delta t^2) \\
&= q^n + \frac{dq}{dt}\Delta t + O(\Delta t^2).
\end{aligned}$$

Wait, you say, that hasn't bought you anything beyond what simple old forward Euler *without* splitting gives you. Aha! Here's where we get a little more sophisticated. Let's assume that the reason we've split $f()$ and $g()$ into separate software modules is that we have special numerical methods that are really good at solving the simpler equations

$$\frac{dr}{dt} = f(r),$$
$$\frac{ds}{dt} = g(s).$$

---

[1]In particular, do not get confused with raising q to the power of n or $n+1$: this is an abuse of notation, but it is so convenient when we add in subscripts for grid indices that it's consistently used in fluid simulation. On the rare occasion that we do raise a quantity to some exponent, we'll very clearly state that: otherwise assume the superscript indicates at what time step the quantity is.

This is precisely the motivation for splitting: we may not be able to easily deal with the complexity of the whole equation, but it's built out of separate terms that we *do* have good methods for. I'll call the special integration algorithms $F(\Delta t, r)$ and $G(\Delta t, s)$. Our splitting method is then

$$\tilde{q} = F(\Delta t, q^n), \qquad (2.6)$$

$$q^{n+1} = G(\Delta t, \tilde{q}). \qquad (2.7)$$

If $F()$ and $G()$ were just forward Euler, then this is exactly the same as Equations (2.4) and (2.5), but the idea is again that they're something better. If you do the Taylor series analysis, you can show we still have a first-order–accurate method[2] but I'll leave that as an exercise.

Splitting really is just the principle of divide-and-conquer applied to differential equations: solving the whole problem may be too hard, but you can split it into pieces that are easier to solve and then combine the solutions.

If you're on the ball, you might have thought of a different way of combining the separate parts: instead of sequentially taking the solution from $F()$ and then plugging it into $G()$, you could run $F()$ and $G()$ in parallel and add their contributions together. The reason we're *not* going to do this but will stick to sequentially working through the steps, is that our special algorithms (the integrators $F()$ and $G()$ in this example) will guarantee special things about their output that are needed as preconditions for the input of other algorithms. Doing it in the *right* sequence will make everything work, but doing it in parallel will mess up those guarantees. We'll talk more about what those guarantees and preconditions are in the next section.

2.2   Splitting the Fluid Equations

We're going to use splitting on the incompressible fluid equations. In particular, we'll separate out the advection part, the body forces (gravity) part, and the pressure/incompressibility part. If viscosity is important, we'll also separate it out: see Chapter 8.

---

[2]There are more complicated ways of doing splitting in fluid dynamics, which can get higher-order accuracy, but for now we won't bother with them. At the time of writing this book, this has remained a sadly overlooked area for improvement within graphics: the first-order time-splitting error can be very significant indeed.

That is, we'll work out methods for solving these simpler equations:

$$\frac{Dq}{Dt} = 0 \qquad \text{(advection)}, \tag{2.8}$$

$$\frac{\partial \vec{u}}{\partial t} = \vec{g} \qquad \text{(body forces)}, \tag{2.9}$$

$$\frac{\partial \vec{u}}{\partial t} + \frac{1}{\rho}\nabla p = 0$$

$$\text{such that} \quad \nabla \cdot \vec{u} = 0. \quad \text{(pressure/incompressibility)} \tag{2.10}$$

We used the generic quantity q in the advection equation because we may be interested in advecting other things, not just velocity $\vec{v}$.

Let's call our algorithm for solving the advection, Equation (2.8), $\texttt{advect}(\vec{u}, \Delta t, q)$: it advects quantity q through the velocity field $\vec{u}$ for a time interval Δt. Chapter 3 will cover how to do this.

For the body force, Equation (2.9), we'll just use forward Euler: $\vec{u} \leftarrow \vec{u} + \Delta t \vec{g}$.

For the pressure/incompressibility part, Equation (2.10), we'll develop an algorithm called $\texttt{project}(\Delta t, \vec{u})$ that calculates and applies just the right pressure to make $\vec{u}$ divergence-free and also enforces the solid wall boundary conditions. Chapter 4 deals with this part (and explains the odd choice of word, "project").

The important precondition/guarantee issue we mentioned in the previous section is that advection should only be done in a divergence-free velocity field. When we move fluid around, if it's going to conserve volume, then the velocity field that we are moving it in must be divergence-free: we covered that already in Chapter 1. So we want to make sure we only run $\texttt{advect}()$ with the output of $\texttt{project}()$: the sequence of our splitting matters a lot!

Putting it together, here is our basic fluid algorithm:

- Start with an initial divergence-free velocity field $\vec{u}^0$.

- For time step $n = 0, 1, 2, \ldots$

  - Determine a good time step Δt to go from time t_n to time t_{n+1}.
  - Set $\vec{u}^A = \texttt{advect}(\vec{u}^n, \Delta t, \vec{u}^n)$.
  - Add $\vec{u}^B = \vec{u}^A + \Delta t \vec{g}$.
  - Set $\vec{u}^{n+1} = \texttt{project}(\Delta t, \vec{u}^B)$.

2.3 Time Steps

Determining a good time-step size is the first step of the algorithm. Our first concern is that we don't want to go past the duration of the current animation frame: if we pick a candidate Δt but find $t_n + \Delta t > t_{\text{frame}}$, then we should clamp it to $\Delta t = t_{\text{frame}} - t_n$ and set a flag that alerts us to the fact we've hit the end of the frame. (Note that checking if $t_{n+1} = t_{\text{frame}}$ is a bad idea, since inexact floating-point arithmetic may mean t_{n+1} isn't exactly equal to t_{frame} even when calculated this way!) At the end of each frame we'll presumably do something special like save the state of the fluid animation to disk, or render it on the screen.

Subject to that clamping, we want to then select a Δt that satisfies any requirements made by the separate steps of the simulation: advection, body forces, etc. We'll discuss these in the chapters that follow. Selecting the minimum of these suggested time steps is generally safe.

However, in some situations we may have a performance requirement that won't let us take lots of small time steps every frame. If we only have time for, say, three time steps per frame, we had better make sure Δt is at least a third of the frame time. This might be larger than the suggested time-step sizes from each step, so we will make sure that all the methods we use can tolerate the use of larger-than-desired time steps—they should generate plausible results in this case, even if they're quantitatively inaccurate.

2.4 Grids

In this numerical section, so far we have only talked about discretizing in time, not in space. While we will go into more detail about this in the subsequent chapters, we'll introduce the basic grid structure here.

In the early days of computational fluid dynamics, Harlow and Welch introduced the marker-and-cell (MAC) method [Harlow and Welch 65] method for solving incompressible flow problems. One of the fundamental innovations of this paper was a new grid structure that (as we will see later) makes for a very effective algorithm.

The so-called *MAC grid* is a *staggered* grid, i.e., a grid where the different variables are stored at different locations. Let's look at it in two dimensions first, illustrated in Figure 2.1. The pressure in grid cell (i, j) is sampled at the center of the cell, indicated by $p_{i,j}$. The velocity is split into its two Cartesian components. The horizontal u-component is sampled

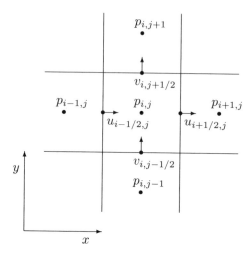

Figure 2.1. The two-dimensional MAC grid.

at the centers of the vertical cell faces, for example indicated by $u_{i+1/2,j}$ for the horizontal velocity between cells (i,j) and $(i+1,j)$. The vertical v-component is sampled at the centers of the horizontal cell faces, for example indicated by $v_{i,j+1/2}$ for the vertical velocity between cells (i,j) and $(i,j+1)$. Note that for grid cell (i,j) we have sampled the *normal* component of the velocity at the center of each of its faces: this will very naturally allow us to estimate the amount of fluid flowing into and out of the cell.

In three dimensions, the MAC grid is set up the same way, with pressure at the grid cell centers and the three different components of velocity split up so that we have the normal component of velocity sampled at the center of each cell face (see Figure 2.2).

We'll go into more detail about why we use this staggered arrangement in Chapter 4, but briefly put it's so that we can use accurate *central differences* for the pressure gradient and for the divergence of the velocity field without the usual disadvantages of the method. Consider just a one-dimensional example: estimating the derivative of a quantity q sampled at grid locations $\ldots, q_{i-1}, q_i, q_{i+1}, \ldots$. To estimate $\partial q/\partial x$ at grid point i without any bias, the natural formula is the first central difference:

$$\left(\frac{\partial q}{\partial x}\right)_i \approx \frac{q_{i+1} - q_{i-1}}{2\Delta x}. \tag{2.11}$$

This is unbiased and accurate to $O(\Delta x^2)$, as opposed to a forward or back-

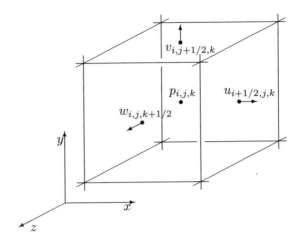

Figure 2.2. One cell from the three-dimensional MAC grid.

ward difference, such as

$$\left(\frac{\partial q}{\partial x}\right)_i \approx \frac{q_{i+1} - q_i}{\Delta x}, \tag{2.12}$$

which is biased to the right and only accurate to $O(\Delta x)$. However, formula
(2.11) has a major problem in that the derivative estimate at grid point i
completely ignores the value q_i sampled there! To see why this is so terrible,
recall that a constant function can be defined as one whose first derivative
is zero. If we require that the finite difference (2.11) is zero, we are allowing
q's that aren't necessarily constant—q_i could be quite different from q_{i-1}
and q_{i+1} and still the central difference will report that the derivative is
zero as long as $q_{i-1} = q_{i+1}$. In fact, a very jagged function like $q_i = (-1)^i$
which is far from constant, will register as having zero derivative according
to formula (2.11). On the other hand, only truly constant functions satisfy
the forward difference (2.12) equal to zero. The problem with formula
(2.11) is technically known as having a non-trivial *null-space*: the set of
functions where the formula evaluates to zero contains more than just the
constant functions it should be restricted to.

How can we get the unbiased second-order accuracy of a central difference without this null-space problem? The answer is by using a staggered
grid: sample the q's at the half-way points, $q_{i+1/2}$ instead. Then we naturally can estimate the derivative at grid point i as

$$\left(\frac{\partial q}{\partial x}\right)_i \approx \frac{q_{i+1/2} - q_{i-1/2}}{\Delta x}. \tag{2.13}$$

This is unbiased and accurate to $O(\Delta x^2)$ but it doesn't skip over any values of q like formula (2.11). So if we set this equal to zero we can only have q constant: the null-space is correct. The MAC grid is set up so that we use this staggered form of the central difference wherever we need to estimate a derivative in the pressure solve (i.e., the incompressibility condition).

The staggered MAC grid is perfectly suited for handling pressure and incompressibility, but it's a little awkward for other uses. For example, if we actually want to evaluate the full velocity vector somewhere, we will always need to use some kind of interpolation even if we're looking at a grid point! At an arbitrary location in space, we'll do separate bilinear or trilinear interpolation for each component of velocity, but since those components are offset from each other we will need to compute a different set of interpolation weights for each component. At the grid locations themselves, this boils down to some simple averaging. In two dimensions these averages are

$$\vec{u}_{i,j} = \left(\frac{u_{i-1/2,j} + u_{i+1/2,j}}{2}, \quad \frac{v_{i,j-1/2} + v_{i,j+1/2}}{2} \right),$$

$$\vec{u}_{i+1/2,j} = \left(u_{i+1/2,j}, \quad \frac{v_{i,j-1/2} + v_{i,j+1/2} + v_{i+1,j-1/2} + v_{i+1,j+1/2}}{4} \right),$$

$$\vec{u}_{i,j+1/2} = \left(\frac{u_{i-1/2,j} + u_{i+1/2,j} + u_{i-1/2,j+1} + u_{i+1/2,j+1}}{4}, \quad v_{i,j+1/2} \right).$$

In three dimensions the formulas are similar:

$$\vec{u}_{i,j,k} = \left(\frac{u_{i-1/2,j,k} + u_{i+1/2,j,k}}{2}, \quad \frac{v_{i,j-1/2,k} + v_{i,j+1/2,k}}{2}, \quad \frac{w_{i,j,k-1/2} + w_{i,j,k+1/2}}{2} \right)$$

$$\vec{u}_{i+1/2,j,k} = \left(u_{i+1/2,j,k}, \quad \frac{\begin{matrix} v_{i,j-1/2,k} + v_{i,j+1/2,k} \\ + v_{i+1,j-1/2,k} + v_{i+1,j+1/2,k} \end{matrix}}{4}, \quad \frac{\begin{matrix} w_{i,j,k-1/2} + w_{i,j,k+1/2} \\ + w_{i+1,j,k-1/2} + w_{i+1,j,k+1/2} \end{matrix}}{4} \right)$$

$$\vec{u}_{i,j+1/2,k} = \left(\frac{\begin{matrix} u_{i-1/2,j,k} + u_{i+1/2,j,k} \\ + u_{i-1/2,j+1,k} + u_{i+1/2,j+1,k} \end{matrix}}{4}, \quad v_{i,j+1/2,k}, \quad \frac{\begin{matrix} w_{i,j,k-1/2} + w_{i,j,k+1/2} \\ + w_{i,j+1,k-1/2} + w_{i,j+1,k+1/2} \end{matrix}}{4} \right)$$

$$\vec{u}_{i,j,k+1/2} = \left(\frac{\begin{matrix} u_{i-1/2,j,k} + u_{i+1/2,j,k} \\ + u_{i-1/2,j,k+1} + u_{i+1/2,j,k+1} \end{matrix}}{4}, \quad \frac{\begin{matrix} v_{i,j-1/2,k} + v_{i,j+1/2,k} \\ + v_{i,j-1/2,k+1} + v_{i,j+1/2,k+1} \end{matrix}}{4}, \quad w_{i,j,k+1/2} \right)$$

Finally, a word is in order about the curious half indices, such as $i+1/2$. These are convenient theoretically and conceptually, fixing the location of the sample points with respect to the grid. However, an implementation obviously should use integer indices. A standard convention is needed, for example:

$$p(\mathtt{i,j,k}) = p_{i,j,k}, \tag{2.14}$$

$$u(\mathtt{i,j,k}) = u_{i-1/2,j,k}, \tag{2.15}$$

$$v(\mathtt{i,j,k}) = v_{i,j-1/2,k}, \tag{2.16}$$

$$w(\mathtt{i,j,k}) = w_{i,j,k-1/2}. \tag{2.17}$$

Then for an $\mathtt{nx} \times \mathtt{ny} \times \mathtt{nz}$ grid, the pressure is stored in an $\mathtt{nx} \times \mathtt{ny} \times \mathtt{nz}$ array, the u component in a $(\mathtt{nx+1}) \times \mathtt{ny} \times \mathtt{nz}$ array, the v component in a $\mathtt{nx} \times (\mathtt{ny+1}) \times \mathtt{nz}$ array, and the w component in a $\mathtt{nx} \times \mathtt{ny} \times (\mathtt{nz+1})$ array.

– 3 –
Advection Algorithms

In the previous chapter we saw that a crucial step of the fluid simulation is solving the advection equation

$$Dq/Dt = 0.$$

We will encapsulate this in a numerical routine

$$q^{n+1} = \texttt{advect}(\vec{u}, \Delta t, q^n),$$

which given a velocity field $\vec{u}$ (discretized on a MAC grid), a time step size Δt, and the current field quantity q^n returns an approximation to the result of advecting q through the velocity field over that duration of time.

It bears repeating here: advection should only be called with a divergence-free velocity field $\vec{u}$, i.e., one meeting the incompressibility constraint. Failure to do so can result in peculiar artifacts.

3.1 Semi-Lagrangian Advection

The obvious approach to solving Dq/Dt for a time step is to simply write out the PDE, e.g., in one dimension:

$$\frac{\partial q}{\partial t} + u \frac{\partial q}{\partial x} = 0$$

and then replace the derivatives with finite differences. For example, if we use forward Euler for the time derivative and an accurate central difference for the spatial derivative we get

$$\frac{q_i^{n+1} - q_i^n}{\Delta t} + u_i^n \frac{q_{i+1}^n - q_{i-1}^n}{2\Delta x} = 0,$$

which can be arranged into an explicit formula for the new values of q:

$$q_i^{n+1} = q_i^n - \Delta t u_i^n \frac{q_{i+1}^n - q_{i-1}^n}{2\Delta x}.$$

At first glance this seems just fine. But there are disastrous problems lurking here!

First off, it turns out that forward Euler is unconditionally *unstable* for this discretization of the spatial derivative: no matter how small we make Δt, it will always eventually blow up! (If you know about the stability region of forward Euler, what's happening is that the eigenvalues of the Jacobian generated by the central difference are pure imaginary, thus always outside the region of stability. If you don't, don't worry: we'll get to a method that works soon enough!)

Even if we replace forward Euler with a more stable time integration technique, in fact even if we were to somehow *exactly* solve the time part of the PDE, the spatial discretization will give us major troubles. Remember from the last chapter that discussion of the problem null-space of standard central differences? Well, it raises its ugly head here too: *high-frequency*[1] jagged components of the solution, like $(-1)^i$, erroneously register as having zero or near-zero spatial derivative, and so don't get evolved forward in time—or at least move much more slowly than the velocity u they should move at. Meanwhile the low frequency components are handled accurately and move at almost exactly the right speed u. Thus the low frequency components end up separating out from the high-frequency components, and you are left with all sorts of strange high-frequency wiggles and oscillations appearing and persisting that *shouldn't be there*!

We won't go into a more rigorous analysis of the problems of simple central differences, but rest assured there is plenty of high-powered numerical analysis, which not only carefully identifies the disease but also supplies a cure with more sophisticated finite difference formulas for the spatial derivative.

We will instead first take a different, simpler, and physically-motivated approach called the *semi-Lagrangian* method. The word Lagrangian should remind you that the advection equation $Dq/Dt = 0$ is utterly trivial in the Lagrangian framework, and if we were using particle system methods it's solved automatically when we move our particles through the velocity field. That is, to get the new value of q at some point $\vec{x}$ in space, we could conceptually just find the particle that ends up at $\vec{x}$ and look up its value of q.

---

[1]By frequency in this context, we mean frequency in space, as if you performed a Fourier transform of the function, expressing it as a sum of sine or cosine waves of different spatial frequencies. The high frequency components correspond to sharp features that vary over a small distance, and the low frequency components correspond to the smooth large-scale features.

We can apply that reasoning on our grid to get the semi-Lagrangian method introduced to graphics by Stam [Stam 99]. We want to figure out the new value of q at a grid point, and to do that in a Lagrangian way we need to figure out the old value of q that the particle that ends up at the grid point possesses. The particle is moving through the velocity field $\vec{u}$, and we know where it ends up—so to find where it started we simply run backwards through the velocity field from the grid point. We can grab the old value of q from this start point, which will be the new value of q at the grid point! But wait, you say, what if that start point wasn't on the grid? In that case we simply interpolate the old value of q from the old values on the grid, and we're done.

Let's go through that again, slowly and with formulas. We'll say that the location in space of the grid point we're looking at is $\vec{x}_G$. We want to find the new value of q at that point, which we'll call q_G^{n+1}. We know from our understanding of advection that if a hypothetical particle with old value q_P^n ends up at $\vec{x}_G$, when it moves through the velocity field for the time step Δt, then $q_G^{n+1} = q_P^n$. So the question is, how do we figure out q_P^n?

The first step is figuring out where this imaginary particle would have started from, a position we'll call $\vec{x}_P$. The particle moves according to the simple ordinary differential equation

$$\frac{d\vec{x}}{dt} = \vec{u}(\vec{x})$$

and ends up at $\vec{x}_G$ after time Δt. If we now run time backwards, we can go in reverse from $\vec{x}_G$ to the start point of the particle—i.e., finding where a particle would end up under the reverse velocity field $-\vec{u}$ "starting" from $\vec{x}_G$. The simplest possible way to estimate this is to use one step of forward Euler:

$$\vec{x}_P = \vec{x}_G - \Delta t\, \vec{u}(\vec{x}_G),$$

where we use the velocity evaluated at the grid point to take a Δt-step backwards through the flow field. It turns out forward Euler is sometimes adequate, but significantly better results can be obtained using a slightly more sophisticated technique such as a higher-order Runge-Kutta method. See Appendix A to review time integration methods. In particular, at least a second-order Runge-Kutta method is recommended as a default, such as

$$\vec{x}_{\text{mid}} = \vec{x}_G - \frac{1}{2}\Delta t\, \vec{u}(\vec{x_G}),$$
$$\vec{x}_P = \vec{x}_G - \Delta t\, \vec{u}(\vec{x}_{\text{mid}}).$$

Here a half-step is taken to get an intermediate position $\vec{x}_{\text{mid}}$ approximating the particle's position halfway along the trajectory. The velocity field is interpolated from the grid at this intermediate location, and that velocity value is used to finally get to $\vec{x}_P$. Depending on how large Δt is—see later in this chapter—it may even be wise to split the trajectory tracing into smaller substeps for better accuracy.

We now know the position where the imaginary particle started; next we have to figure out what old value of q it had. Most likely $\vec{x}_P$ is not on the grid, so we don't have the exact value, but we can get a good approximation by interpolating from q^n at nearby grid points. Trilinear (bilinear in two dimensions) interpolation is often used, though this comes with a serious penalty which we will fix at the end of the chapter.

Putting this together into a formula, our basic semi-Lagrangian formula, assuming the particle-tracing algorithm has tracked back to location $\vec{x}_P$ (typically with RK2 above), is

$$q_G^{n+1} = \texttt{interpolate}(q^n, \vec{x}_P). \tag{3.1}$$

Note that the particle I've described is purely hypothetical. No particle is actually created in the computer: we simply use Lagrangian particles to conceptually figure out the update formula for the Eulerian advection step. Because we are almost using a Lagrangian approach to do an Eulerian calculation, this is called the semi-Lagrangian method.

Just for completeness, let's illustrate this in one dimension again, using linear interpolation for the semi-Lagrangian operations. For grid point x_i, the particle is traced back to $x_P = x_i - \Delta t u$. Assuming this lies in the interval $[x_j, x_{j+1}]$, and letting $\alpha = (x_P - x_j)/\Delta x$ be the fraction of the interval the point lands in, the linear interpolation is $q_P^n = (1-\alpha)q_j^n + \alpha q_{j+1}^n$. So our update is

$$q_i^{n+1} = (1 - \alpha)q_j^n + \alpha q_{j+1}^n.$$

In practice we will need to advect the velocity field, and perhaps additional variables such as smoke density or temperature. Usually the additional variables are stored at the grid cell centers, but the velocity components are stored at the staggered grid locations discussed in the previous chapter. In each case, we will need to use the appropriate averaged velocity, given at the end of the previous chapter, to estimate the particle trajectory.

3.2   Boundary Conditions

If the starting point of the imaginary particle is in the interior of the fluid, then doing the interpolation is no problem. What happens though if the estimated starting point happens to end up outside of the fluid boundaries? This could happen because fluid is flowing in from outside the domain (and the particle is "new" fluid), or it could happen due to numerical error (the true trajectory of the particle actually stayed inside the fluid, but our forward Euler or Runge-Kutta step introduced error that put us outside).

This is really the question of boundary conditions. In the first case, where we have fluid flowing in from the outside, we should know what the quantity is that's flowing in: that's part of stating the problem correctly. For example, if we say that fluid is flowing in through a grating on one side of the domain at a particular velocity $\vec{U}$ and temperature T, then any particle whose starting point ends up past that side of the domain should get velocity $\vec{U}$ and temperature T.

In the second case, where we simply have a particle trajectory that strayed outside the fluid boundaries due to numerical error, the appropriate strategy is to extrapolate the quantity from the nearest point on the boundary—this is our best bet as to the quantity that the true trajectory (which should have stayed inside the fluid) would pick up. Sometimes that extrapolation can be easy: if the boundary we're closest to has a specified velocity we simply use that. For example, for simulating smoke in the open air we could assume a constant wind velocity $\vec{U}$ (perhaps zero) outside of the simulation domain.

The trickier case is when the quantity isn't known *a priori* but has to be numerically extrapolated from the fluid region where it is known. We will go into more detail on this extrapolation in Chapter 6 on water. For now, let's just stick with finding the closest point that is on the boundary of the fluid region and interpolating the quantity from the fluid values stored on the grid near there. In particular, this is what we will need to do for finding velocity values when our starting point ends up inside a solid object, or for free surface flows (water) if we end up in the free space.

Note that taking the fluid velocity at a solid boundary is *not* the same as the solid's velocity in general. As we discussed earlier, the normal component of the fluid velocity had better be equal to the normal component of the solid's velocity, but apart from in viscous flows, the tangential component can be completely different. Thus we usually interpolate the fluid velocity at the boundary and don't simply take the solid velocity. However, for the particular case of viscous flows (or at least, a fluid-solid interaction

that we want to appear viscous and sticky), we can indeed take the shortcut
of just using the solid's velocity instead.

3.3 Time Step Size

A primary concern for any numerical method is whether it is stable: will it
blow up? Happily the semi-Lagrangian approach above is *unconditionally
stable*: no matter how big Δt is, we can never blow up. It's easy to see why:
wherever the particle starting point ends up, we interpolate from old values
of q to get the new values for q. Linear/bilinear/trilinear interpolation
always produces values that lie between the values we're interpolating from:
we can't create larger or smaller values of q than were already present in the
previous time step. So q stays bounded. This is really very attractive: we
can select the time step based purely on the accuracy versus speed trade-off
curve. If we want to run at real-time rates regardless of the accuracy of
the simulation, we can pick Δt equal to the frame duration for example.

In practice, the method can produce some strange results if we are
too aggressive with the time step size. It has been suggested [Foster and
Fedkiw 01] that an appropriate strategy is to limit Δt so that the furthest
a particle trajectory is traced is five grid cell widths:

$$\Delta t \leq \frac{5\Delta x}{u_{max}}, \tag{3.2}$$

where u_{max} is an estimate of the maximum velocity in the fluid. This could
be as simple as the maximum velocity currently stored on the grid. A more
robust estimate takes into account velocities that might be induced due to
acceleration g from gravity (or other body forces like buoyancy) over the
time step. In that case,

$$u_{max} = \max(|u^n|) + \Delta t\,|g|.$$

Unfortunately this estimate depends on Δt (which we're trying to find),
but if we replace Δt with the upper bound from inequality (3.2) we get

$$u_{max} = \max(|u^n|) + \frac{5\Delta x}{u_{max}}|g|.$$

Solving for u_{max} and taking a simple upper bound gives

$$u_{max} = \max(|u^n|) + \sqrt{5\Delta x\,g}.$$

This has the advantage of always being positive, even when the initial velocities are zero, so we avoid a divide-by-zero in inequality (3.2).

In some cases artifacts will still be present with a time step of this size; one possible remedy that avoids the expense of running the entire simulation at a smaller time step is to just trace the trajectories used in semi-Lagrangian advection with several small substeps. If each substep is limited to $|\vec{u}(\vec{x})|\Delta t < \Delta x$, i.e., so that each substep only traverses roughly one grid cell, there is little opportunity for problems to arise. Note that this substep restriction can be taken locally: in fast-moving regions of the fluid more substeps might be used than in slow-moving regions.

3.3.1 The CFL Condition

Before leaving the subject of time-step sizes, let's take a closer look at something called the *CFL condition*. There is some confusion in the literature about what exactly this condition is, so in this section I'll try to set the story straight. This section can be safely skipped if you're not interested in some more technical aspects of numerical analysis.

The CFL condition, named for applied mathematicians R. Courant, K. Friedrichs, and H. Lewy, is a simple and very intuitive necessary condition for convergence. Convergence means that if you repeat a simulation with smaller and smaller Δt and Δx, in the limit going to zero, then your numerical solutions should approach the exact solution.[2]

The solution $q(\vec{x}^{\star}, t^{\star})$ of a time-dependent partial differential equation, such as the advection equation, at a particular point in space $\vec{x}^{\star}$ and time $t^{\star}$ depends on some or all of the initial conditions. That is, if we modify the initial conditions at some locations and solve the problem again, it will change $q(\vec{x}^{\star}, t^{\star})$; at other locations the modifications may have no effect. In the case of the constant-velocity advection equation, the value $q(\vec{x}^{\star}, t^{\star})$ is exactly equal to $q(\vec{x}^{\star} - t^{\star}\vec{u}, 0)$, so it only depends on a single point in the initial conditions. For other PDEs, such as the heat-diffusion equation $\partial q / \partial t = \nabla \cdot \nabla q$, each point of the solution depends on *all* points in the initial conditions. The *domain of dependence* for a point is precisely the set of locations that have an effect on the value of the solution at that point.

---

[2]As an aside, this is a sticky point for the three-dimensional incompressible Navier-Stokes equations, and at the time of this writing nobody has managed to prove that they do in fact have a unique solution for all time. It has already been proven in two dimensions, and in three dimensions up to some finite time; a million-dollar prize has been offered from the Clay Institute for the first person to finish the proof in three dimensions.

Each point of a numerical solution also has a domain of dependence: again, the set of locations in the initial conditions that have an effect on the value of the solution at that point. It should be intuitively obvious that the numerical domain of dependence, at least in the limit, must contain the true domain of dependence if we want to get the correct answer. This is, in fact, the CFL condition: convergence is only possible in general if, in the limit as $\Delta x \to 0$ and $\Delta t \to 0$, the numerical domain of dependence for each point contains the true domain of dependence.

For semi-Lagrangian methods the CFL condition is satisfied if, in the limit, the particle trajectories we trace are close enough to the true trajectories—close enough that we interpolate from the correct grid cells and get the correct dependence. This should hold, since unless we do something terribly wrong, in the limit the particle tracing should converge to the correct trajectories.

That said, for standard explicit finite difference methods for the advection equation, where the new value of a grid point q_i^{n+1} is calculated from a few of the old values at neighboring grid points, i.e., from points only $C\Delta x$ away for a small integer constant C, there is a much more apparent CFL condition. In particular, the true solution is moving at speed $|\vec{u}|$, so the speed at which numerical information is transmitted, i.e., $C\Delta x/\Delta t$, must be at least as fast. That is, for convergence we will require

$$\frac{C\Delta x}{\Delta t} \geq |\vec{u}|,$$

which turns into a condition on the time step:

$$\Delta t \leq \frac{C\Delta x}{|\vec{u}|}. \tag{3.3}$$

Here is where most of the confusion arises. This is often the same, up to a small constant factor, as the maximum stable time step for the method—and in particular, in the original paper by Courant et al. [Courant et al. 28], these were identical. Thus sometimes the CFL condition is confused with a stability condition. In fact, there are methods that are unstable no matter what the time-step size is, such as the forward Euler and central difference scheme that began this chapter.[3] There are also explicit methods that are

---

[3]Interestingly, despite being unconditionally unstable, this method will still converge to the correct solution at a fixed end time T if the initial conditions are adequately smooth and in the limit $\Delta x \to 0$ the time step is reduced as $O(\Delta x^2)$. Taking the time step much smaller than the grid spacing reduces the rate of exponential blow-up to zero in the limit, though of course this is not an efficient method. Naturally it satisfies the CFL condition since it converges.

stable for arbitrary time-step sizes—however, they can't converge to the correct answer unless the CFL condition is met.

To further muddy the waters, there is a related quantity called the *CFL number*, often denoted α. If c is the maximum speed of information propagation in the problem—assuming this concept makes sense, for example in the advection equation we're studying (where $c = \max |\vec{u}|$) or in certain wave equations where it might be termed the "speed of sound"—then the CFL number α of a given discretization is defined from

$$\Delta t = \alpha \frac{\Delta x}{c}. \tag{3.4}$$

Thus the time step we talked about above, inequality (3.2), could be expressed as taking a CFL number of five. The CFL condition for explicit finite difference schemes can be expressed as a limit on the CFL number; similarly the stability of some, though not all, explicit finite difference schemes can be conveniently expressed as another limit on the CFL number. The CFL number by itself is just a useful parameter, not a condition on anything.

3.4   Dissipation

Notice that in the interpolation step of semi-Lagrangian advection we are taking a weighted average of values from the previous time step. That is, with each advection step, we are doing an averaging operation. Averaging tends to smooth out or blur sharp features, a process called *dissipation*. In signal-processing terminology, we have a low-pass filter. A single blurring step is pretty harmless, but if we repeatedly blur every time step, you can imagine there are going to be problems.

Let's try to understand this smoothing behavior more physically. We'll use a technique called *modified PDEs*. The common way of looking at numerical error in solving equations is that our solution gets perturbed from the true solution by some amount: we're only approximately solving the problem. The approach that we'll now use, sometimes also called *backwards error analysis*, instead takes the perspective that we *are* solving a problem exactly—it's just the problem we solved isn't quite the same as the one we started out with, i.e., the problem has been perturbed in some way. Often interpreting the error this way, and understanding the perturbation to the problem being solved, is extremely useful.

To make our analysis as simple as possible, we'll solve the advection problem in one dimension with a constant velocity $u > 0$:

$$\frac{\partial q}{\partial t} + u \frac{\partial q}{\partial x} = 0.$$

We'll assume $\Delta t < \Delta x / u$, i.e., that the particle trajectories span less than a grid cell—the analysis easily extends to larger time steps too, but nothing significant changes. In that case, the starting point of the trajectory that ends on grid point i is in the interval $[x_{i-1}, x_i]$. Doing the linear interpolation between q_{i-1}^n and q_i^n at point $x_i - \Delta t u$ gives

$$q_i^{n+1} = \frac{\Delta t \, u}{\Delta x} q_{i-1}^n + \left(1 - \frac{\Delta t \, u}{\Delta x}\right) q_i^n.$$

We can rearrange this to get

$$q_i^{n+1} = q_i^n - \Delta t \, u \frac{q_i^n - q_{i-1}^n}{\Delta x}, \tag{3.5}$$

which is in fact exactly the Eulerian scheme of forward Euler in time and a one-sided finite difference in space.[4] Now recall the Taylor series for q_{i-1}^n:

$$q_{i-1}^n = q_i^n - \left(\frac{\partial q}{\partial x}\right)_i^n \Delta x + \left(\frac{\partial^2 q}{\partial x^2}\right)_i^n \frac{\Delta x^2}{2} + O(\Delta x^3).$$

Substituting this into Equation (3.5) and doing the cancellation gives

$$q_i^{n+1} = q_i^n - \Delta t \, u \frac{1}{\Delta x} \left(\left(\frac{\partial q}{\partial x}\right)_i^n \Delta x - \left(\frac{\partial^2 q}{\partial x^2}\right)_i^n \frac{\Delta x^2}{2} + O(\Delta x^3) \right)$$

$$= q_i^n - \Delta t \, u \left(\frac{\partial q}{\partial x}\right)_i^n + \Delta t \, u \Delta x \left(\frac{\partial^2 q}{\partial x^2}\right)_i^n + O(\Delta x^2).$$

Up to a second-order truncation error, we can see this is forward Euler in time applied to the *modified PDE*:

$$\frac{\partial q}{\partial t} + u \frac{\partial q}{\partial x} = u \Delta x \frac{\partial^2 q}{\partial x^2}.$$

This is the advection equation with an additional viscosity-like term with coefficient $u\Delta x$! (Recall from the momentum equation of Navier-Stokes

---

[4]If you're interested, note that the side to which the finite difference is biased is the side from which the fluid is flowing. This is no coincidence and makes perfect physical sense—in the real physical world, you get information from upwind, not downwind, directions in advection. In general, biasing a finite difference to the direction that flow is coming from is called *upwinding*. Most advanced Eulerian schemes are upwind-biased schemes that do this with more accurate finite difference formulas.

that viscosity appears as the Laplacian of velocity, which in one dimension is simply the second derivative.) That is, when we use the simple semi-Lagrangian method to try to solve the advection equation *without* viscosity, our results look like we are simulating a fluid *with* viscosity. It's called *numerical dissipation* (or numerical viscosity, or numerical diffusion—they all mean the same thing).

Fortunately the coefficient of this numerical dissipation goes to zero as $\Delta x \to 0$, so we get the right answer in the limit. However, in computer graphics we don't have the patience or supercomputing resources to take Δx extremely small: we want to see good-looking results with Δx as large as possible!

So how bad is it? It depends on what we're trying to simulate. If we're trying to simulate a viscous fluid, which has plenty of natural dissipation already, then the extra numerical dissipation will hardly be noticed—and more importantly, looks plausibly like real dissipation. But, most often we're trying to simulate nearly inviscid fluids, and this is a serious annoyance which keeps smoothing the interesting features like small vortices from our flow. As bad as this is for velocity, in Chapter 6 we'll see it can be much much worse for other fluid variables.

3.5   Reducing Numerical Dissipation

There are many approaches to fixing the numerical dissipation problem. We'll outline one particularly simple, but quite effective, strategy for fixing the semi-Lagrangian method presented so far. As we saw in the last section, the problem mainly lies with the excessive averaging induced by linear interpolation (of the quantity being advected; linearly interpolating the velocity field in which we trace is not the main culprit and can be used as is). Thus, the natural next step is to use sharper interpolation. For example, Fedkiw et al. [Fedkiw et al. 01] proposed using a specially limited form of Catmull-Rom interpolation, which we will explore here.

Underlying Catmull-Rom is cubic Hermite spline interpolation. In one dimension, a cubic Hermite spline simply constructs a cubic polynomial on each interval that matches sampled function values *and* derivatives at the endpoints. That is, the cubic polynomial $p(x)$ on $[x_i, x_{i+1}]$ should satisfy

$$p(x_i) = f_i, \qquad p(x_{i+1}) = f_{i+1},$$
$$\frac{dp}{dx}(x_i) = s_i, \qquad \frac{dp}{dx}(x_{i+1}) = s_{i+1}.$$

Here f_i is the known function value at x_i, and s_i is the known derivative (slope). It's not hard to verify that the cubic[5] is

$$p(x) = f_i + s_i(x - x_i) + \left(\frac{-3f_i + 3f_{i+1}}{\Delta x^2} + \frac{-2s_i - s_{i+1}}{\Delta x} \right)(x - x_i)^2$$
$$+ \left(\frac{2f_i - 2f_{i+1}}{\Delta x^3} + \frac{s_i + s_{i+1}}{\Delta x^2} \right)(x - x_i)^3.$$

Catmull-Rom uses a central finite difference to approximate the derivatives from nearby function values:

$$s_i = \frac{f_{i+1} - f_{i-1}}{2\Delta x}, \qquad s_{i+1} = \frac{f_{i+2} - f_i}{2\Delta x}.$$

Plugging this in, regrouping terms, and substituting

$$\bar{x} = \frac{x - x_i}{\Delta x}$$

gives the following:

$$p(x) = f_{i-1}\left(-\frac{1}{2}\bar{x} + \bar{x}^2 - \frac{1}{2}\bar{x}^3 \right) + f_i\left(1 - \frac{5}{2}\bar{x}^2 + \frac{3}{2}\bar{x}^3 \right)$$
$$+ f_{i+1}\left(\frac{1}{2}\bar{x} + 2\bar{x}^2 - \frac{3}{2}\bar{x}^3 \right) + f_{i+2}\left(-\frac{1}{2}\bar{x}^2 + \frac{1}{2}\bar{x}^3 \right).$$

This can be shown to have cubic accuracy when approximating a smooth function, as opposed to the lower quadratic accuracy of linear interpolation. To extend this to higher dimensions, we simply interpolate along each dimension in turn, in exactly the same way as bi- or trilinear interpolation can be constructed from one-dimensional linear interpolation.

Using Catmull-Rom interpolation in the semi-Lagrangian method for advection boosts the accuracy to second order (from first order for linear interpolation) and significantly reduces the numerical dissipation. However, it doesn't have quite the same guarantees for stability as linear interpolation. The issue is under- or overshooting: near local maximums or minimums in the data, the cubic can go higher or lower than the data points. Whereas linear interpolating between two data points always gives you a number bounded by those data points, Catmull-Rom interpolation might give you something larger or smaller. There is a worry, then, that if used for advection there might be an unstable feedback loop: if each time

---

[5]If you refer back to the paper by Fedkiw et al. [Fedkiw et al. 01], be aware that there are small typos in the quadratic and cubic coefficients, corrected here.

step overshoots the data from the previous time step, the solution might grow exponentially.

A more complicated analysis shows that this *cannot*, in fact, happen for the simple one-dimensional advection problem: it's just as stable as linear interpolation. However, this theoretical analysis doesn't carry over to more general scenarios—it may well still be fully stable, but currently we don't have a proof. Therefore it may be prudent to at least have an option in a simulator to turn on a safety check, a means to detect and correct the under- or overshoot problem. It should be emphasized that directly preventing under- and overshoot this way will cause additional numerical dissipation in the vicinity of local minima and maxima where it is most obvious and least desired: you might not want to use this safety option unless a simulation blows up without it.

Fedkiw et al. [Fedkiw et al. 01] suggest clamping the Catmull-Rom slopes (along each dimension) to zero where they disagree with the sign of the one-sided finite differences: this flattens out the interpolant to prevent under- or overshoot everywhere. However, this can be excessive: evaluating the unmodified Catmull-Rom interpolant at the point we care about may be just fine (lie within the local min and max of the data) even if at other points it under- or overshoots. Generally speaking then, it's preferable to just clamp the interpolated value to lie within the local bounds.

– 4 –
Making Fluids Incompressible

In this chapter we'll look at the heart of a fluid simulation, making the fluid incompressible and simultaneously enforcing boundary conditions: implementation of the routine $\texttt{project}(\Delta t, \vec{u})$ we mentioned earlier in Chapter 2. We'll first cover the classical approach to this and then later talk about boundary condition issues.

The $\texttt{project}$ routine will subtract off the pressure gradient from the intermediate velocity field $\vec{u}$:

$$\vec{u}^{n+1} = \vec{u} - \Delta t \frac{1}{\rho} \nabla p,$$

so that the result satisfies incompressibility inside the fluid:

$$\nabla \cdot \vec{u}^{n+1} = 0$$

and satisfies the solid wall boundary conditions:

$$\vec{u}^{n+1} \cdot \hat{n} = \vec{u}_{\text{solid}} \cdot \hat{n}.$$

Thus, the first thing we need to do is write down the discretization of the pressure update: how do we approximate the pressure gradient on the MAC grid (assuming we know pressure)? After that we'll look at defining the discrete divergence on the MAC grid and, putting the two together, come up with a system of linear equations to solve to find the pressure. We'll cover both the system and an effective way to solve it.

The classical MAC grid approach we'll outline first really only applies to boundaries that are aligned with the grid: it's not obvious how to handle sloped or curved boundaries. We will later find a reinterpretation of the pressure equation that leads to a simple way of handling these irregular boundary conditions accurately and robustly.

4.1   The Discrete Pressure Gradient

The raison d'être of the MAC grid, as we briefly discussed before, is that the
staggering makes accurate central differences robust. For example, where
we need to subtract the $\partial/\partial x$-component of the pressure gradient from the
u-component of velocity, there are two pressure values lined up perfectly on
either side of the u-component just waiting to be differenced. You might
want to keep referring back to Figure 2.1 to see how this works.

So without further ado, here are the formulas for the pressure update
in two dimensions, using the central difference approximations for $\partial p/\partial x$
and $\partial p/\partial y$:

$$u^{n+1}_{i+1/2,j} = u_{i+1/2,j} - \Delta t \frac{1}{\rho} \frac{p_{i+1,j} - p_{i,j}}{\Delta x}, \tag{4.1}$$

$$v^{n+1}_{i,j+1/2} = v_{i,j+1/2} - \Delta t \frac{1}{\rho} \frac{p_{i,j+1} - p_{i,j}}{\Delta x}, \tag{4.2}$$

and in three dimensions, including $\partial p/\partial z$ too:

$$u^{n+1}_{i+1/2,j,k} = u_{i+1/2,j,k} - \Delta t \frac{1}{\rho} \frac{p_{i+1,j,k} - p_{i,j,k}}{\Delta x}, \tag{4.3}$$

$$v^{n+1}_{i,j+1/2,k} = v_{i,j+1/2,k} - \Delta t \frac{1}{\rho} \frac{p_{i,j+1,k} - p_{i,j,k}}{\Delta x}, \tag{4.4}$$

$$w^{n+1}_{i,j,k+1/2} = w_{i,j,k+1/2} - \Delta t \frac{1}{\rho} \frac{p_{i,j,k+1} - p_{i,j,k}}{\Delta x}. \tag{4.5}$$

Note that these pressure updates apply to every velocity component that
borders a grid cell that contains fluid. One of the trickiest parts of making
the pressure solve is keeping track of which velocity and pressure samples
are "active," so it's good to keep this in mind or perhaps keep a diagram
near you when you program.

In later sections we'll work out how to determine the pressure in the
grid cells that contain fluid. However, we immediately have a problem with
the formulas above. On boundary faces of the fluid region, they involve
pressures in grid cells that lie *outside* of the fluid region. Thus, we need to
specify our pressure boundary conditions. We will for now assume that grid
cells can be simply classified as fluid cells (ones that contain fluid), solid
cells (ones that are fully occupied by a solid), or air cells (ones that have
nothing in them—as in free surface water simulations). We'll postpone
dealing with cells that are only partially filled with solid and/or fluid: for
now we'll assume our solids line up with the grid perfectly, and we ignore
the exact mix of air and water in grid cells at the free surface and just label
them as fluid cells.

The easier pressure boundary condition is at a free surface, as in water simulation. Here we assume that the pressure is simply zero outside the fluid: in our update formulas we replace the $p_{i,j,k}$'s that lie in air cells with zero. This is called a *Dirichlet* boundary condition if you're interested in the technical lingo: Dirichlet means we're directly specifying the value of the quantity at the boundary.

The more difficult pressure boundary condition is at solid walls. Since the solid-wall boundaries line up with the grid cell faces, the component of velocity that we store on those faces is in fact $\vec{u} \cdot \hat{n}$. In this case, subtracting the pressure gradient there should enforce the boundary condition $\vec{u}^{n+1} \cdot \hat{n} = \vec{u}_{\text{solid}} \cdot \hat{n}$. This works out to be a specification of the normal derivative of pressure (which technically is known as a *Neumann* boundary condition). By substituting in the pressure update this turns into a simple linear equation to solve for the pressure inside the solid wall. For example, supposing grid cell (i, j) was fluid and grid cell $(i+1, j)$ was solid, we would update $u_{i+1/2,j}$ with

$$u_{i+1/2,j}^{n+1} = u_{i+1/2,j} - \Delta t \frac{1}{\rho} \frac{p_{i+1,j} - p_{i,j}}{\Delta x},$$

and we know that $u_{i+1/2,j}^{n+1}$ actually is u_{solid}. Rearranging the update equation gives

$$p_{i+1,j} = p_{i,j} + \frac{\rho \Delta x}{\Delta t} \left(u_{i+1/2,j} - u_{\text{solid}} \right). \tag{4.6}$$

When we actually update the velocity in the code, rather than bothering to substitute in this pressure, we can simply set velocities on solid-boundary faces equal to the solid normal velocity. However, Equation (4.6) will be necessary in deriving the equations that define pressure in the interior.

An odd point about the boundary conditions that needs to be mentioned here is that we typically figure out the solid grid cell pressure for each boundary face *independently*. That is, if a solid grid cell has two or more faces adjacent to fluid cells, we are going to calculate two or more completely independent pressure values for the cell! If this seems weird just remember that properly speaking, at the continuum level, fluid pressure isn't defined in the interior of the solid: we just have the pressure gradient at the boundary of the solid. Numerically it's convenient to express that as a finite difference (it fits in with all the other formulas) but the pressure we talk about inside that solid grid cell is really just a convenient figment of our mathematical imagination: in fact, they are sometimes called *ghost values*. All that counts is the pressure difference on the boundary faces. Therefore we don't store pressure explicitly inside the solid grid cell (since

```
scale = dt / (rho*dx);
loop over i,j,k where cell(i,j,k)==FLUID:
    u(i,j,k) -= scale * p(i,j,k);
    u(i+1,j,k) += scale * p(i,j,k);
    v(i,j,k) -= scale * p(i,j,k);
    v(i,j+1,k) += scale * p(i,j,k);
    w(i,j,k) -= scale * p(i,j,k);
    w(i,j,k+1) += scale * p(i,j,k);
loop over i,j,k where cell(i,j,k)==SOLID:
    u(i,j,k) = usolid(i,j,k);
    u(i+1,j,k) = usolid(i+1,j,k);
    v(i,j,k) = vsolid(i,j,k);
    v(i,j+1,k) = vsolid(i,j+1,k);
    w(i,j,k) = wsolid(i,j,k);
    w(i,j,k+1) = wsolid(i,j,k+1);
```

Figure 4.1. Pseudocode for the pressure update.

there could be multiple values for it) but instead just use formulas like Equation (4.6) whenever we need to know the pressure difference across a boundary face.

Using the same convention for storage from Chapter 2, Equations (2.14)–(2.17), the pressure update can be translated into code similar to Figure 4.1. Note that instead of looping over velocity locations and updating them with pressure differences, we are looping over pressure values and updating the velocities they affect. Also, we use the trick of directly setting solid wall velocities instead of working it out as a pressure update. The terms such as usolid(i,j,k) may well be replaced with simple expressions rather than actually stored in an array.

Boundary conditions can be complicated and are the usual culprit when bugs show up. It could be worth your time going over this section slowly, with a drawing of the MAC grid (like Figure 2.1) in front of you, looking at different configurations of solid, fluid, and air cells until you feel confident about all this.

4.2   The Discrete Divergence

Now for the easy part of the chapter! In the continuum case, we want our fluid to be incompressible: $\nabla \cdot \vec{u} = 0$. On the grid, we will approximate this

```
scale = 1 / dx;
loop over i,j,k where cell(i,j,k)==FLUID:
    rhs(i,j,k) = -scale * (u(i+1,j,k)-u(i,j,k)
                          +v(i,j+1,k)-v(i,j,k)
                          +w(i,j,k+1)-w(i,j,k));
```

Figure 4.2. Calculating the negative divergence, which will become the right-hand side of the linear system for pressure.

condition with finite differences and require that the divergence estimated at each fluid grid cell be zero for $\vec{u}^{n+1}$.

Remember the divergence in two dimensions is

$$\nabla \cdot \vec{u} = \frac{\partial u}{\partial x} + \frac{\partial v}{\partial y}$$

and in three dimensions is

$$\nabla \cdot \vec{u} = \frac{\partial u}{\partial x} + \frac{\partial v}{\partial y} + \frac{\partial w}{\partial z}.$$

Using the obvious central differences (take a look at the MAC grid again), we approximate the two-dimensional divergence in fluid grid cell (i, j) as

$$(\nabla \cdot \vec{u})_{i,j} \approx \frac{u_{i+1/2,j} - u_{i-1/2,j}}{\Delta x} + \frac{v_{i,j+1/2} - v_{i,j-1/2}}{\Delta x} \tag{4.7}$$

and in three dimensions, for fluid grid cell (i, j, k) as

$$(\nabla \cdot \vec{u})_{i,j,k} \approx \frac{u_{i+1/2,j,k} - u_{i-1/2,j,k}}{\Delta x} + \frac{v_{i,j+1/2,k} - v_{i,j-1/2,k}}{\Delta x}$$
$$+ \frac{w_{i,j,k+1/2} - w_{i,j,k-1/2}}{\Delta x}. \tag{4.8}$$

In terms of the storage convention used earlier, with divergence stored in the same way as pressure, this can be implemented as in the pseudocode of Figure 4.2. It turns out (see below) that we actually are more interested in the negative of divergence, so we store that in a vector we will call rhs (standing for the right-hand side of a linear system).

Note that we are only ever going to evaluate divergence for a grid cell that is marked as fluid. For example, our fluid simulation is not concerned with whether solids are changing volume or not.

Another way of interpreting the discrete divergence we have defined here is through a direct estimate of the total rate of fluid entering or exiting the grid cell. Remember that this (in the exact continuum setting) is just the integral of the normal component of velocity around the faces of the grid cell:

$$\iint_{\partial\text{cell}} \vec{u} \cdot \hat{n}.$$

This is the sum of the integrals over each grid cell face. Since we have the normal component of velocity stored at the center of each face, we can estimate the integral easily by just multiplying the normal component by the area of the face (though be careful with signs here—in the above integral the normal is always outwards-pointing, whereas the velocity components stored on the grid always are for the same directions, as shown in Figure 2.1, for example). After rescaling, this leads to exactly the same central difference formulas—I'll let you work this out for yourself if you're interested. This numerical technique, where we directly estimate the integral of a quantity around the faces of a grid cell instead of looking at the differential equation formulation, is called the *finite volume* method—more on this at the end of the chapter.

Finally we can explain why the MAC grid is so useful. If we used a regular *collocated* grid, where all components of velocity were stored together at the grid points, we would have a difficult time with the divergence. If we used the central difference formula, for example,

$$(\nabla \cdot \vec{u})_{i,j} \approx \frac{u_{i+1,j} - u_{i-1,j}}{2\Delta x} + \frac{v_{i,j+1} - v_{i,j-1}}{2\Delta x},$$

then we have exactly the null-space issues we mentioned back in Chapter 2. Some highly divergent velocity fields such as $\vec{u}_{i,j} = ((-1)^i, (-1)^j)$ will evaluate to zero divergence. Therefore, the pressure solve won't do anything about correcting them, and so high-frequency oscillations in the velocity field may persist or even grow unstably during the simulation. There are two possible fixes to get around this while still using a collocated grid. The first is to use a biased, one-sided difference approximation—and while this works, it does introduce a peculiar bias to the simulation that can be disturbingly obvious. The second is to filter out the high-frequency divergent modes (i.e., smooth the velocity field) before doing the pressure solve, to explicitly get rid of them—unfortunately, our major goal is to *avoid* numerical smoothing wherever possible, so this isn't a good idea for animation either. Thus we stick to the MAC grid.

4.3 The Pressure Equations

We now have the two ingredients we will need to figure out incompressibility: how to update velocities with the pressure gradient and how to estimate the divergence.

Recall that we want the final velocity, $\vec{u}^{n+1}$ to be divergence-free inside the fluid. To find the pressure that achieves this, we simply substitute the pressure-update formulas for $\vec{u}^{n+1}$, Equations (4.1) in 2D and (4.3) in 3D, into the divergence formula, Equation (4.7) in 2D and (4.8) in 3D. This gives us a linear equation for each *fluid* grid cell (remember we only evaluate divergence for a grid cell containing fluid), with the pressures as unknowns. There are no equations for solid or air cells, even though we may refer to pressures in them (but we know *a priori* what those pressures are in terms of the fluid cell pressures).

Let's write this out explicitly in 2D for fluid grid cell (i, j):

$$\frac{u_{i+1/2,j}^{n+1} - u_{i-1/2,j}^{n+1}}{\Delta x} + \frac{v_{i,j+1/2}^{n+1} - v_{i,j-1/2}^{n+1}}{\Delta x} = 0,$$

$$\frac{1}{\Delta x}\left[\left(u_{i+1/2,j} - \Delta t\frac{1}{\rho}\frac{p_{i+1,j} - p_{i,j}}{\Delta x}\right)\right.$$

$$-\left(u_{i-1/2,j} - \Delta t\frac{1}{\rho}\frac{p_{i,j} - p_{i-1,j}}{\Delta x}\right)$$

$$+\left(v_{i,j+1/2} - \Delta t\frac{1}{\rho}\frac{p_{i,j+1} - p_{i,j}}{\Delta x}\right)$$

$$\left.-\left(v_{i,j-1/2} - \Delta t\frac{1}{\rho}\frac{p_{i,j} - p_{i,j-1}}{\Delta x}\right)\right] = 0,$$

$$\frac{\Delta t}{\rho}\left(\frac{4p_{i,j} - p_{i+1,j} - p_{i,j+1} - p_{i-1,j} - p_{i,j-1}}{\Delta x^2}\right) =$$

$$-\left(\frac{u_{i+1/2,j} - u_{i-1/2,j}}{\Delta x} + \frac{v_{i,j+1/2} - v_{i,j-1/2}}{\Delta x}\right). \quad (4.9)$$

And now in 3D for fluid grid cell (i, j, k):

$$\frac{u^{n+1}_{i+1/2,j,k} - u^{n+1}_{i-1/2,j,k}}{\Delta x} + \frac{v^{n+1}_{i,j+1/2,k} - v^{n+1}_{i,j-1/2,k}}{\Delta x} + \frac{w^{n+1}_{i,j,k+1/2} - w^{n+1}_{i,j,k-1/2}}{\Delta x} = 0,$$

$$(4.10)$$

$$\frac{1}{\Delta x} \left[\left(u_{i+1/2,j,k} - \Delta t \frac{1}{\rho} \frac{p_{i+1,j,k} - p_{i,j,k}}{\Delta x} \right) \right.$$

$$- \left(u_{i-1/2,j,k} - \Delta t \frac{1}{\rho} \frac{p_{i,j,k} - p_{i-1,j,k}}{\Delta x} \right)$$

$$+ \left(v_{i,j+1/2,k} - \Delta t \frac{1}{\rho} \frac{p_{i,j+1,k} - p_{i,j,k}}{\Delta x} \right)$$

$$- \left(v_{i,j-1/2,k} - \Delta t \frac{1}{\rho} \frac{p_{i,j,k} - p_{i,j-1,k}}{\Delta x} \right)$$

$$+ \left(w_{i,j,k+1/2} - \Delta t \frac{1}{\rho} \frac{p_{i,j,k+1} - p_{i,j,k}}{\Delta x} \right)$$

$$\left. - \left(w_{i,j,k-1/2} - \Delta t \frac{1}{\rho} \frac{p_{i,j,k} - p_{i,j,k-1}}{\Delta x} \right) \right] = 0,$$

$$\frac{\Delta t}{\rho} \left(\frac{\begin{matrix} 6p_{i,j,k} - p_{i+1,j,k} - p_{i,j+1,k} - p_{i,j,k+1} \\ - p_{i-1,j,k} - p_{i,j-1,k} - p_{i,j,k-1} \end{matrix}}{\Delta x^2} \right) =$$

$$- \left(\frac{u_{i+1/2,j,k} - u_{i-1/2,j,k}}{\Delta x} + \frac{v_{i,j+1/2,k} - v_{i,j-1/2,k}}{\Delta x} + \frac{w_{i,j,k+1/2} - w_{i,j,k-1/2}}{\Delta x} \right). \quad (4.11)$$

Observe that Equations (4.9) and (4.11) are numerical approximations to the *Poisson* problem $-\Delta t/\rho \nabla \cdot \nabla p = -\nabla \cdot \vec{u}$.

If a fluid grid cell is at the boundary, recall that the new velocities on the boundary faces involve pressures outside the fluid that we have to define through boundary conditions: we need to use that here. For example, if grid cell $(i, j + 1)$ is an air cell, then we replace $p_{i,j+1}$ in Equation (4.9) with zero. If grid cell $(i+1, j)$ is a solid cell, then we replace $p_{i+1,j}$ with the value we compute from the boundary condition there, as in formula (4.6).

Assuming $(i - 1, j)$ and $(i, j - 1)$ are fluid cells, this would reduce the equation to the following:

$$\frac{\Delta t}{\rho} \left(\frac{4p_{i,j} - \left[p_{i,j} + \frac{\rho \Delta x}{\Delta t} \left(u_{i+1/2,j} - u_{\text{solid}} \right) \right] - 0 - p_{i-1,j} - p_{i,j-1}}{\Delta x^2} \right)$$

$$= - \left(\frac{u_{i+1/2,j} - u_{i-1/2,j}}{\Delta x} + \frac{v_{i,j+1/2} - v_{i,j-1/2}}{\Delta x} \right),$$

$$\frac{\Delta t}{\rho} \left(\frac{3p_{i,j} - p_{i-1,j} - p_{i,j-1}}{\Delta x^2} \right) =$$

$$- \left(\frac{u_{i+1/2,j} - u_{i-1/2,j}}{\Delta x} + \frac{v_{i,j+1/2} - v_{i,j-1/2}}{\Delta x} \right) + \left(\frac{u_{i+1/2,j} - u_{\text{solid}}}{\Delta x} \right).$$

We can observe a few things about this example that hold in general and how this will let us implement it in code. First, for the air cell boundary condition, we simply just delete mention of that p from the equation. Second, for the solid cell boundary condition, we delete mention of that p but also reduce the coefficient in front of $p_{i,j}$, which is normally four, by one—in other words, the coefficient in front of $p_{i,j}$ is equal to the number of non-solid grid cell neighbors (this is the same in three dimensions). Third,

```
scale = 1 / dx;
loop over i,j,k where cell(i,j,k)==FLUID:
    if cell(i-1,j,k)==SOLID:
        rhs(i,j,k) -= scale * (u(i,j,k) - usolid(i,j,k));
    if cell(i+1,j,k)==SOLID:
        rhs(i,j,k) += scale * (u(i+1,j,k) - usolid(i+1,j,k));

    if cell(i,j-1,k)==SOLID:
        rhs(i,j,k) -= scale * (v(i,j,k) - vsolid(i,j,k));
    if cell(i,j+1,k)==SOLID:
        rhs(i,j,k) += scale * (v(i,j+1,k) - vsolid(i,j+1,k));

    if cell(i,j,k-1)==SOLID:
        rhs(i,j,k) -= scale * (w(i,j,k) - wsolid(i,j,k));
    if cell(i,j,k+1)==SOLID:
        rhs(i,j,k) += scale * (w(i,j,k+1) - wsolid(i,j,k+1));
```

Figure 4.3. Modifying the right-hand side to account for solid velocities.

we increment the negative divergence measured on the right-hand side with a term involving the difference between fluid and solid velocity. This can be implemented in code as an additional loop to modify rhs, as shown in Figure 4.3.

4.3.1 Putting It In Matrix-Vector Form

We have now defined a large system of linear equations for the unknown pressure values. We can conceptually think of it as a large coefficient matrix, A, times a vector consisting of all pressure unknowns, p, equal to a vector consisting of the *negative* divergences in each fluid grid cell, b (with appropriate modifications at solid wall boundaries):

$$Ap = b. \tag{4.12}$$

In the implementation we have discussed so far, of course, p and b are logically stored in a two or three-dimensional grid structure (since each entry corresponds to a grid cell).

We needn't store A directly as a matrix. Notice that each row of A corresponds to one equation, i.e., one fluid cell. For example, if grid cell (i, j, k) is fluid, then there will be a row of the matrix that we can label with the indices (i, j, k). The entries in that row are the coefficients of all the pressure unknowns in that equation: almost all of these are zero except possibly for the seven entries corresponding to $p_{i,j,k}$ and its six neighbors, $p_{i\pm1,j,k}$, $p_{i,j\pm1,k}$, and $p_{i,j,k\pm1}$. (In two dimensions there are at most four neighbors of course.) We only have non-zeros (i, j, k) and its fluid cell neighbors. It is of course pointless to store all the zeros: this is a *sparse* matrix.

Let's take a closer look at A. In the equation for (i, j, k), the coefficients for neighboring fluid cells are all equal to $-\Delta t/(\rho \Delta x^2)$, and if there are $n_{i,j,k}$ fluid- or air-cell neighbors the coefficient for $p_{i,j,k}$ is $n_{i,j,k}\Delta t/(\rho \Delta x^2)$.

One of the nice properties of the matrix A is that it is symmetric. For example, $A_{(i,j,k),(i+1,j,k)}$, the coefficient of $p_{i+1,j,k}$ in the equation for grid cell (i, j, k), has to be equal to $A_{(i+1,j,k),(i,j,k)}$. Either it's zero if one of those two cells is not fluid, or it's the same non-zero value. This symmetry property will hold even with the more advanced discretization at the end of the chapter. Thus we only have to store half of the non-zero entries in A, since the other half are just copies!

This leads us to the following structure for storing A. In two dimensions, we will store three numbers at every grid cell: the diagonal entry $A_{(i,j),(i,j)}$ and the entries for the neighboring cells in the positive directions,

```
scale = dt / (rho*dx*dx);
loop over i,j,k:
  if cell(i,j,k)==FLUID and cell(i+1,j,k)==FLUID:
    Adiag(i,j,k) += scale;
    Adiag(i+1,j,k) += scale;
    Aplusi(i,j,k) = -scale;
  else if cell(i,j,k)==FLUID and cell(i+1,j,k)==EMPTY:
    Adiag(i,j,k) += scale;

  if cell(i,j,k)==FLUID and cell(i,j+1,k)==FLUID:
    Adiag(i,j,k) += scale;
    Adiag(i,j+1,k) += scale;
    Aplusj(i,j,k) = -scale;
  else if cell(i,j,k)==FLUID and cell(i,j+1,k)==EMPTY:
    Adiag(i,j,k) += scale;

  if cell(i,j,k)==FLUID and cell(i,j,k+1)==FLUID:
    Adiag(i,j,k) += scale;
    Adiag(i,j,k+1) += scale;
    Aplusk(i,j,k) = -scale;
  else if cell(i,j,k)==FLUID and cell(i,j,k+1)==EMPTY:
    Adiag(i,j,k) += scale;
```

Figure 4.4. Setting up the matrix entries for the pressure equations.

$A_{(i,j),(i+1,j)}$ and $A_{(i,j),(i,j+1)}$. We could call these entries Adiag(i,j), Aplusi(i,j), and Aplusj(i,j) in our code. In three dimensions, we would similarly have Adiag(i,j,k), Aplusi(i,j,k), Aplusj(i,j,k), and Aplusk(i,j,k). When we need to refer to an entry like $A_{(i,j),(i-1,j)}$ we use symmetry and instead refer to $A_{(i-1,j),(i,j)}$ =Aplusi(i-1,j). See Figure 4.4 for pseudocode to set up the matrix in this structure.

4.3.2   The Conjugate Gradient Algorithm

The matrix A is a very well-known type of matrix, sometimes referred to as the five- or seven-point Laplacian matrix, in two or three dimensions, respectively. It has been exhaustively studied, serves as the subject of countless numerical linear algebra papers, and is the prototypical first example of a sparse matrix in just about any setting. More effort has been put into solving linear systems with this type of matrix than probably all other sparse matrices put together! We won't look very far into this

vast body of work, beyond one particular algorithm that is both fairly efficient and extremely simple to implement, even for irregular domains, called
MICCG(0), or more fully *modified incomplete Cholesky conjugate gradient,
level zero*. Quite a mouthful! Let's go through it slowly.

One of the many properties that A has is that it is *symmetric positive
definite* (SPD). Technically this means that $q^T A q > 0$ for any non-zero
vector q.

Actually, before going on I should be a little more careful. A might
just be symmetric positive semi-definite, meaning that $q^T A q \geq 0$ (with
zero achieved for some non-zero q). If there is some fluid region entirely
surrounded by solid walls, with no empty air cells, then A will not be
strictly positive definite. In that case, A is singular in fact—it doesn't have
an inverse. That doesn't necessarily mean there isn't a solution, however.
If the divergences (the right-hand side) satisfy a *compatibility condition*
then life is good and there is a solution. The compatibility condition is
simply that the velocities of the solid walls are compatible with the fluid
contained within being incompressible—i.e., the fluid-solid boundary faces
have wall velocities that add up to zero, so that the flow in is balanced
by the flow out—we will discuss how to ensure that this is the case at the
end of the chapter. In fact, not only will there be a solution, but there are
infinitely many solutions! You can take any solution for pressure and add
an arbitrary constant to it and get another solution, it turns out. However,
when we take the pressure gradient for the velocity update, the constants
cancel so we don't actually care which solution we get. They're all good.

One particularly useful algorithm for solving symmetric positive semi-
definite linear systems is called the *conjugate gradient* algorithm, usually
abbreviated as CG. It's an iterative method, meaning that we start with
a guess at the solution and in each iteration improve on it, stopping when
we think we are accurate enough. CG chooses the iterative updates to the
guess to minimize a particular measure of the error and thus can be guaranteed to converge to the solution eventually. Another very nice aspect of
CG, as compared to Gaussian elimination for example, is that each iteration only involves multiplying A by a vector, adding vectors, multiplying
vectors by scalar numbers, and computing a few dot-products—all of which
are very easy to code, and most of which can be done with calls to highly
optimized standard libraries (more on this below).

The problem with CG, however, is that the larger the grid, the longer it
takes to converge. It can be shown that the number of iterations it takes to
converge to some desired accuracy is proportional to the width of the grid:
the maximum number of grid cells in any one direction. In practice, when

limited to a small number of iterations even simpler algorithms such as *Gauss-Seidel* (not covered here) tend to be significantly better than plain CG. However, there is a trick up our sleeve that can speed this up, called *preconditioning*. *Preconditioned conjugate gradient* (PCG) is what we will be using.

More generally, CG takes more iterations the further A is from being the identity matrix, I. It should be immediately obvious that solving a system with the identity matrix is pretty easy—the solution of $Ip = b$ is just $p = b$! How exactly we measure how far A is from the identity is beyond the scope of this book—something called the *condition number* of A. The idea behind preconditioning is that the solution of $Ap = b$ is the same as the solution of $MAp = Mb$ for any invertible matrix M. If M is *approximately* the inverse of A, so that MA is really close to being the identity matrix, then CG should be able to solve the preconditioned equations $MAp = Mb$ really fast. PCG is just a clever way of applying CG to these preconditioned equations without actually having to form them.

Before we actually get to the details of PCG, we need to talk about convergence. When do we know to stop? How do we check to see that our current guess is close enough to the solution? Ideally we would just measure the norm of the difference between our current guess and the exact solution—but of course that requires knowing the exact solution! So we will instead look at a vector called the *residual*:

$$r_i = b - Ap_i.$$

That is, if p_i is the ith guess at the true solution, the ith residual r_i is just how far away it is from satisfying the equation $Ap = b$. When we hit the exact solution, the residual is exactly zero.[1] Therefore, we stop our iteration when the norm of the residual is small enough, below some tolerance.

That brings us to the next question: how small is small enough? And what norm do you use to measure r_i? Think back to what r_i means physically. These equations resulted from deriving that $b - Ap$ is the negative of the finite difference estimate of the divergence of $\vec{u}^{n+1}$, which we want to be zero. Thus the residual measures exactly how much divergence there will be in the velocity field after we've updated it with our current estimate of the pressure. It seems sensible, then, to take the infinity norm of the residual (the maximum absolute value of any entry) and compare that to

---

[1] In fact, it's not hard to see that the residual is just A times the error: $r_i = A(p_{\text{exact}} - p_i)$.

some small number `tol`, so that we know the worst case of how compressible our new velocity field could possibly be. The dimensions of `tol` are one over time: $O(1/\texttt{tol})$ is a lower bound on how long it will take our inexact velocity field to compress the fluid by some fraction. Thus `tol` probably should be inversely proportional to the time length of our simulation. In practice, this either doesn't vary a lot (a few seconds for most shots) or we are doing interactive animation with a potentially infinite time length—so in the end we just pick an arbitrary small fixed number for `tol`, like 10^{-6} s^{-1}. (The s^{-1} is one over seconds: remember again that this quantity has dimensions one over time.) Smaller tolerances will result in less erroneous divergence but will take more iterations (and time) to compute, so there's a clear trade-off in adjusting this number up or down.[2] This is particularly important since typically most of the time in a fluid simulation is spent in the pressure solver: this is the code that usually demands the most optimizing and tuning.

Typically we will also want to guard against inexact floating-point arithmetic causing the algorithm not to converge fully, so we stop at a certain maximum number of iterations. Or, we may have a real-time constraint that limits the number of iterations we can use. Setting this constraint is another case of trade-offs: starting out your simulator with the value 100 is reasonable.

A final issue is what the initial guess for pressure should be. One nice thing about PCG is that if we start with a good guess, we can get to an acceptable solution much faster. In some circumstances, say when the fluid has settled down and isn't changing much, the pressure from the last time step is a very good guess for the next pressure: it won't change much either. However, these situations usually can easily be solved from an initial guess of all zeros also. In the more interesting cases (and really, why would you be simulating fluids that are just sitting still?), the pressure can change significantly from one time step to the next, or in fact may be defined on different grid cells anyhow (e.g., as liquid moves from one grid cell to another) and can't be used. Therefore we usually use the vector of all zeros as the initial guess.

Pseudocode for the PCG algorithm is shown in Figure 4.5. Be aware that this statement of PCG uses different symbols than most text books: I've tried to avoid the use of letters like x and ρ that have other meanings in the context of fluids.

---

[2]However, one of the great features of PCG is that the rate of convergence tends to accelerate the further along you go: reducing the tolerance may not slow things down as much as you think.

- Set initial guess $p = 0$ and residual vector $r = b$ (If $r = 0$ then return p)
- Set auxiliary vector $z = \texttt{applyPreconditioner}(r)$, and search vector $s = z$
- $\sigma = \texttt{dotproduct}(z, r)$
- Loop until done (or maximum iterations exceeded):
  - Set auxiliary vector $z = \texttt{applyA}(s)$
  - $\alpha = \sigma/\texttt{dotproduct}(z, s)$
  - Update $p \leftarrow p + \alpha s$ and $r \leftarrow r - \alpha z$
  - If $\max |r| \leq \texttt{tol}$ then return p
  - Set auxiliary vector $z = \texttt{applyPreconditioner}(r)$
  - $\sigma_{\text{new}} = \texttt{dotproduct}(z, r)$
  - $\beta = \sigma_{\text{new}}/\sigma$
  - Set search vector $s = z + \beta s$
  - $\sigma = \sigma_{\text{new}}$
- Return p (and report iteration limit exceeded)

Figure 4.5. The preconditioned conjugate gradient (PCG) algorithm for solving $Ap = d$.

Note that PCG needs storage for an "auxiliary" vector z and a "search" vector s (the same size as p, b, and r), and calls subroutine $\texttt{applyA}$ to multiply the coefficient matrix A times a vector and subroutine $\texttt{applyPreconditioner}$ to multiply M by a vector (which we will talk about next). Also note that the new residual in each iteration is incrementally updated from the previous residual—not only is this more efficient than calculating it from scratch each time, but it in fact tends to reduce the number of iterations required due to some interesting round-off error interactions. Since PCG tends to be the most time-consuming part of the simulation, it pays to use optimized $BLAS$[3] routines for the vector operations here. Finally, it's worth noting that although most of the rest of the fluid simulator may be effectively implemented using 32-bit single precision

---

[3]The BLAS, or basic linear algebra subroutines, provide a standardized API for simple operations like dot-products, scaling and adding vectors, multiplying dense matrices, etc. Every significant platform has at least one implementation, which generally is intensely optimized, making full use of vector units, cache prefetching, multiple cores, and the like. It can be very difficult (if not impossible without using assembly language) to match the efficiency attained by the BLAS for vectors of any appreciable size, so it generally pays to exploit it.

floating-point numbers, 64-bit double precision is *strongly* recommended for PCG—at the very least, for the scalars (in particular when accumulating the dot-products[4]). Single precision rounding errors can cause a significant slow-down in convergence.

4.3.3 Incomplete Cholesky

We still have the question of defining the preconditioner. From the standpoint of convergence the perfect preconditioner would be A^{-1}, except that's obviously far too expensive to compute. The true ideal is something that is both fast to compute and apply and is effective in speeding up convergence, so as to minimize the total solution time.

There are many, many choices of preconditioner, with more being invented each year. Our default choice, though, is quite an old preconditioner from the *incomplete Cholesky* (IC) family. It's both simple to implement and fairly efficient, and it is quite robust in handling irregular domains (like the shape of a liquid splash). Its chief problems are that it's hard to parallelize effectively and that it's not optimally scalable (the number of iterations required for PCG steadily increases with grid size); more complex approaches such as *domain decomposition* or *multigrid* may become useful if you want to scale up your simulator to run on large problems on multi-core machines or clusters, but these methods lie beyond the scope of this book.

Recall how you might directly solve a system of linear equations with Gaussian elimination. That is, you perform row reductions on the system until the matrix is upper-triangular, and then use back substitution to get the solution one entry at a time. Mathematically, it turns out that this is equivalent to factoring the matrix A as the product of a lower- and an upper-triangular matrix and then solving the triangular systems one after the other. In the case of a symmetric positive definite A, we can actually do it so that the two triangular matrices are transposes of each other:

$$A = LL^T.$$

This is called the *Cholesky* factorization. The original system $Ap = b$ is the same as $L(L^Tp) = b$, which we can solve as

$$\begin{aligned} \text{solve} \quad Lq &= b \quad \text{with forward substitution,} \\ \text{solve} \quad L^Tp &= q \quad \text{with backward substitution.} \end{aligned} \tag{4.13}$$

---

[4]If you do use single precision floating-point values for your vectors (pressure, etc.), you should investigate the BLAS routine dsdot to compute the dot-product in double precision.

The main reason that we don't use this method is that although A has very few non-zeros, L can have a lot. In three dimensions the amount of *fill-in* (extra non-zeros in L) is particularly bad; *direct solvers* that take this approach generally fail on 3D problems from lack of memory.

Incomplete Cholesky tackles this problem with a very simple idea: whenever the Cholesky algorithm tries to create a new non-zero in a location that is zero in A, cancel it—keep it as zero. On the one hand, the resulting L is just as sparse as A, and memory is no longer an issue. On the other hand, we deliberately made errors: $A \neq LL^T$ now. *However*, hopefully the incomplete factorization is close enough to A that doing the solves in Equation (4.13) is close enough to applying A^{-1} so that we have a useful preconditioner for PCG!

Technically, performing incomplete Cholesky only allowing non-zeros in L where there are non-zeros in A is called level zero: IC(0). There are variations that allow a limited number of non-zeros in other locations, but we will not broach that topic here.

To make this more precise, IC(0) constructs a lower-triangular matrix L with the same non-zero pattern as the lower triangle of A, such that $LL^T = A$ wherever A is non-zero. The only error is that LL^T is non-zero in some other locations where A is zero.

Assume we order our grid cells (and the corresponding rows and columns of A) lexicographically, say along the i-dimension first, then the j-dimension, and finally the k-dimension.[5] Suppose we split A up into its strict lower triangle F and diagonal D:

$$A = F + D + F^T.$$

Then, it can be shown for the particular A we're solving—though we won't show it here—that the IC(0) factor L is of the form

$$L = FE^{-1} + E,$$

where E is a diagonal matrix. That is, all we need to compute and store are the diagonal entries of L, and we can infer the others just from A!

Crunching through the algebra gives the following formulas for computing the entries along the diagonal of E. In two dimensions,

$$E_{(i,j)} = \sqrt{A_{(i,j),(i,j)} - (A_{(i-1,j),(i,j)}/E_{(i-1,j)})^2 - (A_{(i,j-1),(i,j)}/E_{(i,j-1)})^2}.$$

---

[5]It turns out that the order in which we take the dimensions doesn't actually change anything for IC(0) applied to our particular matrix.

In three dimensions,

$$E_{(i,j,k)} =$$

$$\sqrt{\begin{aligned} & A_{(i,j,k),(i,j,k)} - \left(A_{(i-1,j,k),(i,j,k)}/E_{(i-1,j,k)}\right)^2 \\ & - \left(A_{(i,j-1,k),(i,j,k)}/E_{(i,j-1,k)}\right)^2 - \left(A_{(i,j,k-1),(i,j,k)}/E_{(i,j,k-1)}\right)^2. \end{aligned}}$$

In these equations, we replace terms referring to a non-fluid cell (or cell that lies off the grid) with zero. Also note that the superscript two is an exponent, nothing to do with time steps: those entries of E are squared.

4.3.4 Modified Incomplete Cholesky

Incomplete Cholesky is a great preconditioner that can effectively reduce our iteration count when solving the pressure equations and is often the default choice when preconditioning any general matrix. But, for almost no extra cost, we can do better for our particular A! A slight tweak to IC, *modified* incomplete Cholesky (MIC), scales significantly better: if our grid is n grid cells wide, we'll only need $O(n^{1/2})$ iterations, with a fairly low hidden constant. Modified incomplete cholesky works exactly like incomplete Cholesky, except instead of discarding those unwanted non-zeros, we account for them by adding them to the diagonal of L.

To make this more precise, MIC(0) constructs a lower-triangular matrix L with the same non-zero pattern as the lower triangle of A, such that

- The off-diagonal non-zero entries of A are equal to the corresponding ones of (LL^T).

- The sum of each row of A is equal to the sum of each row of (LL^T).

This boils down to a slightly different calculation for the diagonal entries: the modified L is also equal to $FE^{-1} + E$, just for a different E. In two dimensions,

$$E_{(i,j)} = \sqrt{\begin{aligned} & A_{(i,j),(i,j)} - \left(A_{(i-1,j),(i,j)}/E_{(i-1,j)}\right)^2 - \left(A_{(i,j-1),(i,j)}/E_{(i,j-1)}\right)^2 \\ & - A_{(i-1,j),(i,j)} A_{(i-1,j),(i-1,j+1)}/E_{(i-1,j)}^2 \\ & - A_{(i,j-1),(i,j)} A_{(i,j-1),(i+1,j-1)}/E_{(i,j-1)}^2 \end{aligned}}$$

In three dimensions,

$$E_{(i,j,k)} = \sqrt{\begin{aligned}
& A_{(i,j,k),(i,j,k)} - \left(A_{(i-1,j,k),(i,j,k)}/E_{(i-1,j,k)}\right)^2 \\
& - \left(A_{(i,j-1,k),(i,j,k)}/E_{(i,j-1,k)}\right)^2 - \left(A_{(i,j,k-1),(i,j,k)}/E_{(i,j,k-1)}\right)^2 \\
& - A_{(i-1,j,k),(i,j,k)} \\
& \quad \times \left(A_{(i-1,j,k),(i-1,j+1,k)} + A_{(i-1,j,k),(i-1,j,k+1)}\right)/E^2_{(i-1,j,k)} \\
& - A_{(i,j-1,k),(i,j,k)} \\
& \quad \times \left(A_{(i,j-1,k),(i+1,j-1,k)} + A_{(i,j-1,k),(i,j-1,k+1)}\right)/E^2_{(i,j-1,k)} \\
& - A_{(i,j,k-1),(i,j,k)} \\
& \quad \times \left(A_{(i,j,k-1),(i+1,j,k-1)} + A_{(i,j,k-1),(i,j+1,k-1)}\right)/E^2_{(i,j,k-1)}
\end{aligned}}$$

If you're curious, the intuition behind MIC (and why it outperforms IC) lies in a Fourier analysis of the problem. If you decompose the error as a superposition of Fourier modes, some low frequency (smooth) and some

- Set tuning constant $\tau = 0.97$ and safety constant $\sigma = 0.25$
- For i=1 to nx, j=1 to ny, k=1 to nz:
  - If cell (i,j,k) is fluid:
    - Set $e = \mathtt{Adiag}_{i,j,k} - \left(\mathtt{Aplusi}_{i-1,j,k} * \mathtt{precon}_{i-1,j,k}\right)^2$
      $$- \left(\mathtt{Aplusj}_{i,j-1,k} * \mathtt{precon}_{i,j-1,k}\right)^2$$
      $$- \left(\mathtt{Aplusk}_{i,j,k-1} * \mathtt{precon}_{i,j,k-1}\right)^2$$
      $$-\tau \Big[\mathtt{Aplusi}_{i-1,j,k} * \left(\mathtt{Aplusj}_{i-1,j,k}\right.$$
      $$\left. + \mathtt{Aplusk}_{i-1,j,k}\right)$$
      $$* \mathtt{precon}^2_{i-1,j,k}$$
      $$+ \mathtt{Aplusj}_{i,j-1,k}$$
      $$* \left(\mathtt{Aplusi}_{i,j-1,k} + \mathtt{Aplusk}_{i,j-1,k}\right)$$
      $$* \mathtt{precon}^2_{i,j-1,k}$$
      $$+ \mathtt{Aplusk}_{i,j,k-1}$$
      $$* \left(\mathtt{Aplusi}_{i,j,k-1} + \mathtt{Aplusj}_{i,j,k-1}\right)$$
      $$* \mathtt{precon}^2_{i,j,k-1}\Big]$$
  - If $e < \sigma \mathtt{Adiag}_{i,j,k}$, set $e = \mathtt{Adiag}_{i,j,k}$
  - $\mathtt{precon}_{i,j,k} = 1/\sqrt{e}$

Figure 4.6. The calculation of the MIC(0) preconditioner in three dimensions.

high frequency (sharp), it turns out IC is only effective at removing the high-frequency components of error. On the other hand, MIC is forced to match the action of A on the lowest frequency mode of all, the constant, and thus is more effective at all frequencies.[6]

In practice, you can squeeze out even better performance by taking a weighted average between the regular incomplete Cholesky formula and the modified one, typically weighting with 0.97 or more (getting closer to 1 for larger grids). See Figure 4.6 for pseudocode to implement this in three dimensions. We actually compute and store the *reciprocals* of the diagonal entries of E in a grid variable called `precon`, to avoid divides when applying the preconditioner.

The pseudocode in Figure 4.6 additionally has a built-in safety tolerance. In some situations, such as a single-cell–wide line of fluid cells surrounded by solids, IC(0) and MIC(0) become exact—except that A is singular in this case: the exact Cholesky factorization doesn't exist.

- (First solve $Lq = r$)
- For i=1 to nx, j=1 to ny, k=1 to nz:
  - If cell (i, j, k) is fluid:
    - Set
      $$t = r_{i,j,k} - \texttt{Aplusi}_{i-1,j,k} * \texttt{precon}_{i-1,j,k} * q_{i-1,j,k}$$
      $$- \texttt{Aplusj}_{i,j-1,k} * \texttt{precon}_{i,j-1,k} * q_{i,j-1,k}$$
      $$- \texttt{Aplusk}_{i,j,k-1} * \texttt{precon}_{i,j,k-1} * q_{i,j,k-1}$$
    - $q_{i,j,k} = t * \texttt{precon}_{i,j,k}$
- (Next solve $L^T z = q$)
- For i=nx down to 1, j=ny down to 1, k=nz down to 1:
  - If cell (i, j, k) is fluid:
    - Set
      $$t = q_{i,j,k} - \texttt{Aplusi}_{i,j,k} * \texttt{precon}_{i,j,k} * z_{i+1,j,k}$$
      $$- \texttt{Aplusj}_{i,j,k} * \texttt{precon}_{i,j,k} * z_{i,j+1,k}$$
      $$- \texttt{Aplusk}_{i,j,k} * \texttt{precon}_{i,j,k} * z_{i,j,k+1}$$
    - $z_{i,j,k} = t * \texttt{precon}_{i,j,k}$

Figure 4.7. Applying the MIC(0) preconditioner in three dimensions ($z = Mr$).

---

[6]Continuing this train of thought, looking for methods that work well on all frequency components of the error can lead to multigrid that explicitly solves the equations at multiple resolutions.

This is manifested by hitting a zero or—when rounding error is factored in—very small value for e, and it can safely be cured by replacing that small value with, for example, the diagonal entry from A. This safety check also comes in handy if you want to solve more general linear systems, where the incomplete Cholesky factorization (and even more so the modified incomplete Cholesky factorization) may fail to exist without this check.

All that's left is how to apply the preconditioner, that is perform the triangular solves. This is outlined in Figure 4.7 for three dimensions.

Finally, before going on, I should note that the nesting of loops is an important issue for performance. Due to cache effects, it's far faster if you can arrange your loops to walk through memory sequentially. For example, if $p_{i,j,k}$ and $p_{i+1,j,k}$ are stored next to each other in memory, then the i loop should be innermost.

4.4 Projection

The $\texttt{project}(\Delta t, \vec{u})$ routine does the following:

- Calculate the negative divergence b (the right-hand side) with modifications at solid wall boundaries.
- Set the entries of A (stored in $\texttt{Adiag}$, etc.).
- Construct the MIC(0) preconditioner.
- Solve $Ap = b$ with MICCG(0), i.e., the PCG algorithm with MIC(0) as preconditioner.
- Compute the new velocities $\vec{u}^{n+1}$ according to the pressure-gradient update to $\vec{u}$.

We still haven't explained *why* this routine is called $\texttt{project}$. You can skip over this section if you're not interested.

If you recall from your linear algebra, a projection is a special type of linear operator such that if you apply it twice, you get the same result as applying it once. For example, a matrix P is a projection if $P^2 = P$. It turns out that our transformation from $\vec{u}$ to $\vec{u}^{n+1}$ is indeed a linear projection.[7]

If you want, you can trace through the steps to establish the linearity: the entries of b are linear combinations of the entries of $\vec{u}$, the pressures

---

[7]Technically speaking, if we have non-zero solid wall velocities then this is an affine transformation rather than a linear one, but it still is a projection. For the purpose of simplicity, we'll ignore this case here.

$p = A^{-1}b$ are linear combinations of the entries of d, and the new velocities $\vec{u}^{n+1}$ are linear combinations of $\vec{u}$ and p.

Physically, it's very obvious that this transformation has to be a projection. The resulting velocity field, $\vec{u}^{n+1}$, has discrete divergence equal to zero. So if we repeated the pressure step with this as input, we'd first evaluate $b = 0$, which would give constant pressures and no change to the velocity.

4.5   More Accurate Curved Boundaries

Reducing the geometry of the problem to just labeling grid cells as solid, fluid, or air can introduce major artifacts when the boundaries are actually at an angle or curved. For example, a solid slope becomes (in the eyes of the simulator) a sequence of flat stair steps: obviously water flows down stairs very differently than down an inclined slope. If you render an inclined slope but your water pools at regular intervals along it instead of flowing down, it looks terrible. As a general rule of thumb, you can only expect physically plausible motion for things the simulator can "see" (i.e., those that are taken into account in the numerical discretization of the physics), not details to which only the renderer has access.

To close out this chapter, we will focus on the issue of accurately accounting for solid boundaries that don't line up with the grid, as it also reveals an alternative and very useful view of the pressure projection step. Later, in Chapter 6 on water, we will also look at a more accurate treatment of the free surface.

The tricky part of handling solids that don't line up with the MAC grid is that the normal component of velocity is no longer conveniently stored on the grid: attempts to interpolate that component from the staggered u-, v-, and w-values and then constrain the interpolant to match the solid velocity have met with limited success.

One interesting approach is to replace the grid with an unstructured tetrahedral mesh, with a boundary that matches up with the solid surfaces: see for example Feldman et al. [Feldman et al. 05]. However, this carries with it the overhead of constructing and working with an unstructured mesh and requires that the mesh scale down to the smallest features you want to see present in the simulation. As we'll see soon, we can get around these problems with just a regular Cartesian grid if we rethink our discretization.

4.5.1 The Finite Volume Method

One solution is to be found in the *finite volume* method, mentioned earlier. Here we discretize the integral form of the incompressibility condition:

$$\iint_{\partial C} \vec{u} \cdot \hat{n} = 0,$$

where ∂C is the boundary of a *control volume* C. In particular, in the interior of the flow, we take each grid cell as a control volume and approximate the boundary integral over each face of the cell as the area Δx^2 of the face times the normal component of velocity stored at the face center. At the boundary, it gets more interesting: if a solid wall cuts through a grid cell, we take just the fluid part of the cell as the control volume. This means that the area of some of the faces will be reduced to just the fraction of each face that lies in the fluid. In addition, a term corresponding to the part of the solid wall boundary that cuts through the cell can be added. The equation for such a *cut cell* is then

$$\begin{aligned}
-A_{i-1/2,j,k}u_{i-1/2,j,k} + A_{i+1/2,j,k}u_{i+1/2,j,k} \\
-A_{i,j-1/2,k}v_{i,j-1/2,k} + A_{i,j+1/2,k}v_{i,j+1/2,k} \\
-A_{i,j,k-1/2}w_{i,j,k-1/2} + A_{i,j,k+1/2}w_{i,j,k+1/2} \\
+A_{\text{solid}}(\vec{u}_{\text{solid}} \cdot \hat{n}) = 0,
\end{aligned} \tag{4.14}$$

where the A terms are the (possibly fractional) face areas. Plugging in the same pressure gradient as before results in a symmetric positive semidefinite linear system of the same structure as before (and solvable with exactly the same code) but with modified non-zero entries near boundaries.

It's worth pointing out that in this discretization, unlike the voxelized version from earlier on, pressures inside the solid walls—precisely those that are involved in velocity updates near the wall—appear as actual unknowns in the equations and cannot be simply eliminated as ghost values as before. Indeed, it's these extra unknowns that ultimately allow a more accurate solution.

However, this use of pressures inside the walls also means that this approach can't perfectly handle thin solids, solids that are thinner than a grid cell—including most models of cloth, for example. Ideally there should be no direct coupling of pressures or velocities on either side of a fixed, thin solid. In these cases the voxelized pressure-solve approach, which only uses ghost pressures across solid wall faces, may be preferable—refer to Guendelman et al. [Guendelman et al. 05] for a full description of using voxelized thin solids in fluid simulations.

Another case where the finite volume approach is less than satisfactory is for small objects, on the order of one grid cell. Depending on exactly where they lie relative to the grid, they may block a face and thus have a big impact on the pressure solve or may not intersect any face and be entirely invisible to the pressure solve. This is similar to the aliasing problem that can occur when using simple point samples to image small objects that may randomly appear or not in the image depending on where they lie with respect to the point samples. It is thus desirable to have a more volumetric approach that can somehow average over the interior of each grid cell.

4.5.2   The Variational Approach

There is indeed another approach with this and some other particularly appealing properties which we will take in this book. This is the variational form of the pressure projection introduced by Batty et al. [Batty et al. 07]. It too ends up creating a linear system of the same structure, with pressure unknowns inside the walls but derives slightly different coefficients in the matrix.

One intuition behind this method begins with our fluid-blob mental picture, which we introduced in Chapter 1. The pressure force, responsible for making sure blobs don't crowd together and overlap or that vacuums don't open up between blobs, is essentially a *contact* force. In the incompressible limit, we have eliminated sound waves, which means this contact force must be perfectly inelastic: no compression or rebound is permitted. Going back to the basics of collision processing between regular particles, you may remember that a perfectly inelastic contact force is one that dissipates as much kinetic energy as possible (whereas a perfectly *elastic* contact conserves kinetic energy). Try working it out for yourself! Take two particles, with masses m_1 and m_2, pre-contact velocities $\vec{u}_1^{old}$ and $\vec{u}_2^{old}$, and a contact impulse $J\hat{n}$ between them (acting in the normal direction). The post-contact velocities are

$$\vec{u}_1^{\mathrm{new}} = \vec{u}_1^{\mathrm{old}} + \frac{1}{m_1}J\hat{n},$$

$$\vec{u}_2^{\mathrm{new}} = \vec{u}_2^{\mathrm{old}} - \frac{1}{m_2}J\hat{n}.$$

Therefore the change in kinetic energy due to the contact impulse is

$$\Delta KE = \left(\tfrac{1}{2}m_1\|\vec{u}_1^{\text{new}}\|^2 + \tfrac{1}{2}m_2\|\vec{u}_2^{\text{new}}\|^2\right) - \left(\tfrac{1}{2}m_1\|\vec{u}_1^{\text{old}}\|^2 + \tfrac{1}{2}m_2\|\vec{u}_2^{\text{old}}\|^2\right).$$

Here and in the following, the superscript "2" indicates squaring. If you find the scalar J that minimizes ΔKE (dissipating the most energy possible), you will find it causes a perfectly inelastic collision with $\vec{u}_1^{\text{new}} \cdot \hat{n} = \vec{u}_2^{\text{new}} \cdot \hat{n}$.

Generalizing this to incompressible fluids, we begin with the kinetic energy of a fluid, an integral version of the familiar $\tfrac{1}{2}mv^2$:

$$KE = \iiint_\Omega \tfrac{1}{2}\rho\|\vec{u}\|^2.$$

Here Ω is the fluid-filled domain. Note that we have included the density ρ inside the integral to be able to handle variable density fluids—this will come in handy later on in the book.

The change in energy can be measured as the difference in kinetic energy and, if solid wall boundaries are present, the work exchanged between the solid and the fluid. The first term, based on the intermediate velocity $\vec{u}$ and the pressure-updated final velocity $\vec{u}^{n+1}$, is

$$\iiint_\Omega \tfrac{1}{2}\rho\|\vec{u}^{n+1}\|^2 - \iiint_\Omega \tfrac{1}{2}\rho\|\vec{u}\|^2.$$

The work exchanged between the fluid and the solid is equal to the integral of applied force dotted with the displacement (over the solid boundary S). The force term, per unit area, is nothing more than pressure times the normal direction, $p\hat{n}$, using here the convention that the normal points out from the fluid into the solid. The displacement can be estimated as $\Delta t\vec{u}_{\text{solid}}$ (note that this term then vanishes if the solid is not moving!). Adding this in gives the total change in kinetic energy of the system:

$$\Delta KE = \iiint_\Omega \tfrac{1}{2}\rho\|\vec{u}^{n+1}\|^2 - \iiint_\Omega \tfrac{1}{2}\rho\|\vec{u}\|^2 + \iint_S p\hat{n} \cdot \Delta t\vec{u}_{\text{solid}}.$$

Finally, we seek out the pressure, constrained to be zero on the free surface part of the boundary F, that minimizes this (i.e., dissipates the maximum possible energy). As is shown in Appendix B, such a pressure exactly solves the regular PDE-form of the incompressibility projection:

$$\nabla \cdot \frac{\Delta t}{\rho} \nabla p = \nabla \cdot \vec{u}, \qquad \text{inside } \Omega;$$

$$p = 0, \qquad \text{on } F; \qquad (4.15)$$

$$\frac{\Delta t}{\rho} \nabla p \cdot \hat{n} = \vec{u} \cdot \hat{n} - \vec{u}_{\text{solid}} \cdot \hat{n}, \qquad \text{on } S.$$

This is true even if the density of the fluid varies throughout the domain. For a derivation, see Appendix B. The most important thing about this equivalence is that the solid wall boundary condition doesn't explicitly appear in the minimization form: this will let us capture it in the discretization with ease.

4.5.3 The Discrete Minimization

Our approach is to discretize the change in kinetic energy ΔKE, based on the usual MAC grid velocity field and discrete pressure update, and then solve for the discrete pressure that minimizes the discrete energy.

We'll begin with the internal kinetic energy of the fluid. Writing it out in components we have

$$KE = \iiint_\Omega \tfrac{1}{2}\rho \left(u^2 + v^2 + w^2 \right)$$

$$= \iiint_\Omega \tfrac{1}{2}\rho u^2 + \iiint_\Omega \tfrac{1}{2}\rho v^2 + \iiint_\Omega \tfrac{1}{2}\rho w^2.$$

We will approximate each of these three integrals separately; let's focus on the first, involving u^2. We'll break it up into a sum over cells centered on each of the u samples, which as you recall are stored at staggered locations $(i+1/2, j, k)$. Note that these are offset from the usual grid cells centered on (i, j, k), so we will call them u-cells. Finally, we need the volume $V_{i+1/2,j,k}$ of the fluid contained in each u-cell and the average fluid density $\rho_{i+1/2,j,k}$ in the u-cell (we'll discuss how to find this average for the variable density case later; for now you can just treat it as a constant ρ). Our final approximation of the u^2 integral is

$$\iiint_\Omega \tfrac{1}{2}\rho u^2 \approx \sum_{i,j,k} \tfrac{1}{2}\rho_{i+1/2,j,k} V_{i+1/2,j,k} u^2_{i+1/2,j,k}.$$

The other integrals, of $\frac{1}{2}\rho v^2$ and $\frac{1}{2}\rho w^2$, can be similarly approximated using the fluid volumes $V_{i,j+1/2,k}$ and $V_{i,j,k+1/2}$ and average densities in the similarly defined v- and w-cells. Just as with the finite volume discretization, the new kinetic energy, based on the updated velocities everywhere the cell volumes are non-zero, will probably involve pressures inside solids.

While the cell volumes entirely in the interior of the fluid are exactly Δx^3 (and are zero when entirely outside of the fluid), they pose an interesting problem where solids cut through the grid. Exact clipping formulas for polyhedra are available, though devilishly hard to get right. However, it is not essential that the answers are exact: as will become obvious below, the voxelized discretization that began the chapter corresponds to choosing either 0 or Δx^3 as the weight in a binary fashion. Anything more accurate— even just using the same binary decisions but summed over a $2\times2\times2$ supersampling of each cell—will help significantly, and extremely high accuracy may be pointless as other errors in the discretization will dominate. Later in Chapter 6, when we cover signed distance functions, we will find some particular simple approximations that nevertheless can be quite accurate for smooth geometry.

Continuing on, let's turn to the work exchanged with solids. Presented above it is a surface integral, which is a bit clumsy to discretize on a volume grid. Therefore, we change it to a volume integral with the divergence theorem:

$$W = \iint_S p\hat{n} \cdot \Delta t \vec{u}_{\text{solid}} = \Delta t \iiint_\Omega \nabla \cdot (p\vec{u}_{\text{solid}}).$$

This may appear strange at first sight: the solid velocity isn't defined in the fluid! However, the theorem holds true for any reasonable extrapolation of solid velocity into the fluid and poses no difficulty for numerical implementation: either the velocity is naturally defined everywhere, as is the case for rigid motions, or can be extrapolated as the velocity on the closest point of the object's surface. This volume integral still isn't quite in a convenient form, since on the MAC grid we store pressures at different locations than velocity. Thus we use the product rule of differentiation to get

$$W = \Delta t \iiint_\Omega \nabla p \cdot \vec{u}_{\text{solid}} + \Delta t \iiint_\Omega p\nabla \cdot \vec{u}_{\text{solid}}.$$

It should be pointed out that the second integral, involving the divergence of solid velocity, is exactly zero for rigid-body motions.

Now we'll take the same approach to discretizing the work as in discretizing the kinetic energy, introducing also the volume of fluid $V_{i,j,k}$ in a p-cell, which is the usual grid cell with a pressure value at its center. The discrete estimate of work is

$$W \approx \Delta t \sum_{i,j,k} V_{i+1/2,j,k} \frac{p_{i+1,j,k} - p_{i,j,k}}{\Delta x} u_{i+1/2,j,k}^{\text{solid}}$$

$$+ \Delta t \sum_{i,j,k} V_{i,j+1/2,k} \frac{p_{i,j+1,k} - p_{i,j,k}}{\Delta x} v_{i,j+1/2,k}^{\text{solid}}$$

$$+ \Delta t \sum_{i,j,k} V_{i,j,k+1/2} \frac{p_{i,j,k+1} - p_{i,j,k}}{\Delta x} w_{i,j,k+1/2}^{\text{solid}}$$

$$+ \Delta t \sum_{i,j,k} V_{i,j,k} p_{i,j,k} \left(\frac{u_{i+1/2,j,k}^{\text{solid}} - u_{i+1/2,j,k}^{\text{solid}} + v_{i,j+1/2,k}^{\text{solid}} - v_{i,j+1/2,k}^{\text{solid}}}{\Delta x} \right.$$

$$\left. + \frac{w_{i,j,k+1/2}^{\text{solid}} - w_{i,j,k+1/2}^{\text{solid}}}{\Delta x} \right).$$

$$(4.16)$$

With this we are set: just from the various cell volumes we have a good discretization of the total change in energy of the system.

The next step, conceptually, is to take this change in energy as a function of the (still unknown) discrete pressure values and subsequently solve for the discrete pressure that minimizes it. We are thus discretizing the minimization form of the pressure projection, not the PDE form, and therefore needn't worry about the solid wall boundaries: they will take care of themselves automatically!

It's not hard to see that pressure values appear only linearly in the work W, linearly in the updated fluid velocities, and thus quadratically in the discrete kinetic energy—in fact, the discrete kinetic energy is just a weighted sum of squares, and since the weights are non-negative (because the fluid density and the cell volumes are non-negative), we expect the problem to be well-posed—modulo the compatibility condition, that the integral of the normal component of solid velocities should be zero in the absence of free surfaces, which we will return to in the last section. To find the minimizing pressure all we need do is take the gradient of the change in energy with respect to the pressure values, set it to zero, and solve the resulting linear system.

Let's take the derivative of the change in energy with respect to pressure $p_{i,j,k}$ and set it to zero:

$$\frac{\partial KE^{n+1}}{\partial p_{i,j,k}} - \frac{\partial KE}{\partial p_{i,j,k}} + \frac{\partial W}{\partial p_{i,j,k}} = 0.$$

Pressure doesn't appear in the middle term, the intermediate kinetic energy, so that term drops out. Referring back to the discrete sums above, we get the following gigantic equation:

$$\rho_{i+1/2,j,k} V_{i+1/2,j,k} \frac{\Delta t}{\rho_{i+1/2,j,k}\Delta x} \left(u_{i+1/2,j,k} - \frac{\Delta t}{\rho_{i+1/2,j,k}} \frac{p_{i+1,j,k} - p_{i,j,k}}{\Delta x} \right)$$

$$- \rho_{i-1/2,j,k} V_{i-1/2,j,k} \frac{\Delta t}{\rho_{i-1/2,j,k}\Delta x} \left(u_{i-1/2,j,k} - \frac{\Delta t}{\rho_{i-1/2,j,k}} \frac{p_{i,j,k} - p_{i-1,j,k}}{\Delta x} \right)$$

$$+ \rho_{i,j+1/2,k} V_{i,j+1/2,k} \frac{\Delta t}{\rho_{i,j+1/2,k}\Delta x} \left(v_{i,j+1/2,k} - \frac{\Delta t}{\rho_{i,j+1/2,k}} \frac{p_{i,j+1,k} - p_{i,j,k}}{\Delta x} \right)$$

$$- \rho_{i,j-1/2,k} V_{i,j-1/2,k} \frac{\Delta t}{\rho_{i,j-1/2,k}\Delta x} \left(v_{i,j-1/2,k} - \frac{\Delta t}{\rho_{i,j-1/2,k}} \frac{p_{i,j,k} - p_{i,j-1,k}}{\Delta x} \right)$$

$$+ \rho_{i,j,k+1/2} V_{i,j,k+1/2} \frac{\Delta t}{\rho_{i,j,k+1/2}\Delta x} \left(w_{i,j,k+1/2} - \frac{\Delta t}{\rho_{i,j,k+1/2}} \frac{p_{i,j,k+1} - p_{i,j,k}}{\Delta x} \right)$$

$$- \rho_{i,j,k-1/2} V_{i,j,k-1/2} \frac{\Delta t}{\rho_{i,j,k-1/2}\Delta x} \left(w_{i,j,k-1/2} - \frac{\Delta t}{\rho_{i,j,k-1/2}} \frac{p_{i,j,k} - p_{i,j,k-1}}{\Delta x} \right)$$

$$- V_{i+1/2,j,k} \frac{\Delta t}{\Delta x} u^{\text{solid}}_{i+1/2,j,k} + V_{i-1/2,j,k} \frac{\Delta t}{\Delta x} u^{\text{solid}}_{i-1/2,j,k}$$

$$- V_{i,j+1/2,k} \frac{\Delta t}{\Delta x} v^{\text{solid}}_{i,j+1/2,k} + V_{i,j-1/2,k} \frac{\Delta t}{\Delta x} v^{\text{solid}}_{i,j-1/2,k}$$

$$- V_{i,j,k+1/2} \frac{\Delta t}{\Delta x} w^{\text{solid}}_{i,j,k+1/2} + V_{i,j,k-1/2} \frac{\Delta t}{\Delta x} w^{\text{solid}}_{i,j,k-1/2}$$

$$+ V_{i,j,k} \frac{\Delta t}{\Delta x} \left(u^{\text{solid}}_{i+1/2,j,k} - u^{\text{solid}}_{i+1/2,j,k} \right.$$

$$\left. + v^{\text{solid}}_{i,j+1/2,k} - v^{\text{solid}}_{i,j+1/2,k} w^{\text{solid}}_{i,j,k+1/2} - w^{\text{solid}}_{i,j,k,+1/2} \right) = 0.$$

Dividing through by Δt and rearranging gives a familiar (though still gigantic) form for the linear equation:

$$
\begin{aligned}
\frac{\Delta t}{\Delta x^2} &
\left[
\begin{array}{l}
\left(\dfrac{V_{i+1/2,j,k}}{\rho_{i+1/2,j,k}} + \dfrac{V_{i-1/2,j,k}}{\rho_{i-1/2,j,k}} + \dfrac{V_{i,j+1/2,k}}{\rho_{i,j+1/2,k}} + \dfrac{V_{i,j-1/2,k}}{\rho_{i,j-1/2,k}} \right. \\[2mm]
\left. \qquad\qquad + \dfrac{V_{i,j,k+1/2}}{\rho_{i,j,k+1/2}} + \dfrac{V_{i,j,k-1/2}}{\rho_{i,j,k-1/2}} \right) p_{i,j,k} \\[2mm]
- \dfrac{V_{i+1/2,j,k}}{\rho_{i+1/2,j,k}} p_{i+1,j,k} - \dfrac{V_{i-1/2,j,k}}{\rho_{i-1/2,j,k}} p_{i-1,j,k} - \dfrac{V_{i,j+1/2,k}}{\rho_{i,j+1/2,k}} p_{i,j+1,k} \\[2mm]
- \dfrac{V_{i,j-1/2,k}}{\rho_{i,j-1/2,k}} p_{i,j-1,k} - \dfrac{V_{i,j,k+1/2}}{\rho_{i,j,k+1/2}} p_{i,j,k+1} - \dfrac{V_{i,j,k-1/2}}{\rho_{i,j,k-1/2}} p_{i,j,k-1}
\end{array}
\right] \\[4mm]
&= -\frac{1}{\Delta x}
\left[
\begin{array}{l}
V_{i+1/2,j,k} u_{i+1/2,j,k} - V_{i-1/2,j,k} u_{i-1/2,j,k} \\[1mm]
+ V_{i,j+1/2,k} v_{i,j+1/2,k} - V_{i,j-1/2,k} v_{i,j-1/2,k} \\[1mm]
+ V_{i,j,k+1/2} w_{i,j,k+1/2} - V_{i,j,k-1/2} w_{i,j,k-1/2}
\end{array}
\right] \\[4mm]
&+ \frac{1}{\Delta x}
\left[
\begin{array}{l}
(V_{i+1/2,j,k} - V_{i,j,k}) u^{\mathrm{solid}}_{i+1/2,j,k} - (V_{i-1/2,j,k} - V_{i,j,k}) u^{\mathrm{solid}}_{i-1/2,j,k} \\[1mm]
+ (V_{i,j+1/2,k} - V_{i,j,k}) v^{\mathrm{solid}}_{i,j+1/2,k} - (V_{i,j-1/2,k} - V_{i,j,k}) v^{\mathrm{solid}}_{i,j-1/2,k} \\[1mm]
+ (V_{i,j,k+1/2} - V_{i,j,k}) w^{\mathrm{solid}}_{i,j,k+1/2} - (V_{i,j,k-1/2} - V_{i,j,k}) w^{\mathrm{solid}}_{i,j,k-1/2}
\end{array}
\right].
\end{aligned}
$$

Particularly, if you rescale the cell volumes to be dimensionless volume fractions—i.e., 1 for a full fluid cell, 0 for an empty cell—this can be seen to be just a weighted, variable density version of the first discrete equations we derived. Exactly the same matrix structure and PCG algorithm may be employed to solve the system, and of course the pressure gradient used to update the velocities is identical.

4.5.4 More on Volume Fractions

It should be clear from this form of the equations that there may be troubles when volume fractions get too small, particularly considering we are using PCG to only approximately solve the equations. It can be worthwhile to detect fractions less than some tolerance, say 0.01, and either round them up to be equal to the tolerance or round them down to exactly zero. (Of course, if you are using simple $2 \times 2 \times 2$ supersampling to estimate volume fractions, you will never generate fractions between 0 and 1/8.)

The solid velocity terms in the right-hand-side are particularly interesting. Until now we haven't got into the details of how scripted solids can be brought into the simulation. Here it is apparent they can be added in almost a compositing-like fashion, with the volume fractions playing the role of the alpha channel in image compositing. Each solid can estimate the fraction of the cells it leaves open for fluid or other solids, along with the associated velocity values (akin to the RGB channels in image compositing); these are blended together in the natural way, e.g. multiplying the fractions and averaging the velocities according to one minus each fraction, thus allowing several solids to contribute to an average velocity in one grid cell.

Taking this compositing idea even further, there are artistic uses for applying filters such as Gaussian blur on the solid volume fractions (thus "feathering" the hard edges of the solid to soften its impact) or rescaling the fractions to make the solid slightly "transparent" to the fluid. The complement $(1 - V)$ of a blurred/transparent solid gives a soft "mask" in which fluid is gently constrained to stay, which can be particularly useful for controlling fluids in an animation.

4.5.5   Velocity Extrapolation

To finish off the section, here is a reminder that only the velocity samples with non-zero fluid fractions will be updated. The other velocities are untouched by the pressure and thus may be completely unreliable. As mentioned in Chapter 3, advection may rely on interpolating velocity from these untouched values: clearly we need to do something about them. Also, as mentioned earlier, for inviscid flow it's wrong to simply use the solid velocity there: only the normal component of solid velocity has any bearing on the fluid. Therefore it is usual to extrapolate velocity values from the well-defined fluid samples to the rest of the grid; more on this when we cover level sets in Chapter 6.

4.6   The Compatibility Condition

Naturally a fluid in a solid container cannot simultaneously be incompressible and satisfy solid velocity conditions that are acting to change the volume, a simple result of the divergence theorem:

$$\iiint_\Omega \nabla \cdot \vec{u} = \iint_{\partial\Omega} \vec{u} \cdot \hat{n}.$$

This is the compatibility condition, without which the PDE for pressure has no solution. (Note of course that if there is a free surface as well, no condition is needed.)

More precisely, we want the discrete linear system to have a solution. Even if the solid wall velocity does exactly integrate to zero, once discretized on a grid there may be numerical errors that cause the linear solve to fail. Thus we need a routine which can "correct" the right-hand side of the linear system to make it consistent.

We can view this as a pure linear algebra problem, as outlined by Guendelman et al. [Guendelman et al. 05]. That is, given a singular A and a vector b, we want to remove from b any components which lie outside the range of A: the modified linear system $Ax = \bar{b}$ then has a solution. If A is symmetric, which it is in our case, this is equivalent to removing components from b that lie in the null-space of A. Luckily, for the pressure problem on a MAC grid, this null-space is very simple: for every set of connected grid cells with no free surface conditions, there is a null-space basis vector consisting of unit pressures in those voxels. By "connected," we mean with respect to the graph of the matrix A: two grid cells are connected if there is a non-zero entry in A corresponding to the pair; finding these connected sets is a simple graph traversal problem. Note that the sets are necessarily disjoint, so each of the null-space vectors we find is orthogonal to the rest. Therefore we can efficiently remove the incompatibilities in b by orthogonal projection. Boiled down to basics, this simply means adding up the entries of b in the set, dividing by the number of entries, and subtracting this mean off of each entry. It is imperative here to use double precision floating-point in calculating the sum, as otherwise the accumulated rounding errors can seriously undermine the method (necessitating repeating the process and/or subtracting the sum off a single randomly chosen entry). Also note that this process works for both the classic voxelized solve and the more accurate variational method from the previous section. From a physical standpoint, this causes us to find a solution that strikes a balance between respecting the boundary conditions and staying divergence-free.

–II–
Different Types of Fluids

– 5 –
Smoke

5.1 Temperature and Smoke Concentration

The first visual fluid phenomena we will consider is smoke, loosely following the standard reference papers by Foster and Metaxas [Foster and Metaxas 97] and by Fedkiw et al. [Fedkiw et al. 01], with some additional capabilities added. Our fluid in this case is the air in which the smoke particles are suspended. To model the most important effects of smoke, we need two extra fluid variables: the temperature T of the air and the concentration s of smoke particles—what we actually can see. Similar phenomena, such as vapor, can be modeled in much the same way. Generally we'll try to keep to SI units of Kelvin for temperature and keep s a number between 0 (no smoke) and 1 (as thick as possible). Also keep in mind that it's crucial to simulate *all* the air in the simulation, not just the regions with $s > 0$: a lot of the characteristic swirly behavior you see in smoke depends on enforcing the divergence-free constraint in nearby clear regions of air.

Before getting to how these variables will influence the velocity of the air in the next few sections, let's work out how T and s should evolve. It should be immediately apparent that temperature and soot particles are both advected with the fluid, i.e., we'll be using the material derivatives DT/Dt and Ds/Dt to describe them.[1] This gives us the simplest possible equations,

$$\frac{DT}{Dt} = 0,$$
$$\frac{Ds}{Dt} = 0$$

and will be the first step of a numerical method: when we advect $\vec{u}$, we also advect T and s. Typically we would discretize both variables at cell centers, where the pressure values lie.

---

[1] The story for temperature, at least, can be rather more complicated when full thermodynamics are considered. However, the assumption of incompressible fluid flow abstracts away most of the interaction between heat, pressure, density, etc.

The boundary conditions for advection can vary. As we saw earlier, these arise in the semi-Lagrangian method in terms of which values should be used when interpolating from non-fluid grid cells or when tracing outside the bounds of the grid. For insulated solids it makes sense to extrapolate T-values from the nearest point in the fluid; for solids that should conduct their heat to the flow, the solid's own temperature can be used. Unless a solid is a source of smoke, like a fire, and can supply a sensible s-value, it should be extrapolated from the fluid. At open boundaries, both T and s should be taken to be "ambient" values—typically T on the order of 273 K and $s = 0$.

To make things interesting, we generally add volume sources to the domain: regions where, at each time step, we add heat and smoke. In the PDE form this could be represented as

$$\frac{DT}{Dt} = r_T(\vec{x})(T_{\text{target}}(\vec{x}) - T),$$
$$\frac{Ds}{Dt} = r_s(\vec{x}),$$

where r_T and r_s are functions that control the rate at which we add heat and smoke—which should be zero outside of sources—and T_{target} gives the target temperature at a source. This can be implemented at each grid point inside a source as an update after advection:

$$T_{ijk}^{\text{new}} = T_{ijk} + (1 - e^{-r_T \Delta t})(T_{\text{target}} - T_{ijk}),$$
$$s_{ijk}^{\text{new}} = s_{ijk} + r_s \Delta t.$$

For additional detail, all of these source values might be modulated by an animated volume texture. To help avoid excesses due to poor choices of parameters, the smoke concentration might also be capped at a maximum concentration of 1.

Another useful animation control is to allow for decay of one or both fields: multiplying all values in a field by $e^{-d\Delta t}$ for a decay rate d. This isn't particularly grounded in real physics, but it is a simple way to mimic effects such as heat loss due to radiation.

Heat and smoke concentration both can diffuse as well, where very small-scale phenomena such as conduction or Brownian motion, together with slightly larger-scale processes such as turbulent mixing, serve to smooth out steep gradients. This can be modeled with a Laplacian term in the PDE, much like viscosity:

$$\frac{DT}{Dt} = k_T \nabla \cdot \nabla T,$$

$$\frac{Ds}{Dt} = k_s \nabla \cdot \nabla s.$$

Here k_T and k_s are non-negative diffusion constants. These could be discretized with finite differences in the obvious way, for example for temperature:

$$T_{i,j,k}^{\text{new}} = T_{i,j,k} + \Delta t k_T$$
$$\times \frac{T_{i+1,j,k} + T_{i,j+1,k} + T_{i,j,k+1} - 6T_{i,j,k} + T_{i-1,j,k} + T_{i,j-1,k} + T_{i,j,k-1}}{\Delta x^2}.$$

The same boundary conditions used in advection provide values of T (or s) at non-fluid points. However, this update is only stable and free of spurious oscillations if

$$\Delta t \lesssim \frac{\Delta x^2}{6k_T}.$$

If this condition cannot be met (or is so far from being met that breaking up the time step into several smaller substeps that do satisfy the condition is too slow), another simple option is to run a Gaussian blur on the variable. In fact, apart from boundary conditions, the *exact* solution to the so-called *heat equation*

$$\frac{\partial T}{\partial t} = k_T \nabla \cdot \nabla T \tag{5.1}$$

over a time Δt is a convolution with the following Gaussian filter, which in this context is called the *heat kernel*:

$$G(\vec{x}) = \frac{1}{(4\pi k_T \Delta t)^{3/2}} e^{-\frac{\|\vec{x}\|^2}{4k_T \Delta t}}.$$

The convolution can be evaluated efficiently dimension-by-dimension exploiting the separability of the Gaussian filter; see any reference on image processing for details.

Finally, before moving on, it should be noted that although this approach can work well for fairly diffuse situations, the grid resolution limits its ability to handle sharply defined smoke contours. In this case the particle methods discussed later, in Chapter 10, are preferable. Even if smoke concentration is tracked on a grid for the simulation, it still may be preferable to use particles for rendering—running millions of particles through the grid velocity field can provide finer details than really are resolved in the simulation itself!

5.2   Buoyancy

We now turn to the effect that T and s have on velocity. In this section we introduce a simplified buoyancy model commonly used in graphics.

We all know that hot air rises and cool air sinks; similarly it seems plausible that air laden with heavier soot particles will be pulled downwards by gravity. We can model this by replacing the acceleration $\vec{g}$ due to gravity in the momentum equation with a buoyant acceleration

$$\vec{b} = [\alpha s - \beta(T - T_{\text{amb}})]\,\vec{g},$$

where α and β are non-negative coefficients, and T_{amb} is the ambient temperature (say 273 K). Note that we take this proportional to the downward gravity vector—indeed, buoyancy doesn't exist in a zero-G environment. Also note that the formula reduces to zero wherever $s = 0$ and $T = T_{\text{amb}}$, as might be expected.

Since T and s are generally stored at grid cell centers, we need to do some averaging to add the acceleration to the MAC grid velocities, e.g., $T_{i,j+1/2,k} = \frac{1}{2}(T_{i,j,k} + T_{i,j+1,k})$. Alternatively put, when we add buoyancy to the velocity field prior to projection, the contribution of acceleration evaluated at the grid cell center (i, j, k) is equally split between $v_{i,j-1/2,k}$ and $v_{i,j+1/2,k}$.

5.3   Variable Density Solves

Underlying the buoyancy model is the fact that fluid density is a function of temperature and—if we treat the soot as actually dissolved in the air—smoke concentration. Let's begin with just the effect of temperature, for now taking $s = 0$. From the ideal gas law, thermodynamics derives that the density of the air should be

$$\rho_{\text{air}} = \frac{P}{RT}, \tag{5.2}$$

where P is the absolute pressure (say $1.01 \times 10^5 Pa$ in SI units), R is the specific gas constant for air (approximately 287 J/kg K in SI units), and T is the temperature. It should be underscored here that the absolute pressure P we propose using here is approximated as a constant—not coupled with the pressure solve for incompressibility—as otherwise we end up in a significantly more complicated compressible flow model; this has been worked out by Bonner [Bonner 07] in a generalization of the MAC grid incompressible simulation developed in this book, if you are interested.

Adding in some soot of density ρ_{soot} and treating the concentration s as a volume fraction, we can extend this to

$$\rho = \rho_{\text{air}} \left(1 + s \frac{\rho_{\text{soot}} - \rho_{\text{air}}}{\rho_{\text{air}}} \right) \tag{5.3}$$
$$= \rho_{\text{air}}(1 + \alpha s),$$

where we treat the relative density difference $\alpha = (\rho_{\text{soot}} - \rho_{\text{air}})/\rho_{\text{air}}$ as a constant—i.e., the soot has the same thermal expansion as the air. This is of course false, but we consider this error negligible relative to other modeling errors.

At this stage, the buoyancy model from the previous section can be recovered by linearizing Equation (5.3) around standard conditions

$$\rho \approx \rho_0 \left(1 + \alpha s - \frac{1}{T_{\text{amb}}}(T - T_{\text{amb}}) \right)$$
$$= \rho_0 \left[1 + \alpha s - \beta(T - T_{\text{amb}}) \right],$$

where ρ_0 is the smoke-free air density at ambient temperature and $\beta = 1/T_{\text{amb}}$. Plugging it into the momentum equation (where we have multiplied both sides by ρ) gives

$$\rho_0(1 + \alpha s - \beta \Delta T) \frac{D\vec{u}}{Dt} + \nabla p = \rho_0(1 + \alpha s - \beta \Delta T)\vec{g}.$$

The hydrostatic pressure for constant density fluid at rest is $p = \rho_0 \vec{g} \cdot \vec{x}$; write the actual pressure as the sum of this hydrostatic pressure plus a pressure variation p' so that $\nabla p = \rho_0 \vec{g} + \nabla p'$. This simplifies the momentum equation to

$$\rho_0(1 + \alpha s - \beta \Delta T) \frac{D\vec{u}}{Dt} + \nabla p' = \rho_0(\alpha s - \beta \Delta T)\vec{g}.$$

We now make the *Boussinesq* approximation that, assuming $|\alpha s - \beta \Delta T| \ll 1$, we can drop the density variation in the first term, leading to

$$\rho_0 \frac{D\vec{u}}{Dt} + \nabla p' = \rho_0(\alpha s - \beta \Delta T)\vec{g}.$$

Dividing through by ρ_0 gives the buoyancy form of the momentum equation from the previous section. It then becomes clear what α and β "should" be chosen as, though of course these can be left as tunable parameters. (It also makes it clear that the pressure we solve for in the buoyancy model is not the full pressure but actually just the variation above the hydrostatic pressure.)

This is a fine approximation for small density variations. However, for more extreme scenarios that are common in graphics, extra fidelity can be obtained by *not* taking the Boussinesq approximation, i.e., by treating the density as a variable in the pressure solve. Whereas the buoyancy model only generates forces in the vertical direction, the full model can give interesting plumes along any strong pressure gradient, such as radially inwards in rotating regions of the flow.

As a first step before the variable-density solve, Equation (5.3) should be used to determine the fluid density at each velocity sample in the MAC grid. This entails averaging the temperatures and smoke concentrations from the grid cell centers to the grid cell faces, in the usual manner. These u-, v- and w-densities modify the pressure projection in two ways. The pressure update is now

$$u_{i+1/2,j,k}^{n+1} = u_{i+1/2,j,k} + \Delta t \frac{p_{i+1,j,k} - p_{i,j,k}}{\rho_{i+1/2,j,k}\Delta x},$$

$$v_{i,j+1/2,k}^{n+1} = v_{i,j+1/2,k} + \Delta t \frac{p_{i,j+1,k} - p_{i,j,k}}{\rho_{i,j+1/2,k}\Delta x},$$

$$w_{i,j,k+1/2}^{n+1} = w_{i,j,k+1/2} + \Delta t \frac{p_{i,j,k+1} - p_{i,j,k}}{\rho_{i,j,k+1/2}\Delta x},$$

and the coefficients of the matrix A similarly incorporate the densities, as illustrated at the end of Chapter 4.

One possible problem that arises when using the variable-density solve is that the matrix may be *ill-conditioned* when large density variations are present. This means PCG will run for more iterations to return an accurate answer. For reasons of practicality it may therefore be worthwhile to clamp density to a lower bound of, say, 0.05 times the background density ρ_0.

5.4 Divergence Control

If you read the last section critically, you might have noticed we violated conservation of mass. The incompressibility constraint implies that fluid volumes remain constant, but if simultaneously the density is changed, it must mean mass is also changed. Perhaps unsurprisingly, however, most audiences aren't troubled by the violation: fluid motion is adequately complex and hard to predict so that this "problem" isn't usually an issue. That said, the solution to the problem can be generalized to one of the most useful simulation controls in smoke: *divergence control*.

In the thermal expansion problem, fundamentally we do want the fluid to expand as it heats up and contract as it cools off. In other words, where the change in temperature DT/Dt is non-zero, we don't want a divergence-free velocity field. Let's derive exactly what we want.

Consider a region of fluid Ω, currently with volume $V = \iiint_\Omega 1$. After a time step of Δt with velocities $\vec{u}$, suppose it changes volume to $V + \Delta V$. Meanwhile, suppose the average density in the region changes from ρ to $\rho + \Delta\rho$. Conservation of mass requires $\rho V = (\rho + \Delta\rho)(V + \Delta V)$ which, after neglecting the quadratic term, gives

$$\Delta V = -\frac{\Delta\rho}{\rho}V. \tag{5.4}$$

Using the divergence theorem, the change in volume is approximately

$$\Delta V = \iint_{\partial\Omega} \Delta t \vec{u} \cdot \hat{n}$$
$$= \iiint_\Omega \Delta t \nabla \cdot \vec{u}.$$

Considering an infinitesimally small region, and dividing both sides of (5.4) by $V\Delta t$, we get

$$\nabla \cdot \vec{u} = -\frac{1}{\Delta t}\frac{\Delta\rho}{\rho}.$$

This is the divergence we want to enforce in the pressure projection step, where we evaluate the change in density at grid cell centers due to changes in temperature and smoke concentration. For example, if the temperature increases, leading to a decrease in density, we need positive divergence to enact that thermal expansion.

This is still a little sloppy—in addition to the approximations made for the change in mass, there is a lag between the change in density in one time step and the resulting motion of fluid in the divergent velocity field in the next time step—and we certainly can't hope to exactly conserve mass. However, it does expose a more general divergence control in the simulation. Define a control field $d(\vec{x})$ at the grid cell centers equal to the desired rate of fractional volume change $\Delta V/V\Delta t$ throughout the volume of the fluid: we then solve for pressure to enforce that divergence. For the classic voxelized pressure solve, this is as simple as adding d to the fluid cells in the right-hand side of the linear system. For the more accurate variational pressure solve, we include an additional volume-changing work term in the change of energy of the fluid:

$$- \iiint \Delta tpd,$$

which shows up in the rescaled linear system as an addition of $V_{i,j,k}d_{i,j,k}$ to the right-hand side, where $V_{i,j,k}$ is the volume fraction (i.e., scaled between 0 and 1) of the fluid inside the grid cell (i, j, k).

Note that adding an arbitrary divergence control inside a closed domain—one without free surfaces—may lead to an incompatible linear system: if we constrain the fluid to maintain its total volume (the container's volume) but require it to expand or contract in the interior, we end up with no solution. Therefore it is imperative to enforce the compatibility condition, as discussed at the end of Chapter 4 for the right-hand side.

Divergence control can be used much more liberally than just to account for mass balance in thermal expansion. For example, Feldman et al. [Feldman et al. 03] introduced the technique for modeling a large class of explosions: look for more on this, and other techniques that control divergence, in Chapter 7. A constant, or time-varying, positive divergence can be added to the source volume of smoke to make it billow out more; negative divergence inside a target region of space can cause the smoke to be sucked up into the target.

Before leaving the subject of controlling smoke, it should be pointed out that there are, of course, other methods than modifying the divergence. Users may define force fields as additional body forces to coax the air to blow a particular way; these are simply added to the momentum equation much like the buoyancy terms we began with. Fattal and Lischinski [Fattal and Lischinski 04] provide an interesting class of force fields that automatically move smoke to a desired target shape—a particularly useful idea for dealing with characters made out of smoke.

– 6 –
Water

We, in fact, have most of the machinery in place now to simulate water as well. Our starting point is treating water as a fluid with a free surface boundary condition where it's in contact with air. The main new ingredient is geometric: the free surface condition allows the water to change shape, and thus we need to track or capture[1] that shape somehow. Along the way, we'll also cover extrapolation, which until now we've hidden under the rug.

Before jumping in, a note on terminology: the air-water surface or boundary is also often called an *interface*. Most of this chapter is about how to evolve this interface.

6.1 Marker Particles and Voxels

We'll begin with the simplest possible water simulator. Here we'll use the voxelized pressure solve first covered in Chapter 4, which only required us to classify each grid cell as being fluid (i.e., water), empty (i.e., air), or solid. While the solid cells should be straightforward to identify, determining when to switch a cell to fluid or empty as water moves in or out of it due to advection under the velocity field is the tricky part.

This is where we introduce *marker particles*, used all the way back in Harlow and Welch's seminal marker-and-cell paper, which also introduced the MAC grid [Harlow and Welch 65]. We begin the simulation by filling the volume of water with particles and viewing them as a sampling of the water geometry (and if there are sources adding water during the course of the simulation, we seed particles from them as well). Within each advection step we move the particles according to the grid velocity field, so that they naturally follow where the water should be going—using RK2 or better,

---

[1]In some numerical contexts, tracking and capturing are technical terms referring to different approaches to solving this problem: tracking loosely corresponds to methods using explicit descriptions of surfaces, such as meshes, whereas capturing refers to methods built on implicit descriptions of surfaces.

just like we did for semi-Lagrangian trajectory tracing.[2] Finally, we in turn use the marker particles to mark which grid cells are fluid for the pressure solve: any cell containing a marker particle is water, and the rest of the non-solid cells are left empty by default.

This algorithm can be justified conceptually by imagining taking it to the limit, where each individual molecule of water is identified with a marker particle: then the set of grid cells containing marker particles is exactly the set of grid cells containing water.

This raises the question of how densely to sample with marker particles —clearly one per molecule isn't practical! Obviously there should be at least one particle per water grid cell, and to avoid gaps in the fluid randomly opening up during advection we probably want at least double that resolution: four particles per cell in 2D and eight per cell in 3D. However, going above double won't necessarily give much improvement: ultimately these particles will be moved by velocities sampled at the grid resolution, which places a limit on how much detail we can expect in the water geometry. If higher-resolution geometry is required, the simulation grid must be refined too.

The simplest sampling pattern for the marker particles is just to lay them out in a regular grid lattice. However, this can result in peculiar artifacts as the simulation progresses—if the fluid compresses along one axis as it expands along another, the regular grid turns into anisotropic stripe-like patterns, far from a good uniform sampling. Thus we recommend at least jittering the initial grid, as one might do for sampling patterns in rendering.

The first problem apparent with the marker particle approach is in rendering: ultimately we want a smooth surface, describing the boundary between water and air, but right now we only have a mass of points filling the water volume. Clearly we don't want to simply render the water-filled voxels as blocks.

The standard solution is to construct a smooth implicit surface wrapped around the particles. For example, Blinn [Blinn 82] introduced *blobbies*: given the positions of the particles $\{\vec{x}_i\}$ define

$$F(\vec{x}) = \sum_i k \left(\frac{\|\vec{x} - \vec{x}_i\|}{h} \right),$$

---

[2] Just to remind you, for RK2 and many other integrators, we'll need to look up fluid velocity at locations that might not be inside the current water region, necessitating extrapolation. We'll get to that soon.

where k is a suitable smooth kernel function and h is a user parameter intended to be the extent of each particle. A Gaussian might be a reasonable choice for k; a cheaper and simpler alternative would be a spline, such as

$$k(s) = \begin{cases} (1 - s^2)^3 : s < 1, \\ \qquad 0 : s \geq 1. \end{cases}$$

This spline has the advantage that it depends only on s^2, not s, allowing one to avoid taking a square root when evaluating at $s = \|\vec{x} - \vec{x}_i\|/h$. The extent h should generally be several times the average inter-particle spacing r, for example $h = 3r$, but it can be tweaked as needed. (For our recommended sampling, r is half the grid spacing Δx.) The blobby surface is implicitly defined as the points $\vec{x}$ where $F(\vec{x}) = \tau$ for some threshold τ, or in other words the τ-isocontour or level set of F. A reasonable default for τ is $k(r/h)$, which produces a sphere of radius r for an isolated particle, but this too can be a tweakable parameter.

Unfortunately the blobby surface can have noticeable artifacts, chief among them that it can look, well, blobby. Many water scenarios include expanses of smooth water; after sampling with particles and then wrapping the blobby surface around the particles, generally bumps for each particle become apparent. This is especially noticeable from specular reflections on the water surface, though it can be masked by foam or spray. The bumps can be smoothed out to some extent by increasing the h-parameter—however, this also smooths out or even eliminates small-scale features we *want* to see in the render. Typically there is a hard trade-off involved.

A slight improvement on blobbies is given by Zhu and Bridson [Zhu and Bridson 05], where instead the implicit surface function is given by

$$\phi(\vec{x}) = \|\vec{x} - \bar{X}\| - \bar{r},$$

where $\bar{X}$ is a weighted average of nearby particle locations:

$$\bar{X} = \frac{\sum_i k\left(\frac{\|\vec{x} - \vec{x}_i\|}{h}\right) \vec{x}_i}{\sum_i k\left(\frac{\|\vec{x} - \vec{x}_i\|}{h}\right)}$$

and $\bar{r}$ is a similar weighted average of nearby particle radii:

$$\bar{r} = \frac{\sum_i k\left(\frac{\|\vec{x} - \vec{x}_i\|}{h}\right) r_i}{\sum_i k\left(\frac{\|\vec{x} - \vec{x}_i\|}{h}\right)}.$$

For now we'll take all the particle radii to be the same r, though better
results can be obtained if a particle's radius is actually its distance to the
closest point on the desired water surface—see the paper by Adams et
al. [Adams et al. 07] for an example of how to compute this practically, using a point-based fast marching algorithm similar to Corbett's [Corbett 05].
Finally, the surface is defined as the points $\vec{x}$ where $\phi(\vec{x}) = 0$, the zero isocontour or level set of ϕ. Once again, for an isolated particle this gives
a perfect sphere of radius r. The advantage of this formula over regular blobbies is that it gives somewhat flatter, smoother results where the
particles should be sampling smooth geometry, and it is less sensitive to
non-uniformities in sampling; however, it does have the disadvantage of potentially introducing small-scale "chaff" in concavities (gaps) in the particle
distribution.

Once an implicit surface has been defined, using either formulation, it
may be directly rendered with a raytracer using root-finding along each
ray. However, more commonly—and more efficiently—the implicit surface
function is instead sampled onto a grid. Typically this grid is double or
more the resolution of the simulation grid. Interpolating from the grid values is generally much faster than directly evaluating the formula, so this
can speed up ray tracing. More to the point, marching cubes or related
algorithms can be run on the grid to generate a mesh of the surface, suitable for any renderer. To further reduce bumpy artifacts in the surface,
the values on the grid can be smoothed (essentially by convolving with
a Gaussian blur filter or something similar), or the mesh from marching
cubes can be improved with a mesh-fairing algorithm.

Incidentally, you might be asking why not just start with a mesh in
the first place and move its vertices according to the fluid flow. This does
offer a lot of advantages over the methods covered in this book, but it
has its own set of problems. Typical fluid motion can swirl around in-
definitely, letting two points which are initially very close end up very far
apart: if we connect up points in a mesh, we can expect that before long the
mesh will get tangled and must be reconnected. While volume is preserved
in incompressible flow, surface area certainly may change, which further
necessitates adaptive meshing—adding and deleting elements to maintain
good sampling. Finally topology changes such as a drop of water merging
into another, or a thin sheet separating into a spray of droplets, require
non-trivial alterations to a mesh.[3] Brochu and Bridson [Brochu and Brid-

---

[3]This might be a good place to point out that, technically, the usual Navier-Stokes
equations don't obviously support topology change. If you evolve a path-connected region in a smooth flow, it remains path-connected. To see this, imagine a smooth curve

son 06] have established that these hurdles can be overcome using robust collision methods developed for cloth animation, but at present the implementation difficulty associated with the approach makes other techniques more attractive.

6.2 Level Set Methods

Instead of building an implicit function around particles, then sampling it on a grid for rendering, we can dispense with particles and work with the grid directly. This is the core idea of *level set methods*. Their chief advantage over marker particles is the elimination of blobby artifacts: level sets can easily give you beautifully smooth water surfaces.

Here we'll touch on just the basics we need; readers might look at the book by Osher and Fedkiw [Osher and Fedkiw 02], for example, for a more detailed study of the numerics and applications of level sets.

Define the implicit surface function $\phi_{i,j,k}$ at the centers of simulation grid cells (i.e., in the same locations as pressure, etc.). Tri- or bilinear interpolation can be used to estimate $\phi(\vec{x})$ in between cell centers. The surface is taken to be the points where $\phi(\vec{x}) = 0$; by convention we'll identify the region where $\phi(\vec{x}) < 0$ to be the water, or more generally the inside of the surface, and the region where $\phi(\vec{x}) > 0$ to be the air, or the outside.

This gives us a lot of freedom to choose ϕ: infinitely many functions have the same zero level set. Several arguments can be made that *signed distance* is the most convenient function.

6.2.1 Signed Distance

Given any closed set S of points, the *distance function* for the set is

$$\text{distance}_S(\vec{x}) = \min_{\vec{p} \in S} \|\vec{x} - \vec{p}\|;$$

$\vec{x}(s)$; using the flow map Φ_t which takes initial positions to their positions after being advected up to time t, this curve is advected to $\Phi_t(\vec{x}(s))$, which is also smooth if Φ_t is smooth. In reality, the smoothness underlying Navier-Stokes breaks down as we approach molecular scales, at which point a continuum velocity field makes little sense. Topology changes are ultimately outside of the domain of continuum mechanics. However, numerically we tend not to worry about this issue and simply make the assumption that if a connecting tendril of water gets thinner than a grid cell it breaks apart.

that is, it's the distance to the closest point in S. If S divides space into a well-defined inside and outside, then the *signed distance function* is

$$\phi_S(\vec{x}) = \begin{cases} \text{distance}_S(\vec{x}) : \vec{x} \text{ is outside}, \\ -\text{distance}_S(\vec{x}) : \vec{x} \text{ is inside}. \end{cases}$$

From now on we'll drop the subscript S and just call it $\phi(\vec{x})$. Points exactly on the surface S have distance and signed distance equal to zero, regardless of whether they are included in the inside or outside. (By convention in this book we'll include S with the inside region.) Therefore, both the distance function and the signed distance function can be used to implicitly describe the underling surface: S is the set of points where $\text{distance}_S(\vec{x})$ or $\phi(\vec{x})$ are zero, the zero level set or isocontour.

Signed distance has many useful properties. For example, at some point $\vec{x}$ inside the surface, let $\hat{n}$ be the unit-length direction toward the closest point on the surface. Notice that for positive ϵ small enough, the signed distance $\phi(\vec{x} + \epsilon\hat{n})$ must be $\phi(\vec{x}) + \epsilon$: if I move along this direction $\hat{n}$, my closest point on the surface doesn't change, and my distance to it changes by exactly how much I move. Therefore the directional derivative of ϕ in this direction is 1:

$$\nabla\phi \cdot \hat{n} = 1.$$

Also notice that if I move in any other direction, ϕ cannot change any faster—the fastest way to increase or decrease my distance to the surface is obviously to move along the direction to the closest point. Thus, the gradient of ϕ, which is the direction of steepest ascent, must in fact be the direction $\hat{n}$ to the closest point on the surface:

$$\hat{n} = \nabla\phi.$$

Exactly the same result holds outside the surface. Putting the two previous equations together, we see $\|\nabla\phi\| = 1$ wherever it exists.

It can be shown that in fact signed distance is smooth (i.e., $\nabla\phi$ and higher derivatives exist) everywhere except on the *medial axis*, consisting of points that are equidistant to different parts of the surface, and for reasonable surfaces this is a small, lower-dimensional set indeed—and even on the medial axis, it's still continuous, just with a kink. In particular, if the surface itself is smooth, signed distance is smooth on and near the surface. (In contrast, regular distance has a non-differentiable kink right along S, making it decidedly less attractive numerically.) Another nice feature that falls out of this is that for any point $\vec{x}$, the closest point on the surface is located at $\vec{x} - \phi(\vec{x})\nabla\phi(\vec{x})$.

Also recall from multivariable calculus that, since S is an isocontour of ϕ, the normal to S is parallel to $\nabla\phi$. Knowing that $\|\nabla\phi\| = 1$ and that ϕ is negative in the inside, it's not hard to see that $\nabla\phi$ is in fact exactly the unit-length outward-pointing normal $\hat{n}$. Moreover, $\nabla\phi$ is defined nearly everywhere else, off the surface, and clearly must be the same as the normal $\hat{n}$ at the closest point on S. Thus we can use $\nabla\phi$ as the natural extension of the surface normal.

I should interject here that later, when we use numerical approximations to the signed distance, the gradient $\nabla\phi$ (or finite difference estimates of it) may not be exactly unit length. In this case, it usually makes sense to normalize the result. If you happen to have the bad luck of evaluating it on the medial axis, where signed distance isn't differentiable, there's even a chance that the finite difference might evaluate to zero—in this case typically a default unit length vector such as $(1, 0, 0)$ is used.

It nearly goes without saying that signed distance of course also allows easy inside/outside tests: just check the sign of $\phi(\vec{x})$.

6.2.2   Calculating Signed Distance

Typically we will start the simulation with a known signed distance function (either precomputed, or an analytic function such as $\|\vec{x} - \vec{c}\| - r$ for a sphere centered on $\vec{c}$ with radius r). However, if we are only given the implicit surface with an arbitrary function on a grid, or are constructing it from marker particle data, or are given a triangle mesh of the surface, we need to calculate signed distance.

There are two general approaches: PDE methods that numerically approximate $\|\nabla\phi\| = 1$ (technically known as the Eikonal equation) and geometric methods that instead calculate distances to the surface. There are merits to both approaches, but we will focus on the latter as they are very robust and accurate but also can be simple and quite fast. In particular, we base our method on algorithm 4 in Tsai's article [Tsai 02]. For a recent review of many other algorithms, see the paper by Jones et al. [Jones et al. 06].

The algorithm is given in Figure 6.1. It efficiently propagates information about the surface out to grid points far away, without requiring expensive[4] geometric searches for every single grid point. There are several details to work out: finding the closest points for grid points near the surface, what order to loop over grid points, and determining inside/outside.

---

[4]Expensive either in terms of CPU time for brute-force methods or programmer time for sophisticated fast methods!

- Find the closest points on the surface for the nearby grid points, setting their signed distance values accordingly. Set the other grid points as unknown.
- Loop over the unknown grid points (i, j, k) in a chosen order:
  - Find all neighboring grid points that have a known signed distance and closest surface point.
  - Find the distances from $\vec{x}_{i,j,k}$ to those surface points. If $\vec{x}_{i,j,k}$ is closer than a neighbor, mark the neighbor as unknown again.
  - Take the minimum of the distances, determine if (i, j, k) is inside or outside, and set its signed distance value accordingly.

Figure 6.1. A geometry-based signed distance construction algorithm.

Finding Closest Points. If our input is an implicit surface function already sampled on the grid (but presumably not with signed distance) then we can immediately identify which grid points are near the surface: they are those with a neighbor of a different sign.

The simplest approximation if grid values are already given is to estimate the surface points along the lines between a grid point and its neighbors, by finding where the linear interpolant is zero, and then taking the closest of all these candidate points. This has the advantage of being guaranteed to find reasonable estimates of points on the surface, though they may well not be the closest points, and so accuracy can be less than desired. Also, if the underlying geometry we're trying to recover is curved within a grid cell, the linear-interpolation model can be significantly off, flattening out the curve—and in the process changing the shape of the surface, which is clearly less than ideal.

An alternative for marker particles, with some given radius r, is to compute distance to the particles themselves at nearby grid points and then subtract off r. We can do this efficiently by initializing the grid to some large upper bound on distances, then for each particle, setting the distance of nearby grid points (say within distance $\max(3r, 2\Delta x)$) to the minimum of their current value or distance to the particle, minus r.

Finally, if our geometry is given in the form of a triangle mesh we can adapt the particle approach. Here we loop over the triangles instead of particles, setting grid values within an expanded bounding box around the triangle to the minimum of their current value and the exact distance to the triangle. For full accuracy, rather than storing the closest point alongside the distance on the grid, it's better to store the index of the closest triangle—then when we propagate this to neighboring grid points they can calculate their own exact distance to the triangle. So far this only computes the regular distance function without signs. If the mesh is watertight, then the parity of the number of intersections along a ray cast out from the grid point (say along an axis for convenience) tells us inside/outside and therefore the sign of ϕ: an odd number of intersections indicates inside, an even number outside. However, CG models often come in the form of triangle soup, with holes, self-intersections, and the like. In this case, we refer to the slower but more robust test developed by Houston et al. [Houston et al. 03, Houston et al. 06].

Loop Order. There are two suggestions given in [Tsai 02], one based on the fast marching method [Sethian 96, Tsitsiklis 95] and one based on the fast sweeping method [Zhao 05].

The fast marching method is based on the realization that grid points should get information about the distance to the surface from points that are closer, not the other way around. We thus want to loop over the grid points going from the closest to the furthest. This can be facilitated by storing unknown grid points in a priority queue (typically implemented as a heap) keyed by the current estimate of their distance. We initialize the heap with the neighbors of the known grid points, with their distance values and closest points estimated from those known grid points. We select the minimum and remove it from the priority queue, set it as known, and then update the distance and closest-point information of its unknown neighbors (possibly adding them to or moving them up in the priority queue). And then do that again, and again, until the priority queue is empty. This runs in $O(n \log n)$ time for n unknown grid points.

The fast sweeping method approach takes a different tactic from the fact that information propagates out from closer points to further points. For any grid point, in the end its closest point information is going to come to it from one particular direction in the grid—e.g., from $(i + 1, j, k)$, or maybe from $(i, j - 1, k)$, and so on. To ensure that the information can propagate in the right direction, we thus sweep through the grid points in all possible loop orders: i ascending or descending, j ascending or descending, k ascending or descending. There are eight combinations in three dimensions, four in two dimensions. Each time we sweep through the grid, we include the grid point itself in the list of its neighbors (if the grid point has had a closest point and distance set from a previous sweep—otherwise not). For more accuracy, we can repeat the sweeps again; in practice two times through the sweep gives good results, though more iterations are possible.

The benefit of fast sweeping over fast marching is that it is $O(n)$, requires no extra data structures beyond grids, and thus is extremely simple to implement. However, the fast marching method has a significant advantage in that it permits *narrow-band* methods: that is, if we don't need the signed distance function more than, say, five grid cells away from the surface, we can stop the algorithm once we hit that distance. For example, in our fluid code, if we choose the time step based on the five-grid cell heuristic (3.2), we shouldn't ever go beyond five grid cells from the current surface. In this case, fast marching only takes $O(m \log m)$ time, where m is the number of grid cells set—typically much smaller than the number of grid cells in the whole grid. The remaining grid points can have their ϕ values set to $\pm 5 \Delta x$ in this example.

6.2.3 Moving the Level Set

The most critical part of the simulation is actually moving the surface represented by the level set. The free surface, i.e., the points where $\phi = 0$, should be advected with the fluid velocity: we can simply advect the entire function to capture this. That is, we solve

$$\frac{D\phi}{Dt} = 0. \tag{6.1}$$

Unfortunately, advecting a signed distance field doesn't in general preserve the signed distance property. Thus, we generally need to periodically recalculate signed distance as we have discussed above. Recalculating distance can perturb the interface, though, so we don't want to do this too frequently—perhaps just once a frame.

A worse problem in advection is numerical dissipation. Any small features in the surface—ripples, droplets, thin sheets, etc.—are in danger of being smoothed out of existence. Tri- or bilinear interpolation in a semi-Lagrangian method really is inadequate in this case; at the very least your code should use the sharper Catmull-Rom interpolation, if not other more accurate techniques.

This leads us to a sampling condition of sorts for level sets. Any part of the geometry less than $\sim \Delta x$ in width cannot be reliably captured on the grid: in some configurations it may show up, but after advection it may fall between grid points and disappear, never to return. This is very similar to the Nyquist limit when considering which functions can be reconstructed from a given sampling density. Ideally you should choose your grid size so that the water features you want to resolve are at least $\sim 2\Delta x$ thick.

6.2.4 Boundary Conditions

So far we have avoided discussion of solids, just referring to the water-air surface. This is, unfortunately, probably the messiest part of the operation and has yet to be fully resolved in research. However, something must be decided—once water is in contact with a solid, we need to decide a boundary condition for ϕ at the solid: what values should ϕ take in grid cell centers that lie inside a solid?

One approach is to either join the solid with the air or, less commonly, the water. Taking the former as an example, this means taking ϕ to be zero at both the air-water surface and the solid-water surface, negative only inside the water and positive in both solid and air. This is pleasantly unambiguous, but does give rise to some annoying artifacts. For example in rendering, due to truncation error on the grid, there might be small gaps between the solid and the water that show up as spurious grid-aligned air pockets. One partial remedy is to offset the simulated solid geometry a little inwards from the rendered solid geometry, say by a fraction of a grid cell, to cover potential gaps. However, more troubling is the difficulties this makes when later in this chapter we improve the accuracy of the pressure solve for free surfaces: we'll need to be able to distinguish the solid-water boundary as *not* a free surface.

A possibly superior approach is to extrapolate ϕ from the water-air region into the solid, virtually extending the surface. If done carefully enough this can even enable impressive simulations of surface tension interactions —see Wang et al. [Wang et al. 05]—but is fraught with difficulties. For example, when a water drop is pulled off a solid surface, semi-Lagrangian advection may keep tracking back to negative ϕ values in the wall, making it impossible for water to leave a solid.[5] In any case, at its simplest this can be implemented by extrapolating ϕ from the water-air region into the solid, as discussed in the next section, and then reinitializaing signed distance throughout the whole grid.

---

[5]In fact, this gets at a deeper conundrum, that the solid-wall condition $\vec{u} \cdot \hat{n} = \vec{u}_{\text{solid}} \cdot \hat{n}$ doesn't actually allow for liquids to separate from solids. To "correct" this Foster and Fedkiw [Foster and Fedkiw 01] proposed a simple unsticking trick that only enforces $\vec{u} \cdot \hat{n} \geq \vec{u}_{\text{solid}} \cdot \hat{n}$, which unfortunately fails in several common scenarios; Batty et al. [Batty et al. 07] later demonstrated a more robust, physically consistent, though expensive treatment. This too is an area where the continuum description doesn't quite model reality with its discrete molecules that can separate from a solid surface.

6.3   Extrapolation

Our fluid simulation loop looks like this:

1. If necessary reinitialize the fluid/air signed distance function ϕ to signed distance.

2. Extrapolate the divergence-free velocity field from the last time step outside the fluid, to get an extended velocity field $\vec{u}^n$.

3. Add body forces such as gravity or targetting to get an interim velocity field..

4. Advect the interim velocity field and ϕ in the divergence-free $\vec{u}^n$ velocity field.

5. Solve for and apply pressure to get a divergence-free velocity $\vec{u}^{n+1}$ in the new fluid region.

We now will address the second step, the extrapolation of velocity from inside the fluid. In several other chapters we've made passing reference to extrapolation of other quantities as well, which we will explain here. We'll only use constant extrapolation, i.e., setting a quantity at a point outside the fluid to the value at the closest point on the fluid surface. This was shown to work well for velocity by Enright et al. [Enright et al. 02b] and is generally all we need for this book; if interested you might check out the higher-order generalizations developed by Aslam [Aslam 04]. Also recall that inside solids, we can get more robust treatment of boundary conditions by setting the normal component of the extended velocity field equal to the normal component of the solid (and note that we now have a sensible definition of normal inside the solid volume from the gradient of its signed distance function).

The most straightforward approach to extrapolation is to directly use the closest point definition. In fact, when we constructed signed distance geometrically, we actually stored at each grid point the index of the closest element (either point or triangle) alongside the value of ϕ, making extrapolation a simple matter of copying from those surface points. Of course, when extrapolating velocity we're working on staggered grid locations, not the grid points where we computed closest elements—in that case we can simply average from the neighboring grid cell centers, or find the closest of the two elements stored at the neighboring grid cell centers. This still leaves the question of how to get the values at the surface elements: the usual tri- or bilinear interpolation will involve outside values that we don't yet know. The simplest solution is to view tri- or bilinear interpolation as a particular weighted average of nearby values and simply zero out the weights corresponding to values on the outside (and renormalize the remaining weights).

The only downside to this solution is that if we choose not to reinitialize signed distance every time step—which, given the error this adds to the surface geometry, is a wise choice—we don't necessarily have an up-to-date closest-point index array. An attractive remedy is then to reinitialize signed distance each time step but without modifying the ϕ values close to the surface that actually determine its shape (e.g., those ϕ values less than $2\Delta x$ in magnitude), except once per frame or so when we do full reinitialization.

An alternative espoused by some is to cast extrapolation as a PDE. If we set a quantity equal to the value at the closest point on the surface, then that quantity must be constant along lines normal to the surface, which means its directional derivative along $\nabla\phi$ is zero. In other words, extrapolating a quantity q is equivalent to solving

$$\nabla\phi \cdot \nabla q = 0$$

outside the fluid. This can be discretized with finite differences, biased to the direction towards the surface: for example, to estimate $\partial q/\partial x$ at grid point i, one should select either $(q_{i+1} - q_i)/\Delta x$ or $(q_i - q_{i-1})/\Delta x$ depending on whether ϕ_{i+1} or ϕ_{i-1} is smaller, respectively. The resulting system of linear equations can be solved with variations of the fast marching method or fast sweeping, or directly with sparse matrix methods (in fact, the bias towards the surface forces the linear system to be equivalent to a lower-triangular matrix, which can be solved by forward substitution after topologically sorting the unknowns, all in linear time). However, if ϕ isn't guaranteed to be signed distance, and in particular might not be strictly increasing as you go further from the surface, this can get a little flaky, to say nothing of the complications of handling staggered grid quantities such as velocity.

6.4 More Accurate Pressure Solves

The methods we have developed so far still fall short when it comes to visual plausibility. The culprit is the voxelized treatment of the free surface boundary condition $p = 0$. Even if we can track and render an accurate water surface, so far the core of the simulation—the pressure solve—only sees a block voxelized surface, with some cells marked as water and some as air. Thus the velocity field, and from there the motion and shape of the surface itself, cannot avoid significant voxel artifacts. For example, small "ripples" less than a grid cell high do not show up at all in the pressure solve, and thus they aren't evolved correctly but rather persist statically in the form of a strange displacement texture. Somehow we need to inform the pressure solve about the location of the water-air interface within each grid cell. More precisely, we are going to modify how we compute the gradient of pressure near the water-air interface for updating velocities, which naturally will also change the matrix in the pressure equations.[6]

Our first solution is to use the ghost fluid method, as laid out by Gibou et al. [Gibou et al. 02]. We'll illustrate this by looking at the update to $u_{i+1/2,j,k}$, which in the interior of the water would be

$$u_{i+1/2,j,k}^{n+1} = u_{i+1/2,j,k} - \frac{\Delta t}{\rho_{i+1/2,j,k}} \frac{p_{i+1,j,k} - p_{i,j,k}}{\Delta x}.$$

Suppose further that (i,j,k) is in the water, i.e., $\phi_{i,j,k} \leq 0$, and that $(i+1,j,k)$ is in the air, i.e., $\phi_{i+1,j,k} > 0$ (treating the case where it's the other way around will be obvious). The simple solver before then set $p_{i+1,j,k} = 0$. However, it would be more accurate to say that $p = 0$ at the water-air interface, which is somewhere between (i,j,k) and $(i+1,j,k)$. Linearly interpolating between $\phi_{i,j,k}$ and $\phi_{i+1,j,k}$ gives the location of the interface at $(i + \theta\Delta x, j, k)$ where

$$\theta = \frac{\phi_{i,j,k}}{\phi_{i,j,k} - \phi_{i+1,j,k}}.$$

Linearly interpolating between the real pressure $p_{i,j,k}$ and a fictional "ghost" pressure $p_{i+1,j,k}^G$, then setting it equal to zero at the interface, gives

$$(1-\theta)p_{i,j,k} + \theta p_{i+1,j,k}^G = 0$$

$$\Rightarrow \quad p_{i+1,j,k}^G = -\frac{1-\theta}{\theta}p_{i,j,k}$$

$$= \frac{\phi_{i+1,j,k}}{\phi_{i,j,k}}p_{i,j,k}.$$

Now plug this into the velocity update:

$$u_{i+1/2,j,k}^{n+1} = u_{i+1/2,j,k} - \frac{\Delta t}{\rho} \frac{\frac{\phi_{i+1,j,k}}{\phi_{i,j,k}}p_{i,j,k} - p_{i,j,k}}{\Delta x}$$

$$= u_{i+1/2,j,k} - \frac{\Delta t}{\rho} \frac{\phi_{i+1,j,k} - \phi_{i,j,k}}{\phi_{i,j,k}} \frac{p_{i,j,k}}{\Delta x}.$$

---

[6]Note that this is quite orthogonal to our accurate approach to solid wall boundaries, where we use volume fractions to get better estimates of kinetic energy, independent of how the pressure updates velocity.

The end effect in the matrix is to increase the diagonal. At this point you should probably get worried about the case where $\phi_{i,j,k} = 0$ or is very close to zero—we are dividing by this quantity! To limit the possibility of numerical difficulties we can clamp the coefficient in the pressure update $(\phi_{i+1,j,k} - \phi_{i,j,k})/\phi_{i,j,k}$ to some maximum value, say 10^3.

A closely related solution, more in line with the volume fraction approach we've already used extensively, is to instead modify the fluid density $\rho_{i+1/2,j,k}$ to account for the fractions of the u-cell occupied by water versus air. Compute $\rho_{i+1/2,j,k}$ as the average fluid density in the u-cell, ignoring solids. The ghost fluid method above is in fact equivalent to using $\rho_{\text{air}} = 0$ and estimating the volume fraction from just $\phi_{i,j,k}$ and $\phi_{i+1,j,k}$. We can instead use the true non-zero density of air and better volume estimates, in the same manner we calculate volume fractions for handling solid wall boundary conditions. For example, we can $2 \times 2 \times 2$ supersample ϕ, and in each subcell (of side length $\frac{1}{2}\Delta x$) with an interpolated ϕ value at its center, estimate the fraction occupied by water as

$$\text{volume fraction} \approx \frac{1}{2} - \frac{1}{2}\text{clamp}_{[-1,1]}\left(\frac{4\phi}{\Delta x}\right).$$

and finally average the appropriate subcell fractions to get the volume fractions for each u-, v- and w-cell. Once we have reasonable average densities, we can set $p = 0$ in the grid cells that have no water at all—or, optionally, leave them in. If we do leave them in, we'll have a harder linear system to solve as we are actually solving for pressure in the air as well as the water, but we'll also get zero divergence throughout the grid and not just in the water. This means, for example, that bubbles will behave much more sensibly, approximately conserving their volume.

For all of these solutions it should be emphasized that we need to extrapolate the water-air ϕ into the solid walls. If instead ϕ were always positive in the solid then both of these approaches erroneously treat the solid wall as if it were a free surface, with ugly consequences.

6.4.1 Volume Control

Between iterative solves for pressure, truncation error in level set representations and errors in advection, it is not surprising that a typical water simulation doesn't exactly conserve the volume of water it begins with. Typically the errors are biased to steadily lose volume. Kim et al. [Kim et al. 07] demonstrate a simple correction to this drift by enforcing a non-zero divergence control in the pressure projection step, similar to the correction for conservation of mass discussed in the previous chapter.

6.4.2   Surface Tension

Another subject we'll only briefly touch on is adding surface-tension forces
for small-scale water phenomena. This is, it should be warned, a subject
of ongoing research both within graphics and scientific computing. For example, the test case of running a sphere of water at rest in zero-G with
surface tension (which should result in surface-tension forces exactly can-
celing pressure forces, so velocity remains zero) is surprisingly hard to get
right.

The physical chemistry of surface tension is conceptually simple. Water
molecules are more attracted to other water molecules than to air molecules,
and vice versa. Thus, water molecules near the surface tend to be pulled
in towards the rest of the water molecules and vice versa. In a way they
are seeking to minimize the area exposed to the other fluid, bunching up
around their own type. The simplest linear model of surface tension can
in fact be phrased in terms of a potential energy equal to a surface-tension
coefficient γ times the surface area between the two fluids (γ for water and
air at normal conditions is approximately $0.073 J/m^2$). The force seeks to
minimize the surface area.

The surface area of the fluid is simply the integral of 1 on the boundary:

$$A = \iint_{\partial \Omega} 1.$$

Remembering our signed distance properties, this is the same as

$$A = \iint_{\partial \Omega} \nabla \phi \cdot \hat{n}.$$

Now we use the divergence theorem in reverse to turn this into a volume
integral:

$$A = \iiint_{\Omega} \nabla \cdot \nabla \phi$$

Consider a virtual infinitesimal displacement of the surface, δx. This
changes the volume integral by adding or subtracting infinitesimal amounts
of the integrand along the boundary. The resulting infinitesimal change in
surface area is

$$\delta A = \iint_{\partial \Omega} (\nabla \cdot \nabla \phi) \delta x \cdot \hat{n}.$$

Thus, the variational derivative of surface area is $(\nabla \cdot \nabla \phi) \hat{n}$. Our surface-
tension force is proportional to this, and since it is in the normal direction
we can think of it in terms of a pressure jump at the air-water interface (as

pressure only applies in the normal direction). Since air pressure is zero in our free surface model, we have that the pressure at the surface of the water is

$$p = \gamma \nabla \cdot \nabla \phi.$$

It turns out that that $\kappa = \nabla \cdot \nabla \phi$ is termed the *mean curvature* of the surface, a well-studied geometric quantity that measures how curved a surface is.

This property has been incorporated into the ghost fluid pressure discretization by Kang et al. [Kang et al. 00]. Here, we take the ghost pressures in the air so that we linearly interpolate to $\gamma \kappa$ at the point where $\phi = 0$, rather than interpolating to zero. The mean curvature κ can easily be estimated at that point by using the standard central difference for the Laplacian, on trilinearly interpolated values of ϕ. Though not immediately apparent, there is also a fairly severe stability restriction on the time step, $\Delta t \leq O(\Delta x^{3/2} \sqrt{\rho/\gamma})$, since this is essentially an explicit treatment of the surface-tension forces. Things are also rather more complicated at triple junctions between water, solid, and air; we refer to Wang et al. [Wang et al. 05] for more on this.

– 7 –
Fire

This is a short chapter: while the physics and chemistry of combustion can be extraordinarily complicated, and to this day aren't fully understood, we will boil it down to a very simplified model. Our two main sources in graphics are the papers by Nguyen et al. [Nguyen et al. 02] for thin flames, and those by Melek and Keyser [Melek and Keyser 02] and Feldman et al. [Feldman et al. 03] for volumetric combustion. There are of course many other approaches that avoid fluid simulation and directly model flames procedurally, but we will not cover them in this book.

Combustion is simply a chemical reaction[1] triggered by heat where an oxidizer (like oxygen gas) and a fuel (like propane) combine to form a variety of products, giving out more heat in the process. Thus, at a minimum, our fluid solver will need to be able to track fuel/oxidizer versus burnt products along with temperature—and if it's not a clean flame, we also need smoke concentration to track the resulting soot. In the following sections we'll take a look at two strategies for tracking the fuel/oxidizer appropriate for different classes of combustion.

Just to clarify before proceeding: throughout this chapter we are assuming that both fuel and oxidizer are either themselves gases, or suspended in the air. If you analyze even a wood fire or a candle, you'll find that the flames are the result of gaseous fuel—pyrolyzed from the wood as it heats up, or evaporated wax—not the solid itself directly. Thus when we model a solid (or even liquid) object that is on fire, we treat it as a source emitting gaseous fuel, which then burns. Part of the emission is enforcing a velocity boundary condition $\vec{u} \cdot \hat{n} = \vec{u}_{solid} \cdot \hat{n} + u_{emission}$ similar to the usual moving solid wall boundary condition: gaseous fuel is injected into the grid at this relative velocity $u_{emission}$. In addition, fields describing the presence of fuel (see the following sections) should have the appropriate boundary condi-

---

[1]One of the complexities hidden here is that in most situations in reality, there are actually hundreds of different chemical reactions in play, with a multitude of different chemical species. For example, we all know that the gasoline burned in a car engine doesn't simply combine with the oxygen in the air to produce water and carbon dioxide: a vast range of other chemicals from carbon monoxide to nitrous oxide to all sorts of carbon structures in soot particles end up in the exhaust.

tion for advection. Various authors have looked at further eroding away
the solid or liquid source as it emits gaseous fuel, which is particularly important for thin objects like sheets of paper—see for example the articles
by Melek and Keyser [Melek and Keyser 03] and Losasso et al. [Losasso
et al. 06]. Whether or not (and where) a solid is emitting gaseous fuel is
usually directly specified by the animator, often modulated by an animated
texture to produce more interesting effects, though procedural models simulating the spread of fire according to burn rates or temperature thresholds
can also easily be concocted.

7.1   Thin Flames

Nguyen et al. [Nguyen et al. 02] detail an approach to fire, in which the
region where combustion takes place is modeled as an infinitely thin flame
front, i.e., a surface, not a volume. In addition, it's assumed that fuel and
oxidizer are *premixed* before ignition, as in blow torches—while not really
true for other phenomena where the mixing of fuel and oxidizer is an integral part of the fire (technically known as *diffuse flames*), the simplifying
premixed assumption can still serve just fine for a visually plausible result.

The flame front divides the fluid region into two parts: premixed
fuel/oxidizer on one side and burnt products (and/or background air) on
the other side. To track the flame surface we model it with a level set ϕ
sampled on the grid, as we did for water in Chapter 6.

The first problem to address is how to evolve the flame front: at what
speed does it move? If no combustion were taking place, the flame front
would be nothing more than the material interface between the two fluids—
just like the free surface in water simulation. Thus our first velocity term
is simply the fluid velocity: the flame front is advected along with the flow.
For definiteness (this will be important in a moment) we'll use the velocity
of the unburnt fuel, $\vec{u}_{\text{fuel}}$. However, when combustion is taking place, the
flame front also is "moving:" fuel at the flame surface gets combusted into
burnt products, effectively shrinking the surface inwards. The simplest
model for this is to assume a constant burn speed S, the rate at which the
flame surface burns into the fuel region along the normal direction. Nguyen
et al. [Nguyen et al. 02] suggest a default value of $S = 0.5m/s$. Assuming
that ϕ is negative in the fuel region by convention, this gives our level set
equation

$$\frac{\partial \phi}{\partial t} + \vec{u}_{\text{fuel}} \cdot \nabla \phi = S. \tag{7.1}$$

With $S \neq 0$, note that the volume of the fuel region is *not* conserved, and thus a lot of the worries for tracking level sets for water don't bother us here—just the usual advection approaches can be used as if ϕ were any other scalar, along with an addition of $S\Delta t$ each time step, and perhaps periodic reinitialization to signed distance. Note also that if an object is supposed to be on fire, a boundary condition forcing $\phi \leq 0$ on the burning sections of its surface should be included; otherwise ϕ should be extrapolated into solids to avoid artifacts near the surface, as with liquids.

As an aside, Hong et al. [Hong et al. 07] have more recently added additional detail to this technique by using higher-order non-linear equations for the speed and acceleration of the flame front (rather than keeping it as a constant burn speed S). These promote the formation of "cellular patterns" characteristic of some fires.

The next problem to address is how the fire affects the velocity field. If the density of the burnt products is less than the density of the fuel mix (as is often the case, either due to differences in a specific gas constant or temperature), then conservation of mass demands that the fluid should instantaneously expand when going through the flame front from the fuel region to the burnt-products region. The rate of mass leaving the fuel region per unit area is $\rho_{\text{fuel}}S$, which must match the rate of mass entering the burnt region per unit area, $\rho_{\text{burnt}}(S + \Delta V)$, where ΔV is the jump in the normal component of fluid velocity across the interface. Solving gives

$$\Delta V = \left(\frac{\rho_{\text{fuel}}}{\rho_{\text{burnt}}} - 1 \right) S.$$

Since the tangential component of velocity is continuous across the flame, this means the full velocity satisfies the following jump at the flame front:

$$\vec{u}_{\text{burnt}} = \vec{u}_{\text{fuel}} + \Delta V \hat{n}$$
$$= \vec{u}_{\text{fuel}} + \left(\frac{\rho_{\text{fuel}}}{\rho_{\text{burnt}}} - 1 \right) S\hat{n}, \tag{7.2}$$

where $\hat{n}$ is the normal pointing outward from the fuel region into the burnt region. This naturally defines a *ghost velocity* for use in advection: if you trace through the flame front and want to interpolate velocity on the other side, you need to add or subtract this change in normal velocity for the advection to make sense (where normal, in this case, might be evaluated from the normalized gradient of the level set ϕ wherever you happen to be interpolating). This is one example of the *ghost fluid method* developed by Fedkiw and coauthors.

This expansion also has to be modeled in the pressure projection step, enforcing a non-zero divergence at the flame front—indeed, this is one of the critical visual qualities of fire. The simplest discrete approach is to build Equation (7.2) into the evaluation of divergence that defines the right-hand side of the pressure equation. For example, when evaluating the divergence at a cell where $\phi \leq 0$ (i.e., in the fuel region) then any of the surrounding u-, v-, or w-velocity samples, where the averaged $\phi > 0$ (i.e., in the burnt region) should be corrected by the x-, y- or z-component of $-\Delta V \hat{n}$, respectively. Similarly if $\phi > 0$ at the cell center, then, at surrounding velocity samples where the averaged $\phi \leq 0$, ϕ should be corrected by the appropriate components of $+\Delta V \hat{n}$. This can be interpreted as yet another use for divergence controls. When setting up the matrix in the pressure solve, greater fidelity can be obtained by accounting for the different densities of fuel and burnt products: this shows up as variable densities just as in water or the advanced smoke model discussed earlier in the book. We can estimate the density in, say, a u-cell $(i + 1/2, j, k)$ as a weighted average of ρ_{fuel} and ρ_{burnt}:

$$\rho_{i+1/2,j,k} = \alpha \rho_{\text{fuel}} + (1 - \alpha)\rho_{\text{burnt}},$$

where the weight α could be determined from the level set values $\phi_{i,j,k}$ and $\phi_{i+1,j,k}$:

$$\alpha = \begin{cases} 1 : & \phi_{i,j,k} \leq 0 \text{ and } \phi_{i+1,j,k} \leq 0, \\[2mm] \dfrac{\phi_{i,j,k}}{\phi_{i,j,k} - \phi_{i+1,j,k}} : & \phi_{i,j,k} \leq 0 \text{ and } \phi i + 1, j, k > 0, \\[2mm] 1 - \dfrac{\phi_{i,j,k}}{\phi_{i,j,k} - \phi_{i+1,j,k}} : & \phi_{i,j,k} > 0 \text{ and } \phi i + 1, j, k \leq 0, \\[2mm] 0 : & \phi_{i,j,k} > 0 \text{ and } \phi_{i+1,j,k} > 0. \end{cases}$$

This of course blends very elegantly with the variable density smoke solve, where density is a function of temperature T and the specific gas constant R; this constant R can be taken as different for the fuel region and the burnt-products region.

Speaking of temperature, we don't yet have a model for it. The simplest approach is to keep a constant $T = T_{\text{ignition}}$, the temperature at which combustion starts, inside the fuel region and establish a discontinuous jump to T_{max} on the burnt products side of the flame front. The temperature on the burnt side is advected and dissipated as before for smoke, but using the trick that—just as was done for velocity above—when crossing over the flame front and referring to a temperature on the fuel side, the "ghost" value of $T_{\max}$ is used. Let's make that clear: the actual temperature T in the fuel side is kept constant at T_{ignition}, but when advecting and diffusing T on the burnt side, if reference is made to a T value in the fuel (e.g., when doing interpolation in semi-Lagrangian advection) $T_{\max}$ is used instead. For the extreme temperatures apparent in fires, hot enough to make an incandescent glow, a black-body radiation formula for the decay of T might be used instead of the simple exponential decay mentioned earlier, where the rate of cooling is proportional to the fourth power of the temperature difference

$$\frac{DT}{Dt} = -c\left(\frac{T - T_{\text{ambient}}}{T_{\max} - T_{\text{ambient}}}\right)^4$$

for some cooling constant c defined as a user parameter. After advecting temperature around to get an intermediate $\tilde{T}$ for a time step Δt, this cooling equation can be solved analytically to give

$$T^{n+1} = T_{\text{ambient}} + \left[\frac{1}{(\tilde{T} - T_{\text{ambient}})^3} + \frac{3c\Delta t}{(T_{\max} - T_{\text{ambient}})^4}\right]^{-\frac{1}{3}}.$$

Similar to this treatment of temperature, we can also feed a smoke concentration $s_{\max}$ into the burnt region from the flame front, allowing it to be advected and dissipated as usual. Temperature and smoke concentration can feed into either a buoyancy force (if we make the Boussinesq approximation) or modify density, as discussed in Chapter 5.

The final issue is rendering, which mostly lies outside the scope of this book. The actual flame front itself is sometimes referred to as the "blue core," referring to the spectral emissions made when burning typical hydrocarbons (other fuels give rise to different spectra, giving different colors): the level set itself is a light emitter. For a dirty flame, where soot is produced, the bulk of the visual effect though is the black-body incandescence of the soot particles. That is, light is emitted from the burnt region as well, proportional to the smoke concentration s and following the black-body spectrum for the temperature T. Simultaneously, the soot is somewhat opaque, so light emitted elsewhere should be absorbed at a rate proportional to s. Further scattering effects can be included of course.

7.2 Volumetric Combustion

We now turn to an alternate model where combustion may take place throughout the volume, loosely following Feldman et al. [Feldman et al. 03].

This is appropriate particularly for modeling the fireballs due to deflagration of fuel suspended in the air, whether flammable powder or liquid-fuel mist. It's also slightly simpler to implement than the preceding thin-flame model, since level sets are not involved, yet it can still achieve some of the look of regular flames and thus might be preferred in some instances.

To a standard smoke simulation, which includes temperature T, smoke concentration s, and divergence controls, we add another field F, the concentration of unburnt fuel in each grid cell. The fuel gets advected along with the flow as usual, may be additional diffused, and may be seeded at fuel sources or emitted from boundaries. (In Feldman et al.'s work, fuel is instead represented as the unburnt mass of discrete fuel particles; we'll come back to using particle systems in grid-based fluid solvers in Chapter 10.)

To this we add some simple rules. If the temperature T at a grid cell, following advection and dissipation steps, is above some ignition threshold T_{ignition} and the fuel concentration F is above zero, we burn some of the fuel. At the simplest we reduce F by $z\Delta t$, where z is the burn speed (volume fraction combusted per second), clamping it to zero to avoid negative F. Let ΔF be the change in F; we then increase the smoke concentration s by some amount proportional to ΔF, increase the temperature T also proportional to ΔF, and add an amount to the divergence control proportional to $\Delta F/\Delta t$ (recall the divergence is percent expansion per unit of time, thus we need to divide by Δt). Note that this rule burns the fuel at a constant rate z without regard to the availability of oxidizer; Feldman et al. argue that for suspended particle explosions (coal dust, sawdust, flour, etc.) oxygen availability in the air is never the limiting factor, and thus this rule is justified. However, if need be you could limit the rate based on $1 - s - F$, the volume fraction left for plain air.

Rendering is based on black-body radiation as in the previous section, though here we don't have any representation of the "blue core" available so the rendering possibilities are slightly more limited.

– 8 –
Viscous Fluids

After briefly discussing viscosity in Chapter 1, we dispensed with it and until now have only looked at inviscid simulations. In fact our major problem has been that our numerical methods have too much numerical dissipation which, in the velocity field, looks like viscosity. We now will turn our attention to simulating highly viscous fluids, like molasses, and even variable viscosity fluids where some parts are more viscous than others (perhaps due to heating or cooling, or desired animation effects).

8.1 Stress

To properly understand viscosity and avoid some potential mistakes when handling variable viscosity situations, we need to first understand the concept of stress.

In reality, at least as a first approximation, matter is composed of small particles with mass that interact by applying forces on each other. However, since we're not interested in phenomena at that microscopic scale, in fluid mechanics we make the continuum assumption, that matter is a continuous field with no discrete particles. One way of thinking about this assumption is that we're taking the limit as the particles become infinitesimally small and packed together with infinitesimal space between them. For dynamics this poses the problem that the masses drop to zero, and for accelerations to remain bounded the forces must drop to zero too. To get around this, we measure things in bulk: how much mass there is in a volume of space, or what the net force is on a volume.

While it makes no sense to ask what the mass of a continuum fluid is at a point in space (it has to be zero), we can define the density at any point, which is a useful quantity. By integrating density in a volume we get the total mass of the volume. Similarly it makes no sense to ask what the force on a continuum fluid is at a point in space (it has to be zero), but we can define quantities analogous to density: force densities in a sense, that when integrated over a region give a net force.

We've already seen two examples of force density, body forces (such as gravity) and pressure. These are fundamentally different however: to get the net gravitational force on a volume of fluid you integrate the gravitational body force density $\rho\vec{g}$ over the *volume*, but to get the net pressure force on the volume you integrate the pressure times the normal $p\hat{n}$ over the *surface* of the volume. The difference is that a body force acts over a distance to influence everything inside the volume, whereas other forces (like pressure) can only act locally on the surface of contact. It is these local contact forces that we need to generalize from pressure to figure out viscosity and more exotic fluid effects.

An accepted assumption (verified to be accurate in many experiments), called Cauchy's Hypothesis, is that we can represent the local contact forces by a function of position and orientation only. That is, there is a vector field called *traction*, $\vec{t}(\vec{x}, \hat{n})$, a function of where in space we are measuring it and what the normal to the contact surface there is. It has units of force per area: to get the net contact force on a volume of fluid Ω, we integrate the traction over its surface:

$$\vec{F} = \iint_{\partial\Omega} \vec{t}(\vec{x}, \hat{n}).$$

I'd like to underscore here that this volume can be an arbitrary region containing fluid (or in fact, any continuum substance); e.g., it could be a tiny subregion in the interior of the fluid, or a grid cell, etc.

Once we accept this assumption, it can be proven that the traction must depend linearly on the normal; that is, the traction must be the result of multiplying some matrix by the normal. Technically speaking this is actually a rank-two tensor, not just a matrix, but we'll gloss over the difference for now and just call it a tensor from now on.[1] The tensor is called the *stress tensor*, or more specifically the *Cauchy stress tensor*,[2] which we label σ. Thus we can write

$$\vec{t}(\vec{x}, \hat{n}) = \sigma(\vec{x})\hat{n}.$$

---

[1] Basically a matrix is a specific array of numbers; a rank-two tensor is a more abstract linear operator that can be represented as a matrix when you pick a set of basis vectors with which to measure it. For the purposes of this book, you can think of them interchangeably, as we will always use a fixed Cartesian basis where y is in the vertical direction.

[2] There are other stress tensors, which chiefly differ in the basis in which they are represented. For elastic solids, where it makes sense to talk of a rest configuration to which the object tries to return, it can be convenient to set up a stress tensor in terms of rest-configuration coordinates, rather than the world-space coordinates in which Cauchy stress operates.

Note that the stress tensor only depends on position, not on the surface normal. It can also be proven from conservation of angular momentum that the stress tensor must be symmetric: $\sigma = \sigma^T$.

Since the unit normal has no units, the stress tensor is also measured as force per area, just like traction. However, it's a little harder to interpret; it's easier instead to think in terms of traction on a specific plane of contact.

As a concrete example using continuum materials that are a little easier to experience, put your hand down on a flat desk. The flesh of your hand and the wood of the desk are essentially each a continuum, and thus there is conceptually a stress tensor in each. The net force you apply on the desk with your hand is the integral of the traction over the area of contact. The normal in this case is the vertical vector $(0, 1, 0)$, so the traction at any point is

$$\vec{t} = \sigma \hat{n} = \begin{bmatrix} \sigma_{11} & \sigma_{12} & \sigma_{13} \\ \sigma_{21} & \sigma_{22} & \sigma_{23} \\ \sigma_{31} & \sigma_{32} & \sigma_{33} \end{bmatrix} \begin{bmatrix} 0 \\ 1 \\ 0 \end{bmatrix} = \begin{bmatrix} \sigma_{12} \\ \sigma_{22} \\ \sigma_{32} \end{bmatrix}.$$

Note that the normal force comes from the vertical component σ_{22} of traction—how hard you are pushing down on the desk. The other components of the traction, σ_{12} and σ_{32}, are tangential—how hard you are pushing the desk forwards, backwards, or to the side.

Those tangential forces are due to friction; without it there could only be a normal force. Viscosity is in many ways similar to friction, in particular that a fluid without viscosity only exerts forces in the normal direction. That is, the traction $\vec{t} = \sigma \hat{n}$ in an inviscid fluid is always in the normal direction: it must be parallel to $\hat{n}$. Since this is true for any normal vector, it can be proven that the stress tensor of an inviscid fluid must be a scalar times the identity. That scalar is, in fact, the negative of pressure. Thus, for the inviscid case we have considered up until now, the stress tensor is just

$$\sigma = -p\delta, \tag{8.1}$$

where we use δ to mean the identity tensor. When we model viscosity, we will end up with a more complicated stress tensor.

8.2 Applying Stress

The net force due to stress on a volume Ω of fluid is the surface integral of traction:

$$\vec{F} = \iint_{\partial\Omega} \sigma\hat{n}.$$

We can use the divergence theorem to transform this into a volume integral:

$$\vec{F} = \iiint_\Omega \nabla \cdot \sigma.$$

Note that the notation $\nabla \cdot \sigma$ is the accepted short-hand for the vector whose elements are the divergences of the rows (or columns) of σ:

$$\nabla \cdot \sigma = \begin{bmatrix} \dfrac{\partial \sigma_{11}}{\partial x} + \dfrac{\partial \sigma_{12}}{\partial y} + \dfrac{\partial \sigma_{13}}{\partial z} \\[2mm] \dfrac{\partial \sigma_{21}}{\partial x} + \dfrac{\partial \sigma_{22}}{\partial y} + \dfrac{\partial \sigma_{23}}{\partial z} \\[2mm] \dfrac{\partial \sigma_{31}}{\partial x} + \dfrac{\partial \sigma_{32}}{\partial y} + \dfrac{\partial \sigma_{33}}{\partial z} \end{bmatrix}.$$

Ignoring body forces for simplicity, we set this net force equal to the mass times center-of-mass acceleration:

$$\vec{F} = M\vec{A} = \iiint_\Omega \rho \frac{D\vec{u}}{Dt},$$

i.e., we have an equality between the two volume integrals:

$$\iiint_\Omega \rho \frac{D\vec{u}}{Dt} = \iiint_\Omega \nabla \cdot \sigma.$$

Since this holds for any arbitrary volume, the integrands must be equal:

$$\rho \frac{D\vec{u}}{Dt} = \nabla \cdot \sigma.$$

Adding back in the body force term, we actually have the general momentum equation for a continuum (elastic solids as well as fluids):

$$\frac{D\vec{u}}{Dt} = \frac{1}{\rho}\vec{g} + \frac{1}{\rho}\nabla \cdot \sigma.$$

In the particular case of an inviscid fluid, as we discussed above, the stress tensor is just the negative of pressure times the identity—see Equation (8.1). In this case, it's not hard to see that $\nabla \cdot \sigma$ simplifies to $-\nabla p$, giving the familiar momentum equation.

For general fluid flow, pressure is still a very important quantity, so we will explicitly separate it out from the rest of the stress tensor:

$$\sigma = -p\delta + \tau,$$

where τ is also a symmetric tensor. We will let the pressure term handle the incompressibility constraint and model other fluid behavior with τ.

8.3 Strain Rate and Newtonian Fluids

Viscosity is physically based on the fact that when molecules traveling at different speeds collide or closely interact, some energy may be transferred to vibrational or rotational modes in the molecule—i.e., heat —and thus the difference in center-of-mass velocity between the two molecules is reduced. At the continuum level, the net effect of this is that as a region of fluid slips past another, momentum is transferred between them to reduce the difference in velocity, and the fluids get hotter. The critical thing to note is that this occurs when fluid moves *past* other fluid: in a rigid body rotation there are differences in velocity, but the fluid moves together and there is no viscous effect. Thus we really only care about how the fluid is deforming, i.e., moving non-rigidly.

To measure differences in velocity locally, the natural quantity to consider is the gradient of velocity: $\nabla \vec{u}$. However, mixed up in the gradient is information about the rigid rotation[3] as well as the deformation induced by the flow. We will want to separate out just the deformation part to define viscous stress.

One way to characterize rigid motion is that the dot-product of any two vectors remains constant. (If the two vectors are the same, this is just saying lengths remains constant; for different vectors we're saying the angle between them stays the same.) How much the dot-product between two vectors changes is thus a measure of how fast the fluid is deforming. Let's look at a point $\vec{x}$: in a small time interval Δt it moves to approximately $\vec{x} + \Delta t \vec{u}(\vec{x})$. Now look at two nearby points, $\vec{x} + \Delta \vec{x}$ and $\vec{x} + \Delta \vec{y}$: linearizing appropriately, they approximately move to

$$\vec{x} + \Delta \vec{x} + \Delta t(\vec{u}(\vec{x}) + \nabla \vec{u} \Delta \vec{x})$$
$$\text{and} \quad \vec{x} + \Delta \vec{y} + \Delta t(\vec{u}(\vec{x}) + \nabla \vec{u} \Delta \vec{y}),$$

respectively. The dot-product of the vectors from $\vec{x}$ to these points begins as

$$[(\vec{x} + \Delta \vec{x}) - \vec{x}] \cdot [(\vec{x} + \Delta \vec{y}) - \vec{x}] = \Delta \vec{x} \cdot \Delta \vec{y}$$

and after the time interval is approximately

$$[(\vec{x} + \Delta \vec{x} + \Delta t(\vec{u}(\vec{x}) + \nabla \vec{u} \Delta \vec{x})) - (\vec{x} + \Delta t \vec{u}(\vec{x}))]$$
$$\cdot [(\vec{x} + \Delta \vec{y} + \Delta t(\vec{u}(\vec{x}) + \nabla \vec{u} \Delta \vec{y})) - (\vec{x} + \Delta t \vec{u}(\vec{x}))]$$
$$= [\Delta \vec{x} + \Delta t \nabla \vec{u} \Delta \vec{x}] \cdot [\Delta \vec{y} + \Delta t \nabla \vec{u} \Delta \vec{y}].$$

---

[3]Later in the book, we will take a look at the curl of velocity which is called vorticity, $\vec{\omega} = \nabla \times \vec{u}$; it measures precisely the rotational part of the velocity field.

Then the change in the dot-product, ignoring $O(\Delta t^2)$ terms, is

$$\Delta t \left(\Delta \vec{x} \cdot \nabla \vec{u} \Delta \vec{y} + \Delta \vec{y} \cdot \nabla \vec{u} \Delta \vec{x} \right) = \Delta t \Delta \vec{x}^T \left(\nabla \vec{u} + \nabla \vec{u}^T \right) \Delta \vec{y}.$$

That is, the rate of change of dot-products of vectors in the flow is determined by the symmetric part of the velocity gradient, the matrix $D = \frac{1}{2}(\nabla \vec{u} + \nabla \vec{u}^T)$. This is called the *strain rate tensor* or rate of strain, since it's measuring how fast *strain*—the total deformation of the continuum—is changing.

Incidentally, the rest of the velocity gradient, the skew-symmetric part $\frac{1}{2}(\nabla \vec{u} - \nabla \vec{u}^T)$ naturally has to represent the other source of velocity differences in the flow: rotation. We'll explore this further later in the book.

We'll also immediately point out that for incompressible fluids, which is all we focus on in this book, the trace of D (the sum of the diagonal entries, denoted $\text{tr}(D)$) is simply $\nabla \cdot \vec{u} = 0$.

We are looking for a symmetric tensor τ to model stress due to viscosity; the rate of strain tensor D is symmetric and measures how fast the fluid is deforming. The obvious thing to do is assume τ depends linearly on D. Fluids for which there is a simple linear relationship are called *Newtonian*. Air and water are examples of fluids which are, to a very good approximation, Newtonian. However, there are many liquids (generally with a more complex composition) where a non-linear relationship is essential; they go under the catch-all category of *non-Newtonian* fluids.[4] We won't go into any more detail, but observe that two classes of non-Newtonian fluids, *shear-thickening* and *shear-thinning* fluids, can be easily modeled with a viscosity coefficient η that is a function of $\|D\|_F$, the Frobenius norm of the strain rate:[5]

$$\|D\|_F = \sqrt{\sum_{i,j=1}^{3} D_{i,j}^2}.$$

---

[4]Also sometimes included in the non-Newtonian class are *viscoelastic* fluids, which blur the line between fluid and solid as they can include elastic forces that seek to return the material to an "undeformed" state—in fact these are sometimes best thought of instead as solids with permanent (*plastic*) deformations. You might refer to the article by Goktekin et al. [Goktekin et al. 04] and Irving's thesis [Irving 07] for a fluid-centric treatment in graphics.

[5]Technically this is assuming again that the fluid is incompressible, so the trace of D is zero, which means it represents only *shearing* deformations, not expansions or contractions.

Often a power-law is assumed:

$$\eta = K\|D\|_F^{n-1}, \tag{8.2}$$

where $n = 1$ corresponds to a Newtonian fluid, $n > 1$ a shear-thickening fluid where apparent viscosity increases as you try to deform the fluid faster (e.g., cornstarch suspended in water), and $0 < n < 1$ a shear-thinning fluid where apparent viscosity decreases (e.g., paint). Granular materials such as sand can even be modeled as the limit $n = 0$ of shear-thinning where the magnitude of "viscous" stress depends instead on pressure, not the magnitude of the strain rate, making it more akin to dry Coulomb friction; see Zhu and Bridson [Zhu and Bridson 05] for more on this subject.

Getting back to simple Newtonian fluids, the relationship for incompressible flow is

$$\tau = 2\eta D + \lambda \mathrm{tr}(D)\delta, \tag{8.3}$$

where η is the *coefficient of dynamic viscosity*. The second term, involving $\mathrm{tr}(D) = \nabla \cdot \vec{u}$, is of course zero for incompressible flow for any λ (which is termed the *second coefficient of viscosity*). For compressible flow λ is often taken to be $-\frac{2}{3}\eta$, though theoretically this is only an idealization of monatomic gases. However, for an incompressible fluid we are free to choose λ as we please,[6] and thus for simplicity's sake we'll set $\lambda = 0$.

Plugging this into the momentum equation, we get

$$\frac{D\vec{u}}{Dt} + \frac{1}{\rho}\nabla p = \frac{1}{\rho}\nabla \cdot \left(\eta(\nabla\vec{u} + \nabla\vec{u}^T)\right). \tag{8.4}$$

You may notice that this isn't quite the same as our first statement of the momentum equation, Equation (1.1). It turns out that for the common case where η is constant, the correct equation (8.4) does in fact simplify to Equation (1.1): but be aware, for simulations with variable viscosity, only Equation (8.4) is correct. For example, Equation (1.1) doesn't conserve angular momentum in the variable viscosity case.

---

[6]This isn't quite true: for $\lambda < -\frac{2}{3}\eta$, basic thermodynamics are violated, with viscosity actually accelerating expansion or contraction, increasing the energy of the system. In a numerical method, where divergence probably isn't exactly zero even for incompressible flow, problems are bound to arise.

Let's work through the simplification. If η is constant, then we can take it out from under the divergence:

$$\frac{D\vec{u}}{Dt} + \frac{1}{\rho}\nabla p = \frac{\eta}{\rho}\nabla \cdot (\nabla\vec{u} + \nabla\vec{u}^T)$$

$$= \frac{\eta}{\rho}\left[\nabla \cdot \nabla\vec{u} + \nabla \cdot (\nabla\vec{u}^T)\right]$$

$$= \frac{\eta}{\rho}\left[\nabla \cdot \nabla\vec{u} + \begin{pmatrix} \dfrac{\partial}{\partial x}\dfrac{\partial u}{\partial x} + \dfrac{\partial}{\partial y}\dfrac{\partial v}{\partial x} + \dfrac{\partial}{\partial z}\dfrac{\partial w}{\partial x} \\ \dfrac{\partial}{\partial x}\dfrac{\partial u}{\partial y} + \dfrac{\partial}{\partial y}\dfrac{\partial v}{\partial y} + \dfrac{\partial}{\partial z}\dfrac{\partial w}{\partial y} \\ \dfrac{\partial}{\partial x}\dfrac{\partial u}{\partial z} + \dfrac{\partial}{\partial y}\dfrac{\partial v}{\partial z} + \dfrac{\partial}{\partial z}\dfrac{\partial w}{\partial z} \end{pmatrix}\right]$$

$$= \frac{\eta}{\rho}\left[\nabla \cdot \nabla\vec{u} + \begin{pmatrix} \dfrac{\partial}{\partial x}(\dfrac{\partial u}{\partial x} + \dfrac{\partial v}{\partial y} + \dfrac{\partial w}{\partial z}) \\ \dfrac{\partial}{\partial y}(\dfrac{\partial u}{\partial x} + \dfrac{\partial v}{\partial y} + \dfrac{\partial w}{\partial z}) \\ \dfrac{\partial}{\partial z}(\dfrac{\partial u}{\partial x} + \dfrac{\partial v}{\partial y} + \dfrac{\partial w}{\partial z}) \end{pmatrix}\right].$$

In the last step we simply changed the order of partial derivatives in the last term and regrouped. But now we see that the last term is simply the gradient of $\nabla \cdot \vec{u}$:

$$\frac{D\vec{u}}{Dt} + \frac{1}{\rho}\nabla p = \frac{\eta}{\rho}\left[\nabla \cdot \nabla\vec{u} + \nabla(\nabla \cdot \vec{u})\right].$$

If the flow is incompressible, i.e., $\nabla \cdot \vec{u} = 0$, then the last term is zero and we end up back at Equation (1.1). I emphasize that this only happens when both the viscosity is constant through the flow and the velocity field is incompressible. The second point becomes important numerically since at intermediate stages in our time integration our velocity field may not be discretely incompressible—and then this last term can't be blithely ignored.

Getting back to variable viscosity, some formula needs to be decided for η. For a non-Newtonian fluid, it might be a function of the magnitude of the strain rate, as we have seen. For regular Newtonian fluids it might instead be a function of temperature—assuming we're tracking temperature in the simulation as we saw how to do with smoke and fire—which is most important for liquids. Carlson et al. [Carlson et al. 02] suggest that modeling melting and solidifying (freezing) can be emulated by making the viscosity a low constant for temperatures above a transition zone (centered on the melting point) and a high constant for temperatures below the transition zone (thus giving near-rigid behavior), and smoothly varying between the two in the narrow transition zone itself.

8.4   Boundary Conditions

The two types of boundaries considered in this book are free surfaces and solid walls, and each has particular conditions associated with viscosity.

In the case of a free surface, things are fairly straightforward. On the other side of the boundary there is a vacuum, or another fluid of much smaller density whose effect we assume is negligible. Thus there is nothing with which to transfer momentum: there can be no traction at the free surface. In other words, the boundary condition for the stress at the free surface is

$$\sigma \hat{n} = -p\hat{n} + \tau \hat{n} = 0.$$

Note that if the viscous stress τ is zero, this reduces to $p = 0$ as before; however, this becomes significantly more complex when τ isn't zero.

At solid walls, things are also a little more interesting. Physically speaking once we model viscosity, it turns out the velocity field must be continuous everywhere: if it weren't, viscous transfer of momentum would in the next instant make it smooth again. This results in the so-called *no-slip* boundary condition:

$$\vec{u} = \vec{u}_{\text{solid}},$$

which of course simplifies to $\vec{u} = 0$ at stationary solids. Recall that in the inviscid case, only the normal component of velocities had to match: here we are forcing the tangential components to match as well.

The no-slip condition has been experimentally verified to be more accurate than the inviscid no-stick condition. However, the caveat is that in many cases something called a *boundary layer* develops. Loosely speaking, a boundary layer is a thin region next to a solid where the tangential velocity rapidly changes from $\vec{u}_{\text{solid}}$ at the solid wall to $\vec{u}^{\star}$ at the other side of the layer, where $\vec{u}^{\star}$ is the velocity the inviscid no-stick boundary condition ($\vec{u} \cdot \hat{n} = \vec{u}_{\text{solid}} \cdot \hat{n}$) would have given. That is, the effect of viscous drag at the surface of the solid is restricted to a very small region next to the solid, and can be ignored elsewhere. When we discretize the fluid flow on a relatively coarse grid, that boundary layer may be much thinner than a grid cell, and thus it's no longer a good idea to implement the no-slip condition numerically—we would artificially be expanding the boundary layer to at least a grid cell thick, which would be a much worse approximation than going back to the inviscid no-stick boundary condition. In this case, we have

$$\vec{u} \cdot \hat{n} = \vec{u}_{\text{solid}} \cdot \hat{n},$$

$$(\tau \hat{n}) \times \hat{n} = 0,$$

where the second boundary equation is indicating that the viscous stress causes no tangential traction.

8.5 Implementation

The first simplification we will make is to use time-splitting again, handling viscosity in a separate step from advection, body forces, and pressure projection. While there has been a lot of study of methods that simultaneously treat viscosity and pressure to great advantage, solving the so-called *Stokes problem*, so far in graphics, practitioners have avoided the increased complexity. With splitting, we will include a step that solves, for one time step Δt,

$$\frac{\partial \vec{u}}{\partial t} = \frac{1}{\rho} \nabla \cdot \left(\eta (\nabla \vec{u} + \nabla \vec{u}^T) \right)$$

with any or all of the boundary conditions given above.

Since we are not simultaneously handling viscosity and pressure projection, the question immediately arises: on what intermediate velocity field do we run viscosity? Does it come before or after advection? In all cases errors will be made. For the common case of constant viscosity, however, the attraction of viscosity reducing to a separate Laplacian applied to each component of velocity (instead of coupling all components of velocity together) is obvious—and we have seen that this only is justified if the velocity field is divergence-free. Therefore it is recommended to run viscosity immediately after pressure projection, before body forces and gravity. However, advection *must* use a divergence-free velocity field. Therefore we have two options: apply an additional pressure projection after the viscous stage to get a new divergence-free velocity field; or run advection with the pre-viscous divergence-free velocity field but referring to the post-viscous values. (This is exactly the problem that handling viscosity and pressure projection simultaneously solves, but again we're going to keep with time-splitting.) The second option, cheaper but sometimes of obviously lower quality, can be set up as

- Find $\vec{u}^V$ as the result of viscosity applied to divergence-free velocity field $\vec{u}^n$, using the viscous boundary conditions.

- Advect $\vec{u}^V$ in the divergence-free velocity field $\vec{u}^n$ to get $\vec{u}^A$.

Plate I. A smoke simulation (Chapter 5) using the FLIP particle method (Section 10.4). (*Images courtesy of Hagit Schechter.*)

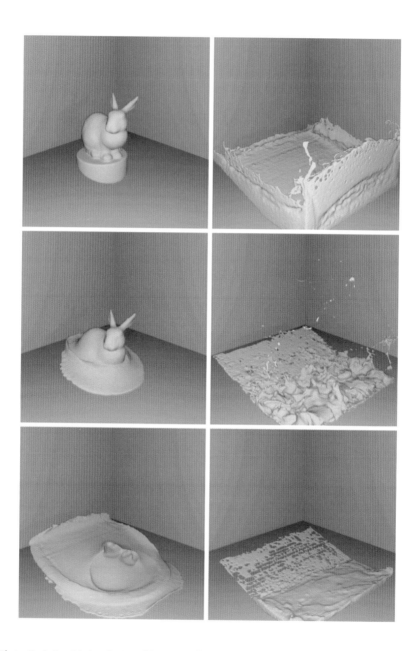

Plate II. A liquid simulation (Chapter 6) using the FLIP particle method (Section 10.4). The classic voxelized pressure solve (Chapter 4) causes grid artifacts: water pools along grid lines on the smooth ramp.

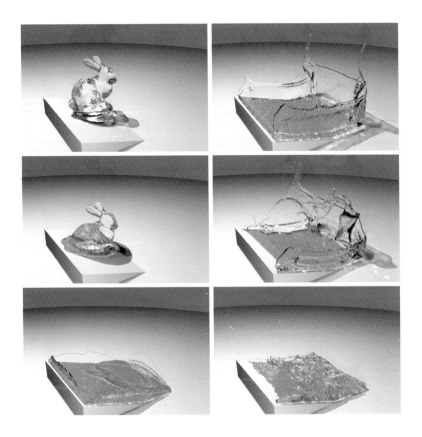

Plate III. A more accurate treatment of solid boundaries in the pressure solve (Section 4.5) cures the grid artifacts of the previous liquid simulation.

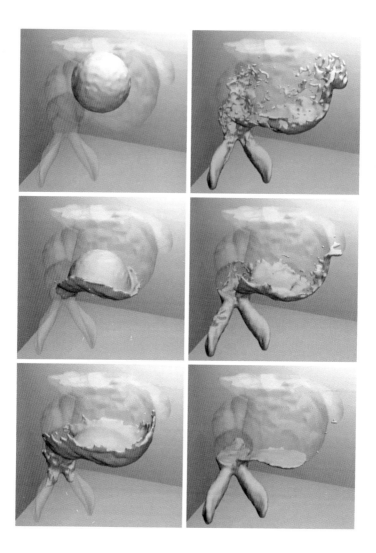

Plate IV. A liquid simulation using the FLIP particle method (Section 10.4) and combining an accurate treatment of the free surface boundary condition (Section 6.4) with an accurate solid boundary treatment (Section 4.5). (*Images courtesy of Christopher Batty.*)

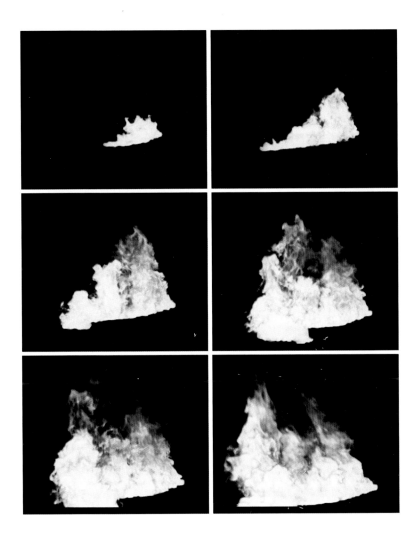

Plate V. Fire simulation, using a volumetric combustion model (Section 7.2) and the FLIP particle method (Section 10.4). (*Images courtesy of Double Negative Visual Effects, simulated and rendered by Jason Harris, Ged Wright and Gavin Graham.*)

Plate VI. Fire simulation, using a volumetric combustion model (Section 7.2) and the FLIP particle method (Section 10.4). (*Images courtesy of Double Negative Visual Effects, simulated and rendered by Jason Harris, Ged Wright and Gavin Graham.*)

- Add body forces to get $\vec{u}^B = \vec{u}^A + \Delta t \vec{g}$.

- Solve for pressure to get a divergence-free $\vec{u}^{n+1} = \text{project}(\vec{u}^B, \Delta t)$ satisfying the inviscid boundary conditions.

Note that there is the possibility that the final velocity field $\vec{u}^{n+1}$ will no longer exactly satisfy the viscous boundary conditions, just the inviscid ones—however, it will be off by at most $O(\Delta t)$, which we can live with.

Now that we have a full time step in place, let's determine how to actually apply viscous forces. Once again staggered grids are our friend. Let's take a look at the contribution to the horizontal component of velocity, given the viscous stress tensor τ:

$$u^V = u^n + \frac{\Delta t}{\rho}\left(\frac{\partial \tau^{11}}{\partial x} + \frac{\partial \tau^{12}}{\partial y} + \frac{\partial \tau^{13}}{\partial z}\right).$$

Since u is located in the grid at, say, $(i+1/2, j, k)$, it's natural to ask for τ^{11} to be at grid cell centers (i, j, k), for τ^{12} to be at the edge-center $(i+1/2, j+1/2, k)$, and for τ^{13} at $(i+1/2, j, k+1/2)$. This gives an elegant discretization:

$$u^V_{i+1/2,j,k} = u^n_{i+1/2,j,k} + \frac{\Delta t}{\rho}\left(\frac{\tau^{11}_{i+1,j,k} - \tau^{11}_{i,j,k}}{\Delta x}\right.$$

$$+ \frac{\tau^{12}_{i+1/2,j+1/2,k} - \tau^{12}_{i+1/2,j-1/2,k}}{\Delta x} + \left.\frac{\tau^{13}_{i+1/2,j,k+1/2} - \tau^{13}_{i+1/2,j,k-1/2}}{\Delta x}\right).$$

Similarly for the other components of velocity:

$$v^V_{i,j+1/2,k} = v^n_{i,j+1/2,k} + \frac{\Delta t}{\rho}\left(\frac{\tau^{12}_{i+1/2,j+1/2,k} - \tau^{12}_{i-1/2,j+1/2,k}}{\Delta x}\right.$$

$$+ \frac{\tau^{22}_{i,j+1,k} - \tau^{22}_{i,j,k}}{\Delta x} + \left.\frac{\tau^{23}_{i,j+1/2,k+1/2} - \tau^{23}_{i,j+1/2,k-1/2}}{\Delta x}\right),$$

$$w^V_{i,j,k+1/2} - w^n_{i,j,k+1/2} + \frac{\Delta t}{\rho}\left(\frac{\tau^{13}_{i+1/2,j,k+1/2} - \tau^{13}_{i-1/2,j,k+1/2}}{\Delta x}\right.$$

$$+ \frac{\tau^{23}_{i,j+1/2,k+1/2} - \tau^{23}_{i,j-1/2,k+1/2}}{\Delta x} + \left.\frac{\tau^{33}_{i,j,k+1} - \tau^{33}_{i,j,k}}{\Delta x}\right).$$

Note that these formulas make use of the symmetry of τ, e.g., $\tau^{12} = \tau^{21}$. In 2D, they simplify the obvious way. But how do we determine the values of τ on the staggered grid, and how do we simplify when viscosity is constant?

8.5.1 Explicit Treatment

The simplest thing of all is to just use central differences on the given velocity field. From the definition $\tau = \eta(\nabla \vec{u} + \nabla \vec{u}^T)$ we get

$$\tau^{11}_{i,j,k} = 2\eta_{i,j,k} \frac{u^n_{i+1/2,j,k} - u^n_{i-1/2,j,k}}{\Delta x}$$

$$\tau^{12}_{i+1/2,j+1/2,k} =$$
$$\eta_{i+1/2,j+1/2,k} \left(\frac{u^n_{i+1/2,j+1,k} - u^n_{i+1/2,j,k}}{\Delta x} + \frac{v^n_{i+1,j+1/2,k} - v^n_{i,j+1/2,k}}{\Delta x} \right)$$

$$\tau^{13}_{i+1/2,j,k+1/2} =$$
$$\eta_{i+1/2,j,k+1/2} \left(\frac{u^n_{i+1/2,j,k+1} - u^n_{i+1/2,j,k}}{\Delta x} + \frac{w^n_{i+1,j,k+1/2} - w^n_{i,j,k+1/2}}{\Delta x} \right)$$

$$\tau^{22}_{i,j,k} = 2\eta_{i,j,k} \frac{v^n_{i,j+1/2,k} - v^n_{i,j-1/2,k}}{\Delta x}$$

$$\tau^{23}_{i,j+1/2,k+1/2} =$$
$$\eta_{i,j+1/2,k+1/2} \left(\frac{v^n_{i,j+1/2,k+1} - v^n_{i,j+1/2,k}}{\Delta x} + \frac{w^n_{i,j+1,k+1/2} - w^n_{i,j,k+1/2}}{\Delta x} \right)$$

$$\tau^{33}_{i,j,k} = 2\eta_{i,j,k} \frac{w^n_{i,j,k+1/2} - w^n_{i,j,k-1/2}}{\Delta x}$$

This can be simplified in the obvious way for 2D.

In the case where η is constant and $\vec{u}^n$ is discretely divergence-free, it's not too hard to verify that just as in the differential equations, the coupling terms between velocity components will drop out, simplifying the whole update to a discrete Laplacian for each velocity component. For brevity, here is just the u-component in 2D:

$$u^V_{i+1/2,j} = u^n_{i+1/2,j}$$
$$+ \frac{\Delta t \eta}{\rho} \left(\frac{u^n_{i+3/2,j} + u^n_{i+1/2,j+1} + u^n_{i-1/2,j} + u^n_{i+1/2,j-1} - 4u^n_{i+1/2,j}}{\Delta x^2} \right),$$

which should look familiar from the discretization of the Laplacian in the pressure problem.

Beyond boundaries, we need ghost velocity values to plug into these formulas. For viscous solid walls with the no-slip condition, it's natural to simply use the solid velocity itself. For free surfaces we have to be a little more careful. The obvious first approach to try is to just extrapolate the velocity into the air, as we have done before, effectively setting $\vec{u}$ at a point in the air to the velocity at the closest point on the surface. Similarly, at an inviscid solid boundary, we can extrapolate the tangential component of fluid velocity into the solid while using the normal component of solid velocity—in fact, Rasmussen et al. [Rasmussen et al. 04] suggest an interesting intermediate condition between inviscid and fully viscous, where a weighted average of the solid's tangential velocity and the fluid's tangential velocity is used.

However, this simple extrapolation induces a non-negligible error. As a thought experiment, imagine a blob of fluid moving rigidly in free flight: it has zero deformation since its internal velocity field is rigid, therefore it should experience no viscous forces—i.e., τ should evaluate to zero, even at the boundary. However, if a rigid rotation is present, τ only evaluates to zero if the ghost velocities keep that same rotation: extrapolating as a constant doesn't, and will induce erroneous viscous resistance at the boundary. Ideally a more sophisticated extrapolation scheme such as linear extrapolation should be used.

That said, at present our first-order time-splitting of advection from pressure also will induce a similar erroneous drag on rotational motion, which we'll discuss in Chapter 9. Reducing one error but not the other is probably not worth the bother, and thus we'll leave this question open for further research.

The chief problem with the method as presented is stability. Unfortunately this method is liable to blow up if Δt is too large. Let's examine a simple 1D model problem to understand why,

$$\frac{\partial q}{\partial t} = k \frac{\partial^2 q}{\partial x^2},$$

where q models a velocity component and k models η/ρ, the kinematic viscosity. Our explicit discretization would give

$$q_i^{n+1} = q_i^n + \Delta t k \frac{q_{i+1}^n - 2q_i^n + q_{i-1}^n}{\Delta x^2}.$$

Consider the highest spatial-frequency component possible in the numerical solution, say $q_i^n = Q^n(-1)^i$. Here Q^n is the time n scalar coefficient multiplying the ± 1 underlying basis function, with grid index i the exponent of (-1). Plug this in to see what Q^{n+1} is:

$$Q^{n+1}(-1)^i = Q^n(-1)^i + \Delta t k \frac{Q^n(-1)^{i+1}_i - 2Q^n(-1)^i + Q^n(-1)^{i-1}}{\Delta x^2}$$

$$= Q^n(-1)^i \left(1 + \frac{\Delta t k}{\Delta x^2}(-1 - 2 - 1)\right)$$

$$= Q^n(-1)^i \left(1 - \frac{4\Delta t k}{\Delta x^2}\right),$$

$$Q^{n+1} = \left(1 - \frac{4\Delta t k}{\Delta x^2}\right) Q^n.$$

This can only exponentially and monotonically decay, as we would expect viscosity to do, if

$$\Delta t < \frac{\Delta x^2}{4k}.$$

Otherwise we end up with q oscillating in time—a physically incorrect vibration—and possibly even exponential *increase*, which is thermodynamically impossible and potentially disastrous numerically.

For the full 3D viscous problem, a similar time step restriction applies:

$$\Delta t < \frac{\Delta x^2 \rho}{12\eta_{max}}. \tag{8.5}$$

This is pretty severe: while we discussed the merit of restricting Δt to be $O(\Delta x)$ to control errors in advection, this possibly reduces it a whole order of magnitude further. More to the point, there is no accuracy requirement to keep Δt this small: the physics of viscous dissipation essentially boils down to the exponential decay of deformation modes, which can be well approximated even with large time steps. In numerical lingo, this means that the problem is *stiff*: accuracy is saying it should be fine to take large Δt, but stability is requiring punishingly small Δt. The usual numerical solution is to use *implicit* time integration.

8.5.2 Implicit Treatment

The simplest implicit time integration scheme is called *backward Euler*. In this case it means rather than evaluating the stress tensor based on the old velocities $\vec{u}^n$, we'll base it on the new velocities $\vec{u}^V$, which of course, we don't know yet, until we get the stress tensor—which again depends on knowing the new velocities. This isn't a paradox: it's merely an *implicit* definition of the new velocities, giving us simultaneous equations we must solve to find them.

Let's first do it with the 1D model problem from the last section. The backward Euler discretization is

$$q_i^{n+1} = q_i^n + \Delta t k \frac{q_{i+1}^{n+1} - 2q_i^{n+1} + q_{i-1}^{n+1}}{\Delta x^2}.$$

This is the ith linear equation: we can complete the system by enforcing, say, no-slip boundary conditions $q_0 = q_{m+1} = 0$, leaving m equations in m unknowns $q_1^{n+1}, \dots q_m^{n+1}$. Rearranging gives

$$-\frac{\Delta t k}{\Delta x^2} q_{i+1}^{n+1} + \left(1 + \frac{2\Delta t k}{\Delta x^2}\right) q_i^{n+1} - \frac{\Delta t k}{\Delta x^2} q_{i-1}^{n+1} = q_i^n.$$

This can now be thought of as a classic matrix-times-unknown-vector-equals-known-vector problem,

$$\left(I + \frac{\Delta t k}{\Delta x^2} A\right) q^{n+1} = q^n,$$

where I is the identity matrix, and A is a tridiagonal matrix with 2 down the main diagonal and -1 along the sub- and super-diagonals:

$$A = \begin{pmatrix} 2 & -1 & & \\ -1 & 2 & -1 & \\ & \ddots & \ddots & \ddots \\ & & -1 & 2 \end{pmatrix}.$$

This is almost the same, up to scaling, as a 1D version of the Poisson problem for pressure, except now we are increasing the positive diagonal entries even further. The matrix is symmetric positive definite—in fact slightly better conditioned than the pressure matrix thanks to the incremented diagonal—and so solving it with PCG works very efficiently.

Does this solve the stability problem? Well, let's rewrite the ith equation again:

$$\left(1 + \frac{2\Delta t k}{\Delta x^2}\right) q_i^{n+1} = \frac{\Delta t k}{\Delta x^2} q_{i+1}^{n+1} + \frac{\Delta t k}{\Delta x^2} q_{i-1}^{n+1} + q_i^n$$

$$\Rightarrow \quad q_i^{n+1} = \left(\frac{\Delta t k/\Delta x^2}{1 + 2\Delta t k/\Delta x^2}\right) q_{i+1}^{n+1} + \left(\frac{\Delta t k/\Delta x^2}{1 + 2\Delta t k/\Delta x^2}\right) q_{i-1}^{n+1}$$

$$+ \left(\frac{1}{1 + 2\Delta t k/\Delta x^2}\right) q_i^n.$$

That is, the new value at a grid point is a weighted average (with guaranteed positive weights, summing to 1) of its neighbors' new values and the old value at that grid point. Here we're including ghost values of q in the boundaries for some of those averages. Therefore, the maximum new value of q has to be less than or equal to the maximum old value of q, and similarly the minimum new value of q has to be greater than or equal to the minimum old value. So unstable growth is impossible. A more detailed analysis further can prove that spurious oscillations (the unphysical vibration we could hit before) are ruled out as well. This is all true no matter how large Δt is taken: it's unconditionally stable and monotone![7]

For the full 3D problem, with constant viscosity, things work out much the same. For each component of velocity independently we need to solve a system with a matrix $I+(\Delta t\eta)/(\rho\Delta x^2)A$ where A is nearly of the same form as the Laplacian matrix in the pressure solve: 6 down the main diagonal and -1 for neighboring grid cells. The one wrinkle we need to address is handling the different boundary conditions. As we said before, at a no-slip solid wall, we can just substitute in the known solid velocity, eliminating that fluid velocity from the equations. Free surfaces and no-stick solid walls are somewhat more tricky. The simplest approach is to use ghost velocity values equal to the neighboring fluid-velocity values. For example, when setting up the $(i+1/2, j, k)$th equation for u in the liquid, where $u_{i+3/2,j,k}$ is in the air, use the ghost value

$$u^G_{i+3/2,j,k} = u_{i+1/2,j,k}$$

instead. Unfortunately, not only does this have the rigid rotation issue that arose in explicit treatment, it's not even convergent for non-grid-aligned boundaries—much the same way the classic voxelized pressure solve fairs poorly on non-grid-aligned boundaries. We leave a solution to this problem for further research. Finally, for no-stick inviscid solid walls, we can substitute in either the solid velocity (if it's the component normal to the grid cell face) or use the ghost-fluid velocity (if it's a component tangential to the grid cell face)—or again, some weighted average of the two for a partially viscous boundary.

Finally we turn to the variable viscosity case. This can also be done implicitly by making the components of τ on the staggered grid depend on the new velocities.[8] We don't want to actually include the τ values as

---

[7]This of course doesn't mean we're necessarily getting the correct answer if Δt is very large—there is still an approximation error. However, a Fourier analysis can show that for large Δt the only "problem" is that the diffusion, the exponential decay of all the deformation modes, is effectively slower than it should be, though it still takes place.

[8]For non-Newtonian fluids where η is a function of the strain rate, defining that implicitly based on the new strain rate makes the equations non-linear; it simplifies life

unknowns in the linear system, however; we eliminate them by plugging in their definition into the velocity equations. This gives three sets of coupled equations, of the form:

$$u_{i+1/2,j,k}^{V} = u_{i+1/2,j,k}^{n} + \frac{\Delta t}{\rho \Delta x^2}$$

$$\times \begin{pmatrix} 2\eta_{i+1,j,k}(u_{i+3/2,j,k}^{V} - u_{i+1/2,j,k}^{V}) \\ -2\eta_{i,j,k}(u_{i+1/2,j,k}^{V} - u_{i-1/2,j,k}^{V}) \\ +\eta_{i+1/2,j+1/2,k}(u_{i+1/2,j+1,k}^{V} - u_{i+1/2,j,k}^{V} + v_{i+1,j+1/2,k}^{V} - v_{i,j+1/2,k}^{V}) \\ -\eta_{i+1/2,j-1/2,k}(u_{i+1/2,j,k}^{V} - u_{i+1/2,j-1,k}^{V} + v_{i+1,j-1/2,k}^{V} - v_{i,j-1/2,k}^{V}) \\ +\eta_{i+1/2,j,k+1/2}(u_{i+1/2,j,k+1}^{V} - u_{i+1/2,j,k}^{V} + w_{i+1,j,k+1/2}^{V} - w_{i,j,k+1/2}^{V}) \\ -\eta_{i+1/2,j,k-1/2}(u_{i+1/2,j,k}^{V} - u_{i+1/2,j,k-1}^{V} + w_{i+1,j,k-1/2}^{V} - w_{i,j,k-1/2}^{V}) \end{pmatrix},$$

$$v_{i,j+1/2,k}^{V} = v_{i,j+1/2,k}^{n} + \frac{\Delta t}{\rho \Delta x^2}$$

$$\times \begin{pmatrix} \eta_{i+1/2,j+1/2,k}(u_{i+1/2,j+1,k}^{V} - u_{i+1/2,j,k}^{V} + v_{i+1,j+1/2,k}^{V} - v_{i,j+1/2,k}^{V}) \\ -\eta_{i-1/2,j+1/2,k}(u_{i-1/2,j+1,k}^{V} - u_{i-1/2,j,k}^{V} + v_{i,j+1/2,k}^{V} - v_{i-1,j+1/2,k}^{V}) \\ +2\eta_{i,j+1,k}(v_{i,j+3/2,k}^{V} - v_{i,j+1/2,k}^{V}) \\ -2\eta_{i,j,k}(v_{i,j+1/2,k}^{V} - v_{i,j-1/2,k}^{V}) \\ +\eta_{i,j+1/2,k+1/2}(v_{i,j+1/2,k+1}^{V} - v_{i,j+1/2,k}^{V} + w_{i,j+1,k+1/2}^{V} - w_{i,j,k+1/2}^{V}) \\ -\eta_{i,j+1/2,k-1/2}(v_{i,j+1/2,k}^{V} - v_{i,j+1/2,k-1}^{V} + w_{i,j+1,k-1/2}^{V} - w_{i,j,k-1/2}^{V}) \end{pmatrix},$$

$$w_{i,j,k+1/2}^{V} = w_{i,j,k+1/2}^{n} + \frac{\Delta t}{\rho}$$

$$\times \begin{pmatrix} \eta_{i+1/2,j,k+1/2}(u_{i+1/2,j,k+1}^{V} - u_{i+1/2,j,k}^{V} + w_{i+1,j,k+1/2}^{V} - w_{i,j,k+1/2}^{V}) \\ -\eta_{i-1/2,j,k+1/2}(u_{i-1/2,j,k+1}^{V} - u_{i-1/2,j,k}^{V} + w_{i,j,k+1/2}^{V} - w_{i-1,j,k+1/2}^{V}) \\ +\eta_{i,j+1/2,k+1/2}(v_{i,j+1/2,k+1}^{V} - v_{i,j+1/2,k}^{V} + w_{i,j+1,k+1/2}^{V} - w_{i,j,k+1/2}^{V}) \\ -\eta_{i,j-1/2,k+1/2}(v_{i,j-1/2,k+1}^{V} - v_{i,j-1/2,k}^{V} + w_{i,j,k+1/2}^{V} - w_{i,j-1,k+1/2}^{V}) \\ +2\eta_{i,j,k+1}(w_{i,j,k+3/2}^{V} - w_{i,j,k+1/2}^{V}) \\ -2\eta_{i,j,k}(w_{i,j,k+1/2}^{V} - w_{i,j,k-1/2}^{V}) \end{pmatrix}.$$

Yes, that's them in all their gory magnificence. It's not too hard to verify that, thanks to our use of the staggered grid, we still get a symmetric positive definite matrix to solve (for all three components of velocity si-

---

a lot to instead *lag* the value of η by basing it on the old strain rate, giving linear equations which nonetheless should give you stability.

multaneously).[9] These of course no longer fit in the same structure we used to stored Laplacian matrices earlier; see Chapter 11 for a discussion of general sparse matrices. However, the real new problem is that some of the off-diagonal entries are now positive instead of all being negative. This causes problems for the simple incomplete Cholesky preconditioners we have developed, when Δt gets too large.

Rasmussen et al. [Rasmussen et al. 04] suggest improving this by splitting up the problem between implicit and explicit parts, recovering the decoupled linear solves with Laplacian-like matrices. In continuous variables this boils down to solving

$$\vec{u}^V = \vec{u}^n + \frac{\Delta t}{\rho} \left(\nabla \cdot \eta \nabla \vec{u}^V \right) + \frac{\Delta t}{\rho} \left(\nabla \cdot \eta \left(\nabla \vec{u}^n \right)^T \right). \tag{8.6}$$

We leave it to the reader to expand out the discretization in this case.

---

[9]Rasmussen et al. [Rasmussen et al. 04] report getting an unsymmetric matrix for this problem, probably due to using collocated velocities all at the grid cell centers. To combine this with the MAC grid for pressure solves, they average the staggered velocities to the grid cell centers for most stages of the time step, then average the grid cell centers back to the staggered locations for the pressure solve. While this continual averaging introduces unwanted numerical dissipation when simulating inviscid flow, for highly viscous fluids it is fairly innocuous.

–III–
More Algorithms

– 9 –
Turbulence

This chapter takes a look at methods aimed to capture more of the fine-scale swirly motion characteristic of turbulence. This is far from a scientific examination of turbulence, and in fact scientific work on the subject tends to concentrate on averaging or smoothing over the details of turbulent velocity fields—whereas we want to get to those details as cheaply as possible, even if they fall short of true accuracy.

9.1 Vorticity

Our first stop is getting at a precise measurement of the "swirliness" characteristic of turbulent flow. That is, at any point in space, we would like to measure how the fluid is rotating. In Chapter 8 on viscosity we saw how the gradient of the velocity field gives a matrix whose symmetric part measures deformation—independent of rigid body motions. It's not surprising then that what's left over, the skew-symmetric part, gives us information about rotation. (And of course, $\vec{u}$ itself without any derivatives tells us the translational component of the motion.)

Let's take a look at a generic rigid motion velocity field in 3D:

$$\vec{u}(\vec{x}) = \vec{U} + \vec{\Omega} \times \vec{x}.$$

Here $\vec{U}$ is the translation, and $\vec{\Omega}$ is the angular velocity measured around the origin. Let's work out the gradient of this velocity field in three dimensions to see how we can extract the angular velocity:

$$\frac{\partial \vec{u}}{\partial \vec{x}} = \frac{\partial}{\partial \vec{x}} \begin{pmatrix} U_1 + \Omega_2 z - \Omega_3 y \\ U_2 + \Omega_3 x - \Omega_1 z \\ U_3 + \Omega_1 y - \Omega_2 x \end{pmatrix}$$

$$= \begin{pmatrix} 0 & -\Omega_3 & \Omega_2 \\ \Omega_3 & 0 & -\Omega_1 \\ -\Omega_2 & \Omega_1 & 0 \end{pmatrix}.$$

Thus for a rigid body rotation, the gradient has no symmetric part—there's no deformation after all—and the skew-symmetric part lets us read out the components of angular velocity directly.

Take a look at the skew-symmetric part of the velocity gradient (in general, not just for rigid body motions):

$$\frac{1}{2}\left(\frac{\partial \vec{u}}{\partial \vec{x}} - \frac{\partial \vec{u}^T}{\partial \vec{x}}\right) = \frac{1}{2}\begin{pmatrix} 0 & \frac{\partial u}{\partial y} - \frac{\partial v}{\partial x} & \frac{\partial u}{\partial z} - \frac{\partial w}{\partial x} \\ \frac{\partial v}{\partial x} - \frac{\partial u}{\partial y} & 0 & \frac{\partial v}{\partial z} - \frac{\partial w}{\partial y} \\ \frac{\partial w}{\partial x} - \frac{\partial u}{\partial z} & \frac{\partial w}{\partial y} - \frac{\partial v}{\partial z} & 0 \end{pmatrix}.$$

Reading off the local measure of angular velocity this represents, just as we saw in the rigid case, we get

$$\vec{\Omega}(\vec{x}) = \frac{1}{2}\left(\frac{\partial w}{\partial y} - \frac{\partial v}{\partial z}, \ \frac{\partial u}{\partial z} - \frac{\partial w}{\partial x}, \ \frac{\partial v}{\partial x} - \frac{\partial u}{\partial y}\right).$$

This is exactly half the curl of the velocity field.

In fact we define *vorticity* $\vec{\omega}$ to be the curl of the velocity field, which will then be twice the local angular velocity. Again, in three dimensions this is a vector:

$$\vec{\omega} = \nabla \times \vec{u}$$

$$= \left(\frac{\partial w}{\partial y} - \frac{\partial v}{\partial z}, \ \frac{\partial u}{\partial z} - \frac{\partial w}{\partial x}, \ \frac{\partial v}{\partial x} - \frac{\partial u}{\partial y}\right).$$

In two dimensions it reduces to a scalar:

$$\omega = \nabla \times \vec{u} = \frac{\partial v}{\partial x} - \frac{\partial u}{\partial y}.$$

This turns out to be one of the most useful "derived" quantities for a fluid flow.

Take the curl of the momentum equation (1.1), assuming constant viscosity:

$$\nabla \times \frac{\partial \vec{u}}{\partial t} + \nabla \times (\vec{u} \cdot \nabla \vec{u}) + \nabla \times \left(\frac{1}{\rho}\nabla p\right) = \nabla \times \vec{g} + \nabla \times \nu\nabla \cdot \nabla \vec{u}.$$

Switching the order of some derivatives, and assuming that density ρ is constant so it can be brought outside the curl for the pressure term, gives

$$\frac{\partial \nabla \times \vec{u}}{\partial t} + \nabla \times (\vec{u} \cdot \nabla \vec{u}) + \frac{1}{\rho}\nabla \times \nabla p = \nabla \times \vec{g} + \nu\nabla \cdot \nabla(\nabla \times \vec{u}).$$

Recalling that the curl of a gradient is automatically zero (see Appendix A for identities such as this) and assuming that $\vec{g}$ is constant or the gradient of some potential, and substituting in vorticity, reduces this to

$$\frac{\partial \vec{\omega}}{\partial t} + \nabla \times (\vec{u} \cdot \nabla \vec{u}) = \nu \nabla \cdot \nabla \vec{\omega}.$$

The advection term can be simplified with some work (and exploiting the divergence-free condition $\nabla \cdot \vec{u} = 0$) to eventually get, in three dimensions:

$$\frac{\partial \vec{\omega}}{\partial t} + \vec{u} \cdot \nabla \vec{\omega} = -\omega \cdot \nabla \vec{u} + \nu \nabla \cdot \nabla \vec{\omega}. \tag{9.1}$$

This is known as the *vorticity equation*, which you can see has the material derivative $D\vec{\omega}/Dt$ on the left-hand side, a viscosity term on the right-hand side, and a new term $\vec{\omega} \cdot \nabla \vec{u}$, which we can write in components as

$$\vec{\omega} \cdot \nabla \vec{u} = \begin{pmatrix} \omega_1 \dfrac{\partial u}{\partial x} + \omega_2 \dfrac{\partial v}{\partial x} + \omega_3 \dfrac{\partial w}{\partial x} \\ \omega_1 \dfrac{\partial u}{\partial y} + \omega_2 \dfrac{\partial v}{\partial y} + \omega_3 \dfrac{\partial w}{\partial y} \\ \omega_1 \dfrac{\partial u}{\partial z} + \omega_2 \dfrac{\partial v}{\partial z} + \omega_3 \dfrac{\partial w}{\partial z} \end{pmatrix}.$$

This term is sometimes called the *vortex-stretching* term from a geometric point of view which we won't get into in this book. In two dimensions, the vorticity equation actually simplifies further: the vortex-stretching term is automatically zero. (This is easy to verify if you think of a 2D flow as being a slice through a 3D flow with u and v constant along the z-direction and $w = 0$.) Here it is in 2D, now written with the material derivative to emphasize the simplicity:

$$\frac{D\omega}{Dt} = \nu \nabla \cdot \nabla \omega. \tag{9.2}$$

In fact, if we are talking about inviscid flow where viscosity is negligible (as we have done throughout this book except in Chapter 8 on highly viscous flow), the 2D vorticity equation reduces simply to $D\omega/Dt = 0$. That is, vorticity doesn't change, but is just advected with the flow.

It turns out you can build an attractive fluid solver based on vorticity, particularly in 2D where the equation is even simpler, though there are decidedly non-trivial complications for boundary conditions and reconstructing the velocity field for advection from vorticity (more on this in the next chapter). For example, Yaeger et al. [Yaeger et al. 86], Gamito et al. [Gamito 95], Angelidis et al. [Angelidis and Neyret 05, Angelidis et al. 06], Park and Kim [Park and Kim 05], and Elcott et al. [Elcott et al.] have all taken this route. However, our chief concern now is in what happens to vorticity in our regular fluid solver, based on velocity and pressure.

In fact we already know that we run the risk of numerical dissipation in our Eulerian advection schemes: we saw that for first-order linear interpolation, the error behaves like additional viscosity, and so it should be no surprise that the vorticity of the velocity field similarly gets dissipated. So far we've dealt with this by increasing the sharpness of the interpolation—though even this doesn't fully avoid dissipation. We will get to a method that can virtually eliminate dissipation in the advection stage in Chapter 10, but this is not the only source of vorticity dissipation.

The other big source lies in the time-splitting algorithm itself. We mentioned before that our algorithm for separately advecting and then projecting velocity is only first-order accurate in time; it turns out this can be a fairly problematic error when attempting to capture small-scale vortices. As a motivating example, imagine starting with just a 2D rigid rotation of constant-density fluid around the origin, say

$$\vec{u}^0 = (-y, x).$$

Ignoring boundary conditions and body forces, the exact solution of the Navier-Stokes equations, given this initial velocity field, is for $\vec{u}$ to stay constant—the rotation should continue at exactly the same speed. However, if we advance it with our time-splitting algorithm, things go wrong. Even with *perfect* error-free advection, for a time step of $\Delta t = \frac{1}{2}\pi$ which corresponds in this velocity field to a counterclockwise rotation of 90°, we get this intermediate velocity field:

$$\vec{u}^A = (x, y).$$

It no longer has any vorticity (easy to check) and moreover is divergent: our advection step transferred all the energy from rotation to expansion. It's not hard to verify that the pressure solution is

$$p = \frac{x^2 + y^2}{2\pi\rho}.$$

After updating the intermediate velocity field with this pressure, we end up with

$$\vec{u}^{n+1} = 0.$$

Oops! The flow comes to a standstill, never to move again. If we had taken a smaller time step it would have just been slowed down, but only in the limit $\Delta t \to 0$ does it approach the vorticity it should be preserving. (If we had taken a larger time step, the fluid might even have reversed direction and rotated the other way!)

In fact, at least when density is constant, since the curl of a gradient is automatically zero the pressure projection stage can't affect the fluid's vorticity: the damage is already done when we advect velocities. With a little more effort, it's not hard to verify that starting with a rigid rotation of vorticity ω, one time step of perfect advection will change that to vorticity $\omega \cos(\omega \Delta t/2)$. If Δt is small enough, this is approximately

$$\omega_{n+1} \approx \left(1 - \frac{\omega_n^2 \Delta t^2}{8}\right) \omega_n.$$

Thus our next step is to look at a way of adding back some of the missing vorticity.

9.2 Vorticity Confinement

The *vorticity confinement* technique developed by Steinhoff and Underhill [Steinhoff and Underhill 94] is a modification of the Navier-Stokes equations by a term that tries to preserve vorticity. Fedkiw et al. [Fedkiw et al. 01] introduced it to graphics, introducing a Δx factor so that in the limit (as the grid is refined) the term disappears and we get back the true fluid solution. The underlying idea is to detect where vortices are located and add a body force to boost the rotational motion around each vortex.

In this context, a vortex is loosely speaking a peak in the vorticity field, a place that's spinning faster than all the fluid nearby. We can construct unit vectors $\vec{N}$ that point to these maximum points simply by normalizing the gradient of $\|\vec{\omega}\|$:

$$\vec{N} = \frac{\nabla \|\vec{\omega}\|}{\|\nabla \|\vec{\omega}\|\|}.$$

Now $\vec{N}$ points towards the center of rotation of a vortex, and $\vec{\omega}$ itself points along the axis of rotation, so to get a force vector that increases the rotation, we just take a cross-product:

$$f_{\text{conf}} = \epsilon \Delta x (\vec{N} \times \vec{\omega}).$$

The ϵ here is a parameter that can be adjusted to control the effect of vorticity confinement. The Δx factor, as mentioned above, makes this physically consistent: as we refine the grid and Δx tends to zero, the erroneous numerical dissipation of vorticity also tends to zero so our fix should too.

Let's step through numerically implementing this. We begin by averaging velocities from the MAC grid to the cell centers (as discussed in Chapter 2) and then use central derivatives to approximate the vorticity:[1]

$$\vec{\omega}_{i,j,k} = \left(\frac{w_{i,j+1,k} - w_{i,j-1,k}}{2\Delta x} - \frac{v_{i,j,k+1} - v_{i,j,k-1}}{2\Delta x}, \right.$$
$$\frac{u_{i,j,k+1} - u_{i,j,k-1}}{2\Delta x} - \frac{w_{i+1,j,k} - w_{i-1,j,k}}{2\Delta x},$$
$$\left. \frac{v_{i+1,j,k} - v_{i-1,j,k}}{2\Delta x} - \frac{u_{i,j+1,k} - u_{i,j-1,k}}{2\Delta x} \right).$$

The gradient of $\|\vec{\omega}\|$ is similarly estimated with central differences at the grid cell centers, for use in defining $\vec{N}$:

$$\nabla\|\vec{\omega}\|_{i,j,k} =$$
$$\left(\frac{\|\vec{\omega}\|_{i+1,j,k} - \|\vec{\omega}\|_{i-1,j,k}}{2\Delta x}, \frac{\|\vec{\omega}\|_{i,j+1,k} - \|\vec{\omega}\|_{i,j-1,k}}{2\Delta x}, \frac{\|\vec{\omega}\|_{i,j,k+1} - \|\vec{\omega}\|_{i,j,k-1}}{2\Delta x} \right).$$

When we normalize this to get $\vec{N}$, we should of course guard against a divide-by-zero by using, for example,

$$\vec{N}_{i,j,k} = \frac{\nabla\|\vec{\omega}\|_{i,j,k}}{\|\nabla\|\vec{\omega}\|_{i,j,k}\| + 10^{-20}M},$$

where M is a characteristic value of units $\mathrm{m^{-1}s^{-1}}$ for the simulation— nothing to be too concerned about; $M = 1/(\Delta x\Delta t)$ is fine just to make sure this scales properly. Finally, we take the cross-product to get f_{conf} at the grid cell centers; we can take the appropriate averages to apply this to the different components of velocity on the MAC grid.

Ideally we would connect the confinement parameter ϵ with the expected numerical dissipation of vorticity. However, this has yet to be done, but in the meantime serves as another tweakable parameter for the simulation. If set too high, the simulation can go quasi-unstable, reducing the velocity field to essentially a random turbulent chaos; more moderate values encourage fine-scale vortices and keep the flow more lively.

---

[1] Note that the null-space problem we discussed earlier isn't particularly alarming here: we just will lack the ability to "see" and boost the very smallest vortices. We still get the benefit of boosting slightly larger ones.

9.3   Procedural Turbulence

Ultimately, there is a practical limit to the resolution a fluid simulator can run at. For an $n \times n \times n$ grid, we obviously require $O(n^3)$ memory—and the hidden constant is a bit hefty, as you can see when you add up all the additional arrays needed for time integration, pressure solves, etc. Furthermore, if we keep Δt proportional to Δx as recommended, and use the MICCG(0) linear solver developed in Chapter 4 which requires $O(\sqrt{n})$ iterations to converge, we end up with the total cost of a simulation scaling like $O(n^{4.5})$. That puts a pretty severe bottleneck on going to higher resolution.

However, real turbulence can show features—vortices—on a huge range of length scales. As a point of reference, for example, turbulence in the atmosphere can span from kilometers down to millimeters. There simply is no practical way to directly simulate with a grid capable of capturing that range ($n \sim 10^5$). However, the turbulent features below a certain length scale tend to lose structure and become isotropic and easily described statistically: if you filter out the large-scale motion of the fluid and zoom in on just the small-scale turbulence, any region looks pretty much like any other region. This is our saving grace. Below the scale of the actual simulation, we can add in procedural models of turbulent velocity fields to fake additional detail. For turbulent smoke, instead of tracking the grid-level smoke concentration field, we instead trace and render millions of marker particles running through this enhanced velocity field (see Rasmussen et al. [Rasmussen et al. 03], for example).

We now take a look at two approaches to generating the required procedural velocity fields. The critical requirements are allowing control over the spectrum of the velocity (i.e., looking at the velocity variation over different length-scales) and making sure the velocity is still divergence-free.

9.3.1   Fourier Synthesis

One of the simpler methods for generating plausible turbulent velocity fields is to do it in Fourier space. If we take the Fourier transform of a velocity field $\vec{u}(\vec{x})$, which we'll assume is periodic over a cube of side length L, we can write it as

$$\vec{u}(\vec{x}) = \sum_{i,j,k=-\infty}^{\infty} \hat{u}_{ijk} e^{\sqrt{-1}2\pi(ix+jy+kz)/L}.$$

Here we're using $\sqrt{-1}$ as a symbol to denote an imaginary number, instead of the more common i or j since this book uses i and j as indices. This Fourier series is also obviously using complex exponentials instead of sines and cosines, which implies the Fourier coefficients $\hat{u}_{ijk}$ may be complex even though $\vec{u}$ is real-valued: this helps to simplify some of the other notation, and more to the point, matches the API of most Fast Fourier Transform packages. Note also that the Fourier coefficients $\hat{u}_{ijk}$ are 3D vectors of complex numbers, not just scalars: you can think of this really being the Fourier transform of u, the separate Fourier transform of v, and the further separate Fourier transform of w all wrapped up into one equation.

In practice, of course, we'll use just a discrete Fourier transform, over an $m \times m \times m$ array of Fourier coefficients. The length L should be chosen large enough that the periodic tiling isn't too conspicuous, but not too large relative to the simulation grid spacing Δx—after all, we won't be able to afford to take m too large, and we want the Fourier grid spacing L/m (the smallest details we'll procedurally add) to be a lot smaller than Δx.

Shinya and Fournier [Shinya and Fournier 92] and Stam and Fiume [Stam and Fiume 93] introduced to graphics perhaps the simplest physically reasonable turbulence model, the Kolmogorov "5/3-law". This states that for fully developed steady-state turbulence, the kinetic energy contained in the Fourier modes of spatial frequency k should scale like $k^{-5/3}$. This means that the (i, j, k) Fourier coefficient should have magnitude on the order of

$$\|\hat{u}_{ijk}\| \sim (i^2 + j^2 + k^2)^{-11/12}$$

for i, j, k large enough (the low spatial frequencies are assumed to not belong to the isotropic turbulence regime.) We can take it, in fact, to be a random vector uniformly sampled from a ball of radius $C(i^2+j^2+k^2)^{-11/12}$, for some user-tunable constant C. The cut-off frequency, below which we keep $\hat{u}_{ijk}$ zero, should be on the order of $L/\Delta x$ or more, so that we don't add procedural details at scales that were captured in the simulation.

The divergence of velocity becomes a simple algebraic operation on the Fourier series:

$$\nabla\vec{u}(\vec{x}) = \sum_{i,j,k=-\infty}^{\infty} \frac{\sqrt{-1}2\pi}{L} [(i,j,k) \cdot \hat{u}_{ijk}] e^{\sqrt{-1}2\pi(ix+jy+kz)/L}.$$

Therefore, $\nabla \cdot \vec{u} = 0$ is equivalent to requiring that each Fourier coefficient $\hat{u}_{ijk}$ is perpendicular to its *wave vector* (i, j, k). Making a velocity field divergence-free then simplifies to just fixing each coefficient individually, subtracting off their component in the radial direction—a simple 3D projection.

Finally, once the Fourier coefficients have been determined, an inverse FFT can be applied on each of the u-, $v-$, and w-components to get a grid of plausible velocities. Note that the velocity vectors are sampled at the grid points, all components together—this is not a staggered MAC grid. Trilinear interpolation can be used between grid points for particle advection.

To animate this velocity field in time, the simplest technique (proposed by Rasmussen et al. [Rasmussen et al. 03]) is just to construct two such velocity fields and then cross-fade back and forth between them. The key observation is that while on its own this method of animation falls short of plausibility (and for that matter, the periodicity of the field is objectionable too), this only is added on top of an already detailed simulation. The extra detail is just needed to break up the smooth interpolation between simulation grid points, not to behave perfectly.

9.3.2 Noise

While Fourier synthesis has many advantages—it's fairly efficient and has a nice theoretical background—it has a few problems too, chief among them being the problem of how to control it in space. If you want the turbulence to be stronger in one region than another, or to properly handle a solid wall somewhere in the flow, simultaneously meeting the divergence-free constraint becomes difficult.

An alternative is to forget about Fourier transforms and instead directly construct divergence-free velocity fields from building blocks such as Perlin noise. We get the divergence-free condition by exploiting vector calculus identities. For example, the divergence of the curl of a vector field is always zero:

$$\nabla \cdot (\nabla \times \vec{\psi}) = 0 \quad \text{for all vector fields } \vec{\psi}$$

and the cross-product of two gradients is always divergence free as well:

$$\nabla \cdot (\nabla \phi \times \nabla \psi) = 0 \quad \text{for all scalar fields } \phi \text{ and } \psi.$$

Kniss and Hart [Kniss and Hart 04] and Bridson et al. [Bridson et al. 07] used the first of these formulas, with $\vec{\psi}$ a vector-valued noise function, and DeWolf [DeWolf 05] used the second with ϕ and possibly ψ scalar noise functions (see also von Funck et al. [von Funck et al. 06] for an application of this identity in geometric modeling).

To get full turbulence, several octaves of noise can be added in either formula, with an appropriate power-law scaling of magnitudes. For example, using the first formula, *curl-noise*, we might take for the vector potential

$$\vec{\psi}(\vec{x}) = \sum_{p=1}^{m} A_p \vec{N} \left(\frac{C2^p \vec{x}}{\Delta x} \right)$$

and then get the velocity field as

$$\vec{u} = \nabla \times \vec{\psi}.$$

The curl here can be approximated with finite differences for convenience, rather than evaluated exactly. The simulation grid Δx appears here to emphasize that this should be done only for length scales below the simulation.

In addition, the amplitude A_p of each octave of noise can be modulated in space, allowing full control over where turbulence should appear. Bridson et al. [Bridson et al. 07] in addition show that ramping A_p down to zero at the boundary of a solid causes the velocity field to meet the solid wall boundary condition.

All of these noise formulations can be animated in time, either using 4D noise functions or, more intriguingly, the FlowNoise method of Perlin and Neyret [Perlin and Neyret 01].

– 10 –
Hybrid Particle Methods

Advection is one of the central themes of fluid simulation in this book. We've already struggled with the excessive numerical dissipation produced by semi-Lagrangian advection with linear interpolation, and improved it significantly with a Catmull-Rom interpolant. Even sharper grid-based methods have been developed—however, all Eulerian schemes have a fundamental limit.

One way of looking at a time step of any Eulerian advection schemes is as follows:

- Begin with the field sampled on a grid.

- Reconstruct the field as a continuous function from the grid samples.

- Advect the reconstructed field.

- Resample the advected field on the grid.

Technically speaking, some Eulerian schemes might use more than just the values sampled on the grid—e.g., multistep time integration will also use several past values of the field on the grid—but these details don't change the gist: the key is the resampling at the end.

The problem is that a general incompressible velocity field, though it preserves volumes, may introduce significant distortions: at any point in space, the advected field may be stretched out along some axes and squished together along others. From a rendering perspective, you might think of this as a local magnification (stretching out) along some axes and a local minification (squishing together) along the others. And just as in rendering, while resampling a stretched out or magnified field doesn't lose any information, resampling a shrunk or minified field *can* lead to information loss. If the advected field has details varying at the grid scale Δx, as soon as those get shrunk in advection, resampling will at best destroy them (or worse, if care is not taken in the numerical method, cause them to alias as spurious lower-frequency artifacts—again, just as in rendering).

It's actually a little worse: the Nyquist limit essentially means that even in a pure translation velocity field with no distortion, the maximum spatial frequency that can be reliably advected has period $4\Delta x$. Higher-frequency signals, even though you might resolve them on the grid at a particular instant in time, cannot be handled in general: e.g., just in one dimension the highest-frequency component you can see on the grid, $\cos(\pi x/\Delta x)$, exactly disappears from the grid once you advect it by a distance of $\frac{1}{2}\Delta x$.

A "perfect" Eulerian scheme would filter out the high-frequency components that can't be reliably resampled at each time step, and a bad one will allow them to alias as artifacts. The distortions inherent in non-rigid velocity fields mean that as time progresses, some of the lower-frequency components get transferred to higher frequencies—and thus must be destroyed. But note that the fluid flow, after squeezing the field along some axes at some point, may later stretch it back out—transferring higher frequencies down to lower frequencies. However, it's too late if the Eulerian scheme has already filtered them out.

At small enough length scales, viscosity and other molecular diffusion processes end up dominating advection: if Δx is small enough, Eulerian schemes can behave perfectly well since the physics itself is effectively band-limiting everything, dissipating information at higher frequencies. This brute-force approach leads to the area called direct numerical simulation (DNS), which comes in handy in the scientific study of turbulence for example. However, since many scenarios of practical interest would require Δx less than a millimeter, DNS is usually far too expensive for graphics work.

A more efficient approach is to use adaptive grids, where the grid resolution is increased where higher resampling density is required to avoid information loss, and decreased where the field is smooth enough that low resolution suffices. This can be done using octrees (see for example Losasso et al. [Losasso et al. 04]) or unstructured tetrahedral meshes (see for example by Feldman et al. [Feldman et al. 05] or Wendt et al. [Wendt et al. 07]). However, these approaches suffer from considerable implementation complexity, increased overhead in execution, and typically lower accuracy compared to regular grids of similar resolution—and still must enforce a maximum resolution that, for practical purposes, tends to be much coarser than the DNS ideal.

This is where the subject of particle methods comes into play. If we store a field on particles that move with the flow, it doesn't matter how the flow distorts the distribution of particles: the advection equation $Dq/Dt = 0$

says the values stored on the particles shouldn't change, and thus there is no filtering and no information loss. In some sense particles are perfect for advection. In fact, we've already seen some uses for marker particles in Chapter 5 for rendering smoke and Chapter 6 for tracking liquids.

Many people have in fact constructed fluid simulators that only use particles with no grids at all, except perhaps as acceleration structures for quickly finding which particles are close together. Just within graphics this includes the seminal work of Miller and Pearce [Miller and Pearce 89], the introduction of smoothed particle hydrodynamics (SPH) to graphics by Desbrun and Cani [Desbrun and Cani 96], further development of SPH for animation for example by Müller et al. [Müller et al. 03], and mesh-free vortex methods by Angelidis and Neyret [Angelidis and Neyret 05] or Park and Kim [Park and Kim 05]. However, while particles are excellent for advection, grids are extremely hard to beat when it comes to efficiently and accurately enforcing incompressibility. Thus we will instead focus on hybrid methods that use particles and grids together, trying to exploit the best of both.

It should also be pointed out, before we get into details, that these particle methods really are only worthwhile for fields with zero diffusion (or viscosity, or conduction, or whatever other name is appropriate for the quantity in question). If there is significant physical diffusion, strong enough to show up on the grid length scale, then using an Eulerian advection scheme should work perfectly well without need for particles. We will in fact take a look at incorporating small amounts of diffusion into particle methods, but the emphasis is on small: for large diffusion you're probably best off sticking to Eulerian methods.

10.1   Particle Advection

The details of a particle-grid method lie in how information is passed back and forth between particles and the grid—which we'll explore for several examples in the rest of this chapter. Underlying all of them, however, is a particle advection stage, where we update particle positions based on the MAC grid velocity field. As we discussed back in Chapter 3, the simplest time integration scheme, forward Euler, really is insufficient. In fact, the requirements for particle advection are probably a bit stricter than for tracing trajectories in semi-Lagrangian advection, since errors in particle advection are accumulated over many time steps instead of being reset each time step as in the semi-Lagrangian method.

The simplest and cheapest method that makes sense to use is a second-order Runge-Kutta integrator, an example of which we introduced before. However, it's actually slightly unstable in regions of rigid rotation: particles will steadily migrate away from the center of rotation, perturbing the distribution. A much better choice, albeit a little more expensive choice, is to use a "three-stage third-order Runge-Kutta scheme:" these *are* stable for rigid rotations as long as Δt isn't too large. There are infinitely many such schemes, but Ralston [Ralston 62] showed the following scheme is probably the best when it comes to minimizing error:

$$\vec{k}_1 = \vec{u}(\vec{x}_n),$$
$$\vec{k}_2 = \vec{u}(\vec{x}_n + \tfrac{1}{2}\Delta t \vec{k}_1),$$
$$\vec{k}_3 = \vec{u}(\vec{x}_n + \tfrac{3}{4}\Delta t \vec{k}_2),$$
$$\vec{x}_{n+1} = \vec{x}_n + \tfrac{2}{9}\Delta t \vec{k}_1 + \tfrac{3}{9}\Delta t \vec{k}_2 + \tfrac{4}{9}\Delta t \vec{k}_3.$$

Here I've ignored the time dependence of the velocity field, which technically reduces the accuracy back to first order in time, just like our overall time-splitting algorithm; the error we care more about here has to do with the variation of velocity in space.

Chapter 3 also mentions the possibility of using substeps in time integration to better control error, say constraining each particle to move roughly Δx each substep. This can easily be incorporated into Runge-Kutta schemes by first evaluating $\vec{u}(\vec{x}_n)$, which will be used regardless of the time-step size and then setting the substep size $\Delta\tau$ to keep $\|\Delta\tau\vec{u}(\vec{x}_n)\|$ below a threshold. Of course, substep sizes must be adjusted so that when you add them up they exactly equal the global time step Δt. A fairly effective solution is given in Figure 10.1.

There's finally also the question of boundaries: what should happen to a particle when it leaves the fluid? For the usual solid wall boundaries, this is presumably just due to small numerical errors, which in the limit should go to zero. The obvious fix if a particle does end up on the other side of a solid wall is to project it out to the closest point on the boundary, perhaps plus a small fraction of Δx back into the fluid. This projection is a trivial operation if the solid is described with a level set and not too difficult for other geometry. The same may be true of a liquid free surface—unless the particles themselves are helping to define where that surface is, in which case they should be free to move. However, for open edges on the grid with a $p = 0$ "free surface" condition, or inflow/outflow boundaries where we specify $\vec{u} \cdot \hat{n}$ to be something different than the solid's normal velocity, it makes sense instead to simply delete particles that stray outside the

- Set substep time $\tau = 0$.
- Set flag `finished` to false.
- While `finished` is false:
  - Evaluate $\vec{u}(\vec{x})$.
  - Find the maximum substep size $\Delta\tau = C\Delta x/(\|\vec{u}(\vec{x})\| + \epsilon)$. ($\epsilon$ is a small number like 10^{-37} used to guard against divide-by-zero.)
  - If $\tau + \Delta\tau \geq \Delta t$:
    - Set $\Delta\tau = \Delta t - \tau$ and `finished` to true.
  - Else if $\tau + 2\Delta\tau \geq \Delta t$:
    - Set $\Delta\tau = \frac{1}{2}(\Delta t - \tau)$
  - Update $\vec{x}$ with RK3 for substep size $\Delta\tau$, reusing the evaluated $\vec{u}(\vec{x})$.
  - Update $\tau \leftarrow \tau + \Delta\tau$.

Figure 10.1. Pseudocode for substepping particle advection, loosely restricting a particle $\vec{x}$ to travel no more than $C\Delta x$ per substep.

fluid. In these cases, however, it might also be critical to add new particles at those boundaries when the velocity field is pulling new fluid into the problem—we'll address this seeding problem in the next section.

10.2 Secondary Particles

Our first sortie is using particles to track secondary fields, such as smoke concentration. In fact, we already suggested running particles through the velocity field as a post-process for more detailed smoke rendering; now we're going to go further and use particles directly in the simulation. We'll stick with the smoke concentration example to begin with.

We will assume each particle, in addition to its position $\vec{x}_p$, has a smoke concentration s_p. This value should represent the concentration of smoke in the volume associated with the particle—more on this in a moment. At it simplest, s_p could be a constant for all particles, but as it can be useful to have smoke steadily dissipate—which can be emulated by reducing each s_p just as we scaled back grid values—it makes sense to track this per particle. At the moment a particle is created, it will take a default initial value S; once s_p has been reduced to below some threshold, the particle can be deleted. For extra variability, the initial S itself could be modulated by an animated volume texture in the emission region.

We now need a way to determine the smoke concentration on the simulation grid from the particle data, for use in the buoyancy law or density calculation. The simplest thing is to sum, at each grid point, the particle values modulated by a kernel function k that only gives weight to nearby particles, normalized by a weight value W which we'll discuss in a moment:

$$s_{i,j,k} = \sum_p s_p \frac{k(\vec{x}_p - \vec{x}_{i,j,k})}{W}. \qquad (10.1)$$

Note the convention in this chapter is to always use p for particle indices and reserve i, j, and k for grid indices: thus $s_{i,j,k}$ is unambiguously the smoke concentration at grid point (i, j, k) which is at position $\vec{x}_{i,j,k}$. Also note that in practice it makes much more sense to order the computation as a loop over particles, each contributing to the nearby grid points:

- Reset all grid $s_{i,j,k}$ values to zero.

- Loop over particle index p:

    - Loop over grid indices i, j, k where $k(\vec{x}_p - \vec{x}_{i,j,k})$ might be non-zero:
        - Add $s_p k(\vec{x}_p - \vec{x}_{i,j,k})/W$ to $s_{i,j,k}$

The kernel function k should be adapted to the grid spacing, just as in rendering—if its support is less than Δx then some particles between grid points may momentarily vanish from the grid (not contribute to any grid points), but if the support is too much larger than Δx, the method becomes inefficient and we'll have blurred away a lot of the desirable sharpness of particle methods. The simplest choice that makes sense is to use the trilinear hat function:

$$k(x, y, z) = h\left(\frac{x}{\Delta x}\right) h\left(\frac{y}{\Delta x}\right) h\left(\frac{z}{\Delta x}\right)$$

$$\text{with} \quad h(r) = \begin{cases} 1 - r & : \quad 0 \leq r \leq 1, \\ 1 + r & : -1 \leq r \leq 0, \\ 0 & : \text{otherwise.} \end{cases}$$

Smoother results can be achieved using higher-order B-splines, for example, though it should be emphasized that the grid values $s_{i,j,k}$ are not going to be rendered so this is probably overkill. Speaking of rendering, it's virtually certain that memory and time constraints dictate that the number of simulation smoke particles will be much less than that required for a high-quality render—though they provide useful data for the renderer, they will have to be augmented with many extra rendering particles in the rendering stage.

So what about the normalization weight W? This is intimately tied up with the sampling density of the particles. Let V be the volume associated with each particle: you can think of it as the limit of a volume of space divided by the number of particles contained within, for uniform sampling. For example, if you initialize with eight particles per grid cell in a smoky region, then $V = \Delta x^3/8$. We can estimate the total amount of smoke in the simulation, i.e., the integral of smoke concentration over the simulation volume, either from the particles as

$$S_{\text{total}} \approx \sum_p s_p V$$

or from the grid as

$$S_{\text{total}} \approx \sum_{i,j,k} s_{i,j,k} \Delta x^3.$$

We now choose W so these two estimates are equal. For the recommended trilinear hat kernel function k (or indeed, any other B-spline), the sum of $k(\vec{x}_p - \vec{x}_{i,j,k})$ over all grid points is exactly one, which nicely simplifies the calculation:

$$\sum_{i,j,k} s_{i,j,k} \Delta x^3 = \sum_{i,j,k} \sum_p s_p \frac{k(\vec{x}_p - \vec{x}_{i,j,k})}{W} \Delta x^3$$

$$= \sum_p s_p \left(\sum_{i,j,k} k(\vec{x}_p - \vec{x}_{i,j,k}) \right) \frac{\Delta x^3}{W}$$

$$= \sum_p s_p \frac{\Delta x^3}{W}.$$

Therefore, we take $W = \Delta x^3/V$, or more simply, the average number of particles per grid cell.

We can of course get a little fancier and introduce a normalization weight W_p per particle, tying into a non uniform particle seeding. This brings up the question of how to seed particles in the first place. There are a lot of possibilities, and not necessarily any single best choice, but we will outline one strategy.

On the initial frame, we use an initial grid-sampled smoke concentration s, and in grid cells where this is non-zero, add W particles with s_p-values interpolated from the grid. Positioning them on a jittered grid works fine for this. In subsequent time steps, each smoke emitter specifies a desired number of new smoke particles per unit time in each grid cell, $r_{i,j,k}$, each with an initial value $S_{i,j,k}$: this corresponds to an increase in smoke concentration of $(\partial s/\partial t)_{i,j,k} = r_{i,j,k}S_{i,j,k}/W$. At inflow boundaries, where we're injecting smoke through a surface, we could make this rate proportional to $\vec{u}\cdot\hat{n}$. If the rate is non-zero in the time step Δt, we try to emit $m = r_{i,j,k}\Delta t$ particles with value $S_{i,j,k}$. That is, we for sure emit the integer part of m and use the fractional part as the probability of emitting one extra particle (i.e., emit the extra particle if a uniform random number from $[0, 1]$ is less than the fractional part of m). For each particle we emit, we choose a random initial position within the cell and a random initial time within the time step: we adjust that position by advecting it the rest of the time step. Including the random time and advection is crucial for avoiding temporal aliasing when velocities are high: without it, you get undesirable strobing patterns.

There is one further small tweak we can add to simulate the effect of a small amount of smoke diffusion. Some non-trivial stochastic calculus shows that diffusing a quantity, i.e., including a Laplacian term $Dq/Dt = k\nabla \cdot \nabla q$, is equivalent in the limit to adding a component of random Brownian motion to particle trajectories (i.e., solving $Dq/Dt = 0$ with a randomly perturbed velocity field). That is, we can add an independent random-walk contribution to each particle's position each time step, such as a random vector chosen uniformly from the sphere of radius $\sqrt{2k\Delta t}$. Obviously this is only an effective technique if the perturbations are reasonably small compared to a grid cell.

Finally, there are several other quantities for which we can use this machinery. Temperature of course can go hand-in-hand with smoke concentration, storing both quantities with each particle. Feldman et al. [Feldman et al. 03] also include unburnt fuel as a particle variable for their volumetric combustion model (see Chapter 7), albeit with a slightly more advanced particle system that gives particles mass and inertia (see Chapter 11).

10.3   Vortex Particles

We now have enough machinery in place to actually build an interesting alternative fluid simulation algorithm, using vorticity as the primary variable. We'll focus on two dimensions, where the vorticity is a scalar and its inviscid equation (from Chapter 9) is breathtakingly simple:

$$\frac{D\omega}{Dt} = 0.$$

This is practically begging for a particle treatment! In this section, we'll go through the basics of the *vortex-particle* method of Chorin [Chorin 73], introduced to graphics by Gamito et al. [Gamito et al. 95].

We'll begin with an initial velocity field, say on a MAC grid, and estimate its vorticity at the grid cell corners:

$$\omega_{i+1/2,j+1/2} = \frac{v_{i+1,j+1/2} - v_{i,j+1/2}}{\Delta x} - \frac{u_{i+1/2,j+1} - u_{i+1/2,j}}{\Delta x}.$$

We then seed particles throughout the entire fluid region (a small number, maybe one or four, per cell) and interpolate the grid vorticity at each. Each particle's vorticity ω_p will stay fixed for the duration of the simulation: all we need to do is advect the particles in the velocity field. Velocity itself needn't be advected, pressure needn't be solved, etc.

Of course, if we don't explicitly simulate velocity, we are left with the tricky question of how to determine the velocity field from just the particles. We begin by transferring the vorticity of the particles to the grid cell corners $\omega_{i+1/2,j+1/2,k+1/2}$ in essentially the same way we transferred smoke concentration in the previous section. Then we solve for the incompressible velocity field that possesses this vorticity.

Recalling an identity we used at the end of Chapter 9, any incompressible velocity field can be represented as the curl of a potential: $\vec{u} = \nabla \times \psi$. In two dimensions ψ is a scalar, and the curl operator simply rotates its gradient by 90 degrees:

$$\vec{u} = \nabla \times \psi = \left(\frac{\partial \psi}{\partial y}, -\frac{\partial \psi}{\partial x} \right).$$

In fact, since the gradient of ψ is then normal to the velocity field, the isocontours of ψ are just the *streamlines* of the flow, and we can call ψ the *streamfunction*. Storing the ψ values at the grid cell corners, we can easily get the discrete velocity field from

$$u_{i+1/2,j} = \frac{\psi_{i+1/2,j+1/2} - \psi_{i+1/2,j-1/2}}{\Delta x},$$

$$v_{i,j+1/2} = -\frac{\psi_{i+1/2,j+1/2} - \psi_{i-1/2,j+1/2}}{\Delta x}.$$

Finally, to determine the streamfunction we solve for one whose velocity field has the desired vorticity:

$$\nabla \times (\nabla \times \psi) = \omega.$$

Directly discretizing this gives

$$\frac{-\psi_{i+3/2,j+1/2} + 2\psi_{i+1/2,j+1/2} - \psi_{i-1/2,j+1/2}}{\Delta x^2}$$
$$+ \frac{-\psi_{i+1/2,j+3/2} + 2\psi_{i+1/2,j+1/2} - \psi_{i+1/2,j-1/2}}{\Delta x^2} = \omega_{i+1/2,j+1/2},$$

which in fact is our usual discretization of the Poisson problem—the same matrix as the pressure solve! (It's easy to verify that in two dimensions, $\nabla \times \nabla \psi = -\nabla \cdot \nabla \psi$.)

For stationary solid wall boundaries, where we want $\vec{u} \cdot \hat{n} = 0$, we will equivalently require that $\nabla \psi \cdot \hat{t} = 0$, where $\hat{t}$ is the normal rotated 90 degrees—i.e., a tangent vector. This means that the tangential derivative of ψ along the boundary should be zero, or in other words, ψ should be equal to a constant value along the solid wall. The constant value can be related to how fast the fluid is rotating around the solid (this can be determined from the initial conditions; in the absence of viscosity it should remain unchanged), but for simplicity we'll just take it to be zero. This can feed into the discretization by simple setting $\psi = 0$ in solids, or more accurately using the ghost fluid method discussed in Chapter 6.

One of the remarkable strengths of this method is that it suffers no numerical dissipation of vorticity whatsoever. It can also be fairly easily extended to include forces such as buoyancy, changing the equation to $D\omega/Dt = \nabla \times \vec{f}$. That said, this method doesn't have the same flexibilities in dealing with moving boundaries, free surfaces, variable densities, controlled divergence, coupled solids, and more. More serious drawbacks come in three dimensions: in addition to the vortex stretching term complicating the equations (a particle's vorticity no longer remains constant), the potential we need to reconstruct the velocity field must be vector-valued. The vector potential equation $\nabla \times \nabla \vec{\psi} = \nabla \times \vec{\omega}$ is significantly larger and harder to solve than the simple pressure Poisson problem, and its boundary conditions are significantly more complex.

In answer to this, Selle et al. [Selle et al. 05] created a method where a regular velocity-pressure three-dimensional fluid simulation is augmented with just a few vortex particles, or "spin particles" to put a distinct label on them, sprinkled in turbulent regions. The spin particles are advected with the flow as before, and to partially account for the vortex-stretching term $\vec{\omega} \cdot \nabla \vec{u}$, have their vorticity vectors essentially rotated (by adding $\Delta t \vec{\omega}_p \cdot \nabla \vec{u}$ and then rescaling to preserve the magnitude). They in turn add to the velocity field with an acceleration term which encourages the flow to spin with that vorticity. This can be understood as a per-particle vorticity confinement term (see Chapter 9). Using some smooth Gaussian-like kernel function ξ around each particle, with support spanning at least a few grid cells, the acceleration from each particle applied to nearby grid-velocity values is taken as

$$\vec{f}_p(\vec{x}) = \epsilon \left(\frac{\vec{x}_p - \vec{x}}{\|\vec{x}_p - \vec{x}\|} \times \vec{\omega}_p \right).$$

The confinement parameter ϵ again can be tuned to get more or less influence from the spin particles.

10.4 Particle-in-Cell Methods

A major part of the numerical viscosity we have battled is due to the Eulerian advection. Techniques such as vorticity confinement and spin particles can partially mitigate this, but as it turns out, we can do even better. In this section, we will replace the velocity advection step $D\vec{u}/Dt = 0$ itself with particle advection.

Simply storing velocity vectors on particles and advecting them around isn't enough, of course: pressure projection to keep the velocity field divergence-free globally couples all the velocities together. Somehow we need to account for particle-particle interactions on top of advection. We'll now take a look at a general class of methods that can efficiently treat particle-particle interaction by way of a grid.

The particle-in-cell (PIC) approach was pioneered at Los Alamos National Laboratory in the early 1950s, though Harlow's 1963 paper [Harlow 63] is perhaps the first journal article describing it.[1] The basic PIC method begins with all quantities—velocities included—stored on particles that sample the entire fluid region. For graphics work, eight particles per grid cell, initialized as usual from a jittered grid, seems to be about right. In each time step, we first transfer the quantities such as velocity from the particles to the grid—perhaps just as we did with smoke concentration earlier in this chapter. All the non-advection terms, such as acceleration due to gravity, pressure projection and resolution of boundary conditions, viscosity, etc., are integrated on the grid, just as in a fully Eulerian solver.

---

[1] Harlow and other team members in the T-3 Division at Los Alamos also created the MAC grid and marker particle method, and pioneered the use of the vorticity-streamfunction formulation used in the previous section, to name just a few of their many contributions to computational fluid dynamics; see the review article by Harlow [Harlow 04] for more on the history of this group.

Finally we interpolate back from the grid to the particles, and then advect the particles in the grid velocity field.

To more accurately do the particle-to-grid transfer, and be more robust in the face of non-uniform particle distributions, it's recommended that at least for velocity the normalization weight W actually be calculated per grid point, making the value at each grid point a weighted average of nearby particle values. For example, the u-component of velocity on the grid ends up as

$$u_{i+1/2,j,k} = \frac{\sum_p u_p k(\vec{x}_p - \vec{x}_{i+1/2,j,k})}{\sum_p k(\vec{x}_p - \vec{x}_{i+1/2,j,k})}, \qquad (10.2)$$

though of course to actually calculate it we instead loop over the particles accumulating both $u_p k(\vec{x}_p - \vec{x}_{i+1/2,j,k})$ and the weight $k(\vec{x}_p - \vec{x}_{i+1/2,j,k})$ on the grid, and then do the divide in a second pass over the grid.

Also note that the particle-to-grid transfer only provides grid values near particles; it may be imperative to extrapolate those grid values out to the rest of the grid as discussed before. If errors in advection or a positive divergence control result in "gaps" between particles opening up on the grid, it may be necessary to include a reseeding stage where new particles are added to grid cells with too few particles (say, less than three), with particle values interpolated from the grid. Similarly particles can be dynamically deleted from grid cells with an excess of particles (say, more than twelve).

While plain PIC worked admirably—albeit only with first-order accuracy—for the compressible flow problems to which it was originally applied, it also suffered from severe numerical dissipation. The problem is that fluid quantities are averaged from particles to the grid, introducing some smoothing, and then the smoothed grid values are interpolated back to the particles, compounding the smoothing. Even if nothing is happening—particles aren't moving at all—a significant amount of smoothing takes place at every time step.

To counteract this, Brackbill and Ruppel [Brackbill and Ruppel 86] developed the fluid implicit particle (FLIP) method, a beautifully simple variation on PIC. In FLIP, instead of interpolating a quantity back to the particles, the *change* in the quantity (as computed on the grid) is interpolated and used to *increment* the particle value, not replace it. Each increment to a particle's value undergoes one smoothing (from interpolation) but that's all: smoothing is not accumulated, and thus FLIP is virtually free of numerical dissipation. In pseudocode, the method can be interpreted as

- Transfer particle values q_p to the grid $q_{i,j,k}$, through equations like (10.1) or (10.2), and extrapolate on the grid as necessary.
- Save the grid values $q_{i,j,k}$.
- Compute all other terms on the grid, such as pressure projection, to get an updated $q_{i,j,k}^{\text{new}}$.
- For each particle, interpolate the change $\Delta q_{i,j,k} = q_{i,j,k}^{\text{new}} - q_{i,j,k}$ from the grid to add it to the particle's value.
- Advect the particles in the grid velocity field.

Zhu and Bridson [Zhu and Bridson 05] introduced FLIP to incompressible flow and demonstrated how effective it can be at producing highly detailed motion on fairly coarse grids. It essentially eliminates all numerical dissipation from advection, though of course the loss of vorticity from our first-order time-splitting remains. At the same time, it is almost trivial to implement, and especially if you are using particles for other tasks (e.g., marker particles for liquid tracking) it is highly recommended.

One issue with FLIP is that it may develop noise. Typically we use eight particles per grid cell, meaning there are more degrees of freedom in the particles than in the grid: velocity fluctuations on the particles may, on some time steps, average down to zero and vanish from the grid, and on other time steps show up as unexpected perturbations. Of course basic PIC doesn't have this problem, since the particle velocities are simply interpolated from the grid there. Therefore it may be useful to actually blend in a small amount of the PIC update with the FLIP update, causing any noise to decay to zero while hopefully not introducing significant dissipation. That is, for some small *regularization* parameter α in the range $[0, 1]$, set the new particle velocities to

$$\vec{u}_p^{\text{new}} = \alpha \operatorname{interp}(\vec{u}_{\text{grid}}^{\text{new}}, \vec{x}_p) + (1 - \alpha) \left[\vec{u}_p^{\text{old}} + \operatorname{interp}(\Delta \vec{u}_{\text{grid}}, \vec{x}_p) \right].$$

When $\alpha = 0$ this is the pure FLIP update; when $\alpha = 1$ it is the basic PIC update.

A little analysis of the numerical dissipation implied by PIC, similar to our analysis of the first-order semi-Lagrangian method back in Chapter 3, shows that we can actually relate α to the kinematic viscosity of the fluid ν:

$$\alpha = \frac{6\Delta t \nu}{\Delta x^2}.$$

Of course, if this formula gives an $\alpha > 1$, you should clamp it to one, use the PIC update (or just a regular Eulerian advection scheme) and probably even add in a viscous step as in Chapter 8.

Another issue with FLIP is that it is limited to first-order accuracy, despite being free of numerical dissipation. This appears to be quite adequate for treating velocity, smoke concentration, temperature, etc., but *not* adequate for advecting level sets (from Chapter 6): the nice smooth surfaces characteristic of level sets depend on either getting high-order accuracy (so that derivatives of ϕ, e.g., the normal field or the curvature of the surface, are handled accurately) or on strong numerical dissipation (though of course this leads to other unacceptable errors). Thus, we are lead to consider one more hybrid particle-grid method, specifically adapted to level sets.

10.5   The Particle Level Set Method

The particle level set (PLS) method, pioneered by Foster and Fedkiw [Foster and Fedkiw 01] and fully developed by Enright et al. [Enright et al. 02a, Enright et al. 02b], is the result of augmenting an Eulerian level set formulation with helper marker particles to track material boundaries, like the free surface of a liquid.[2]

One of the key differences between PLS and other particle-grid hybrid methods that is helpful to have in mind is that the grid-based level set function is the fundamental representation of the quantity here, and the particles are auxiliary. For almost all the other methods in this chapter, the fundamental representation was the field stored on the particles, and this was transferred to the auxiliary simulation grid as needed—with the one exception of the basic particle-in-cell method (*not* FLIP) where the particles are only helpful auxiliaries in advecting around a grid-sampled function. In this respect PLS is very similar to basic PIC, albeit with a much more sophisticated coupling between particles and grid and special seeding/deletion rules. One of the consequences of this is that PLS only will work with geometry that *can* be reliably represented on the grid: it is subject to the same fundamental limits as pure Eulerian methods that we discussed at the start of this chapter. However, signed distance is one case where even the most accurate Eulerian methods tend to fall far short of this limit: pure Eulerian schemes tend to gain accuracy only where the function is smooth, reducing to first order (and related numerical dissipation) at

---

[2]PLS is not as appropriate for non-conservative boundaries, such as the thin flame front we saw in Chapter 7, where other processes actively erode or grow the surface in addition to passive advection. However, in these cases the numerical dissipation that PLS aims to reduce isn't nearly as objectionable, so regular non-particle methods are generally just fine.

points where smoothness is lost, and unfortunately the signed distance function is not smooth at precisely the locations of interesting features that we want to be able to preserve in advection. (Recall that ϕ has a "kink," a discontinuity in its gradient, at places that are equidistant from two or more points on the boundary, i.e., the medial axis: the sharper a surface feature is the closer this kink is to the surface and the more problems pure Eulerian methods have with dissipation no matter how formally accurate they are.) PLS, with help from particles, can achieve nearly the full accuracy possible for a grid-based method and maybe a little bit more...

PLS begins with a grid-sampled level set, $\phi_{i,j,k}$. Noting that it's only the values of ϕ near the zero isocontour that define the surface, we'll concentrate attention on accurately advecting just the grid cells where $|\phi|$ is small enough, say less than $3\Delta x$. Away from these critical grid cells, as long as the advection algorithm doesn't erroneously flip the sign of ϕ, which even the simplest semi-Lagrangian advection guarantees, we don't care how much it diffuses or smears out the values: these can easily be corrected with a distance reinitialization as discussed in Chapter 6.

It is these cells, within a $3\Delta x$ band of the interface, where we'll add particles. To avoid bias, particles are added on *both* sides of the interface, ϕ positive and negative—for a free surface liquid this means there are "air" particles as well as "water" particles. Each particle, in addition to its position, includes its own estimate of the ϕ value, i.e., how far that particle is from the true interface. Since we only need particles near the interface, we can afford a relative dense sampling: in three dimensions, Fedkiw and coauthors recommend seeding 64 per grid cell, perhaps at randomly jittered positions. A particle's initial ϕ_p value can be interpolated from the grid. Finally, to limit the effect of errant particles later on, the particle ϕ_p values are limited to $[0.1\Delta x, 0.5\Delta x]$ in absolute magnitude: particles with smaller interpolated ϕ values shouldn't be seeded at all, and particles at larger distances have their values clamped to $\pm 0.5\Delta x$. More complicated seeding is possible, attracting particles from their initial positions towards a randomly-decided goal isocontour (distance from the interface): see the original paper for details [Enright et al. 02a]. A particle ϕ_p value can be thought of as the signed radius of the particle, with the smaller particles actually touching the surface.

Both the grid level set values and the particles are advected forward each time step. In smooth regions it's expected they will continue to agree, but in more interesting regions the particles should be much more accurate. Thus a series of error-correction passes are applied, where the particles attempt to correct numerical dissipation errors in the grid, but features that ultimately cannot be represented on the grid are removed from the particles.

This error-correction process begins with identifying *escaped particles*: particles where ϕ interpolated from the grid is a different sign from their own ϕ_p and of larger magnitude. These are cases where an air particles ended up inside the water, or a water particle ended up inside the air, and have gone further than their own radius. We expect that for all other particles, the grid representation is probably smoother and more accurate, and thus should have precedence. The escaped particles are then used to build a corrected level set. The positive escaped particles are considered as one set E^+, defining ϕ^+ on the grid as the max of the regular grid ϕ and the distance to the union of the escaped positive particles:

$$\phi_{i,j,k}^+ = \max(\phi_{i,j,k}, \min_{p \in E^+} \|\vec{x}_{i,j,k} - \vec{x}_p\| - \phi_p).$$

This can be efficiently computed for the grid cells near escaped positive particles by looping over the particles, adjusting the values on the grid nearby each. Similarly the negative escaped particles E^- build a corrected version ϕ^-:

$$\phi_{i,j,k}^- = \min(\phi_{i,j,k}, -\min_{p \in E^-} \|\vec{x}_{i,j,k} - \vec{x}_p\| - |\phi_p|).$$

Finally, the two corrected versions ϕ^+ and ϕ^- are reconciled by taking $\phi^{\text{corrected}}$ to be whichever of the two has least magnitude at each grid point, as that presumably is the one with information most relevant to the true interface.

At this point the corrected ϕ is reinitialized to signed distance, as it may be quite far from a true distance function now. This may of course perturb the surface again, smoothing out features, and so the particles are used to correct this version again. It is this corrected-reinitialized-recorrected grid representation that we now take as the final level set: it should be numerically close to signed distance and should contain all features that can still be represented on the grid after advection. It's now the turn of the particles to be corrected: particles that still register as escaped are deleted (more on this in a moment) and the rest take their new radii from interpolating ϕ from the grid and clamping to the allowed range of magnitudes $[0.1\Delta x, 0.5\Delta x]$.

Finally, since the velocity field might have stretched apart the initial dense sampling near the interface, or sucked in some particles deep into the fluid where they are now essentially useless, a periodic reseeding step is required: in grid cells further than $3\Delta x$ from the interface, all particles are deleted, and otherwise if the grid cell has fewer than 64 particles it is topped up with new randomly seeded particles. This kind of reseeding becomes especially important, and delicate, when solids enter into the picture: to allow water to separate from a solid surface (allowing air to fill the newly created gap) particles will have to be seeded as soon as the water moves away, but when water remains in contact with a solid we *don't* want any particles as they will interfere with the proper extrapolation of the water ϕ into the solid. Rasmussen et al. [Rasmussen et al. 04] discuss this issue to some extent, though a completely robust treatment still remains a research problem.

The one final comment is the status of truly escaped particles. The simplest thing that makes sense is to just delete them: otherwise they run the risk of later flickering back into being when they pass close enough to a grid point, and then disappearing again, giving rise to severely distracting grid-aligned strobing artifacts. They no longer give information that can be reliably represented on the grid and thus have no more direct use in the simulation. However they do still represent *some* information, though it's perhaps difficult to interpret strictly physically. Foster and Fedkiw [Foster and Fedkiw 01] suggest instead of deleting them, transforming them into a secondary particle system such as tiny water droplets following ballistic motion until they hit the level set again; many subsequent authors and practitioners have found similar uses for the escaped particles.

– 11 –
Coupling Fluids and Solids

We have covered in some detail earlier (Chapter 4) how to incorporate moving solid-wall boundary conditions in a simulation. The assumption there was that the solids followed an immutable scripted path: the fluid can't push back on them to change their motion. This chapter is focused on providing this two-way coupling.

11.1 One-Way Coupling

However, before going into two-way coupling, let's take a quick look at the other one-way coupling: solids that take their motion from the fluid, but don't affect it. This is particularly useful for solids that are much lighter than the fluid or much smaller than the features of the flow. In fact we have already seen this, tracing marker particles in the velocity field of the fluid for smoke animation. Here the position $\vec{x}_i$ of each particle simply followed the fluid velocity field:

$$\frac{d\vec{x}_i}{dt} = \vec{u}(\vec{x}_i, t). \tag{11.1}$$

This is also useful for small objects, or even particle systems representing foam, drifting in water, perhaps with a step projecting them to stay on the water surface.

One step up from marker particles are rigid bodies that take their motion from the fluid. In addition to moving their centers of mass with Equation (11.1), we need to update their orientations. Recalling the the vorticity of the flow $\vec{\omega} = \nabla \times \vec{u}$ is twice the angular velocity of the fluid at any given point, we simply integrate the rigid body position using $\frac{1}{2}\vec{\omega}$. For example, using a unit-length quaternion $\hat{q}_i$ to represent the orientation, we could update it over a time step Δt with

$$\tilde{q}_i = \left(1, \tfrac{1}{4}\Delta t\vec{\omega}\right)\hat{q}_i^n,$$
$$\hat{q}_i^{n+1} = \frac{\tilde{q}_i}{\|\tilde{q}_i\|}.$$

Take note of the factor of $\frac{1}{4}$: this is $\frac{1}{2}$ from the quaternion integration formula and another $\frac{1}{2}$ to get angular velocity from vorticity. Advancing orientations in this manner is useful not just for actual rigid bodies but also for oriented particles that carry a local coordinate system—see Rasmussen et al. [Rasmussen et al. 03] for an example in constructing highly detailed smoke plumes from explosions, where each particle carries a volumetric texture.

More generally, we might want solids to have some inertia, with the effect of the fluid felt in terms of force, not velocity. As we know, there are two forces in effect in a fluid: pressure and viscous stress. The second is perhaps more important for very small objects.

The net force due to viscosity is the surface integral of viscous traction, the viscous stress tensor times the surface normal:

$$\vec{F} = -\iint_{\partial S} \tau \hat{n}.$$

Here I take S to be the volume of the solid and ∂S to be its boundary—this is a slight change of notation from earlier chapters where S represented the solid surface. The normal here points *out* of the solid and *into* the fluid, leading to the negative sign. In one-way coupling, the viscous boundary condition $\vec{u} = \vec{u}_{\text{solid}}$ isn't present in the simulation and thus the fluid's viscous stress tensor isn't directly usable. Indeed, the assumption underlying one-way coupling is that the solid objects don't have an appreciable effect on the fluid at the resolution of the simulation. However, we can imagine that *if* the solid were in the flow, there would be a small *boundary layer* around it in which the velocity of the fluid rapidly alters to match the solid velocity: the gradient of velocity in this region gives us the viscous stress tensor. The actual determination of this boundary layer and exactly what average force results is in general unsolved. We instead boil it down to simple formulas, with tunable constants. For small particles in the flow, we posit a simple drag force of the form:

$$\vec{F}_i = D(\vec{u} - \vec{u}_i).$$

Here D is proportional to the fluid's dynamic viscosity coefficient, and might be a per-particle constant, or involve the radius or cross-sectional area of the object, or might even introduce a non-linearity such as being proportional to $\|\vec{u} - \vec{u}_i\|$—in various engineering contexts all of these have been found to be useful. For flatter objects, such as leaves or paper, we might constrain the normal component of the velocity to match the fluid and only apply a weak (if not zero) viscous force in the tangential direction.

If we are further interested in solids with orientation, the net torque on an object due to viscosity is likewise

$$\vec{T} = -\iint_S (\vec{x} - \vec{x}_i) \times (\tau \hat{n}),$$

where $\vec{x}_i$ is the center of mass of the object, and similarly we can't hope to derive a perfect physical formula for it. Instead we can posit simple formulas now based on the difference between the angular velocity of the solid and half the vorticity of the fluid:

$$\vec{T} = E\left(\tfrac{1}{2}\vec{\omega} - \vec{\Omega}\right).$$

The proportionality E can be tuned similar to D and may even be generalized to a matrix incorporating the current rotation matrix of the object if the solids are far from round.

The effect of pressure is a little simpler. The net force in this case is

$$\vec{F} = -\iint_{\partial S} p\hat{n} = -\iiint_S \nabla p,$$

where we have used the divergence theorem to convert it into an integral of the pressure gradient over the volume occupied by the solid. For small objects, we can evaluate ∇p from the simulation at the center of mass and multiply by the object's volume to get the force. Note that for water sitting still (and assuming a free surface pressure of zero), the hydrostatic pressure is equal to $\rho_{\text{water}}|g|d$ where d is depth below the surface, giving a gradient of $-\rho_{\text{water}}\vec{g}$. Multiplying this by the volume that the object displaces, we get the mass of displaced water, leading to the usual buoyancy law.

The torque due to pressure is

$$T = -\iint_{\partial S} (\vec{x} - \vec{x}_i) \times (p\hat{n}).$$

If p is smooth enough throughout the volume occupied by the solid—say it is closely approximated as a constant or even linear function—this integral vanishes, and there is no torque on the object; we needn't model it. Do note that in the case of water sitting still, the pressure is *not* smooth across the surface—it can be well approximated as a constant zero above the surface, compared to the steep linear gradient below—and thus a partially submerged object can experience considerable torque from pressure. In the partially submerged case, the integral should be taken (or approximated) over the part of the solid below the water surface.

11.2   Weak Coupling

For objects large or heavy enough to significantly affect the fluid flow, but light enough to be affected in turn by the fluid, we need methods for simulating both in tandem. One common approach to implementing this two-way coupling is sometimes termed *weak coupling*. In this scheme, we interleave the solid- and fluid-simulation steps. At its simplest, we get the following algorithm for each time step:

- Advect the fluid, and update the solid positions (and orientations if relevant).

- Integrate non-coupled forces into all velocities (e.g., gravity, internal elasticity forces).

- Solve for the pressure to make the fluid incompressible, enforcing the solid-wall boundary condition with the current solid velocities held fixed.

- Update the solid velocities from forces due to the new fluid pressure and from contact/collision.

More complicated schemes are of course possible, e.g., with repeated alternations between fluid and solid or with substeps to get higher accuracy for the internal elastic forces, but the essence of weak coupling remains: one pressure solve for fluid treats the solid velocities as fixed, and one update to solid velocities treats the fluid pressure as fixed.

In terms of implementation, we have already covered the fluid aspect of this problem since, from the point of view of the fluid solver, the solid is always treated as fixed as before.[1] All that needs to be added is the fluid-to-solid stage, where fluid forces are applied to the solid.

For a rigid object, the fluid-to-solid coupling amounts to finding the net force and torque due to the fluid, which we have seen in surface integral form in the previous section. If the geometry of the solid objects is tesselated finely enough (i.e., on a scale comparable to the grid spacing Δx) these surface integrals can be directly approximated with numerical quadrature. For example, if the object surface is represented by a triangle mesh, the force could be as simple as summing over the triangles the product of triangle area with pressure interpolated at the centroid of the triangle,

---

[1]Though as Guendelman et al. [Guendelman et al. 05] point out, if the solids are thin, care must be taken in advection—in the semi-Lagrangian approach, if a particle trajectory is traced back *through* a solid, the fluid velocity at the interfering solid wall should be used, interpolated in a one-sided way only from the correct side of the solid; for particle methods, collision detection should be used to ensure particles don't pass through solid walls.

and if relevant, the viscous stress tensor times the triangle normal. The torque can similarly be approximated. However, in other circumstances (e.g., objects tesselated at a very different scale, or thin curves such as rope) these surface integrals can be inconvenient. We can then transform the surface integral to volume integrals, which can be approximated directly on the grid. For example, for pressure the net force is

$$\vec{F} = -\iint_{\partial S} p\hat{n} = -\iiint_S \nabla p \qquad (11.2)$$

and the net torque is

$$\vec{T} = -\iint_{\partial S} (\vec{x} - \vec{x}_C)p\hat{n} = \iiint_S \nabla \times [(\vec{x} - \vec{x}_X)p] , \qquad (11.3)$$

where $\vec{x}_C$ is the center of mass. The volume integrals can be broken up into sums over the appropriate grid cells, using the appropriate volume fractions (which are approximated for the pressure solve anyhow).

This general approach has met with success in many graphics papers (e.g., [Takahashi et al. 02, Guendelman et al. 05]) and is quite attractive from a software architecture point of view—the internal dynamics of fluids and solids remain cleanly separated, with new code only for integrating fluid forces applied to solids—but does suffer from a few problems that may necessitate smaller than desirable time steps. For example, if we start with a floating solid initially resting at equilibrium: after adding acceleration due to gravity all velocities are $\Delta t\vec{g}$, the fluid pressure solve treats this downward velocity at the solid surface as a constraint and thus leads to non-zero fluid velocities, and finally the pressure field (perturbed from hydrostatic equilibrium) doesn't quite cancel the velocity of the solid; the solid sinks to some extent, and the water starts moving. These errors are proportional to the time-step size and thus of course can be reduced, but at greater expense.

11.3   The Immersed Boundary Method

A somewhat stronger coupling scheme is epitomized by the immersed boundary method (the classic reference is the review article by Peskin [Peskin 02]). Here we give the fluid pressure solve leeway to change the solid velocity by, in effect, momentarily pretending the solid is also fluid (just of a different density). In particular, rather than impose the solid velocity as boundary conditions for the fluid pressure solve, we add the mass and velocity of the solid to the fluid grid and then solve for pressure throughout the whole domain. The usual fluid fractions are used as weights in determining the average density and average velocity in each u-, v-, and w-cell, and then the fractions actually used in determining the pressure equations are full. (Incidentally, this approach was in fact combined with the approach of the previous section in the paper of Guendelman et al. [Guendelman et al. 05], where this pressure is used instead of the less accurate pressure of the classic voxelized pressure solve to update the solid's velocity.)

A related method, the rigid fluid approach of Carlson et al. [Carlson et al. 04], simplifies the solve somewhat by moreover assuming the density of the solid to be the same as the fluid and adding a corrective buoyancy force as a separate step, recovering a rigid body's velocity directly from averaging the velocity on the grid after the pressure solve (i.e., finding the average translational and angular velocity of the grid cells the solid occupies) rather than integrating pressure forces over the surface of the body. This can work extremely well if the ratio of densities isn't too large.

For inviscid flow, simply averaging the solid and fluid velocities in mixed cells as is typically done in the immersed boundary method may lead to excessive numerical dissipation. Recall that the tangential velocity of the solid is not coupled to the tangential velocity of the fluid: only the normal components are connected for inviscid flows. When averaging the full velocities together we are, in essence, constraining the fluid to the viscous boundary condition $\vec{u} = \vec{u}_{\text{solid}}$. Therefore it is recommended if possible to extrapolate the tangential component of fluid velocity into the cells occupied by the solid and only average the normal component of the solid's velocity onto the grid. For very thin solids, such as cloth, this is particularly simple since extrapolation isn't required—just a separation of the solid velocities into normal and tangential components.

This approach helps reduce some of the artifacts of the previous weak-coupling method, but it doesn't succeed in all cases. For example, starting a simulation with a floating object resting at equilibrium still ends up creating false motion, since in the pressure solve the solid object appears to be an odd-shaped wave on the fluid surface.

11.4 General Sparse Matrices

Before getting into strong coupling, where we compute fluid and solid forces simultaneously, we need to take a brief diversion to generalize our sparse matrix capabilities: the regular structure of the matrices used up until now will not accommodate the addition of solids.

There are several possible data structures for storing and manipulating general sparse matrices. The one we will focus on is sometimes called *compressed sparse row* (or CSR) format. Here each row of the matrix is stored as an array of non-zero values and their associated column indices. We'll actually use two variations of CSR, a simple dynamic version (that makes adding new non-zeros when dynamically constructing a matrix fairly efficient) and a static version that gives better performance in PCG.

In dynamic CSR, the array for each sparse row is stored independently with an associated length. To support adding new non-zeros relatively efficiently, we may allocate extra storage for these arrays and keep track of the total available; when the extra space runs out, we can reallocate the array with double the size. This is the strategy taken in the C++ STL `vector` container for example. Often people will further maintain the arrays in order sorted by column index, making it more efficient to find entries or add two sparse rows together.

However multiplying the sparse matrix by a dense vector, the core of PCG, loses some efficiency with this approach: each sparse row might be scattered in memory leading to poor cache usage. Therefore, after constructing a matrix using the dynamic CSR structure, we convert it to a static CSR structure. Here just three arrays are defined, ensuring that all matrix non-zeros are contiguous in memory:

- a floating-point array `value` containing all non-zero values ordered row by row,

- an integer array `colindex` of the same length containing the corresponding column indices, and

- an integer array `rowstart` of length $n+1$ (for an $n \times n$ matrix) indicating where each sparse row begins in `value` and `colindex`—an extra entry at the end points just past the end of the `value` and `colindex` arrays (i.e., contains the number of non-zeros in the matrix).

The small overhead of converting a dynamic CSR matrix to static format is generally well worth it for PCG, bringing the cost back in line with our earlier grid-based method.

You may recall that with our grid version of the matrix we optimized the storage by exploiting symmetry, in some sense just storing the upper (or lower) triangle of the matrix. This is generally not worthwhile with CSR: it considerably complicates matrix operations.

```
for i = 0 to n-1
  y(i) = 0
  for j = rowstart(i) to rowstart(i+1)-1
    y(i) += value(j)*x(colindex(j))
```

Figure 11.1. Pseudocode for multiplying an $n \times n$ static CSR matrix with a dense vector, $y = Ax$.

It is fairly straightforward to multiply a static CSR sparse matrix with a dense vector; see Figure 11.1 for pseudocode. It's another matter to generalize the incomplete Cholesky preconditioner and associated triangular solves. It turns out, for general sparsity patterns, that the previous simplification of only having to compute diagonal entries (and reusing the off-diagonal entries of A) doesn't hold, and furthermore the modified incomplete Cholesky factorization cannot be computed with the same loop-ordering presented earlier. It is more natural, in fact, to compute $R = L^T$ in CSR format (or equivalently, L in a compressed sparse column format). All that said, we can still define the regular incomplete factor from the previous properties:

- R is upper triangular, and $R_{i,j} = 0$ wherever $A_{i,j} = 0$,
- $(R^T R)_{i,j} = A_{i,j}$ wherever $A_{i,j} \neq 0$,

- Set tuning constant $\tau = 0.97$ and safety constant $\sigma = 0.25$.
- Copy the upper triangle of A into R (including the diagonal).
- For $k = 0$ to $n - 1$ where $R_{k,k} \neq 0$:
  - If $R_{k,k} < \sigma A_{k,k}$ then set $R_{k,k} \leftarrow \sqrt{A_{k,k}}$, otherwise set $R_{k,k} \leftarrow \sqrt{R_{k,k}}$.
  - Rescale the rest of the k'th row of R: $R_{k,j} \leftarrow \frac{R_{k,j}}{R_{k,k}}$ for stored entries with $j > k$.
  - Loop over $j > k$ where $R_{k,j}$ is stored:
    - Set $\delta = 0$ (where we keep a sum of the elements we drop).
    - Loop over $i > k$ where $R_{k,i}$ is stored:
      - If $R_{j,i}$ is stored, set $R_{j,i} \leftarrow R_{j,i} - R_{k,i}R_{k,j}$, otherwise $\delta \leftarrow \delta + R_{k,i}R_{k,j}$.
    - Set $R_{j,j} \leftarrow R_{j,j} - \tau\delta$.

Figure 11.2. The calculation of the MIC(0) preconditioner R for general matrices A, using CSR format.

- (First solve $R^T z = r$).
- Copy $z \leftarrow r$.
- For $i = 0$ to $n - 1$ where $R_{i,i} \neq 0$:
  - Set $z_i \leftarrow \frac{z_i}{R_{i,i}}$.
  - Loop over $j > i$ where $R_{i,j}$ is stored:
    - Set $z_j \leftarrow z_j - R_{i,j} z_i$.
- (Next solve $R z^{\text{new}} = z$ in place).
- For $i = n - 1$ down to 0, where $R_{i,i} \neq 0$:
  - Loop over $j > i$ where $R_{i,j}$ is stored:
    - Set $z_i \leftarrow z_i - R_{i,j} z_j$.
  - Set $z_i \leftarrow \frac{z_i}{R_{i,i}}$.

Figure 11.3. Applying the MIC(0) preconditioner in CSR format to get $z = (R^T R)^{-1} r$.

and the modified factor from:

- R is upper triangular, and $R_{i,j} = 0$ wherever $A_{i,j} = 0$,

- $(R^T R)_{i,j} = A_{i,j}$ wherever $A_{i,j} \neq 0$ with $i < j$ (i.e. off the diagonal),

- each row sum $\sum_j (R^T R)_{i,j}$ matches the row sum $\sum_j A_{i,j}$ of A.

Without going into the picky but obvious details of using the format, Figure 11.2 presents pseudocode to construct R, with the same parameters as before, and Figure 11.3 demonstrates how to apply the preconditioner by solving with R and R^T.

11.5 Strong Coupling

Strong coupling has been most thoroughly worked out for the rigid body case, with an inviscid fluid (just pressure); this is where we will end the chapter. Let's work out the equations for the continuous case before proceeding to discretization.

First we'll define some notation for a rigid body:

- $\vec{X}$ the center of mass of the rigid body,

- $\vec{V}$ its translation velocity,

- $\vec{\Omega}$ its angular velocity,

- $\vec{L}$ its angular momentum,

- m its mass, and

- I its inertia tensor.

(Extending this to multiple rigid bodies is straightforward.) We saw the net force and torque on the body due to pressure above, which gives us the following updates:

$$\vec{V}^{n+1} = \vec{V} - \frac{\Delta t}{m} \iint_{\partial S} p\hat{n}, \tag{11.4}$$

$$\vec{\Omega}^{n+1} = \vec{\Omega} - \Delta t I^{-1} \iint_{\partial S} \left(\vec{x} - \vec{X}\right) \times p\hat{n}. \tag{11.5}$$

The velocity of the solid at a point $\vec{x}$ on the surface is

$$\vec{u}_{\text{solid}}(\vec{x}) = \vec{V} + \Omega \times \left(\vec{x} - \vec{X}\right),$$

which then appears in the boundary conditions for the usual pressure problem:

$$\nabla \cdot \frac{\Delta t}{\rho} \nabla p = \nabla \cdot \vec{u} \qquad \text{in the fluid,}$$

$$\left(\vec{u} - \frac{\Delta t}{\rho} \nabla p\right) \cdot \hat{n} = \vec{u}_{\text{solid}}^{n+1} \cdot \hat{n} \qquad \text{on } \partial S.$$

A free surface boundary condition $p = 0$ may also be included.

As an aside, though not immediately apparent in this form, the linear operator that maps $(\vec{V}, \vec{\Omega})$ to the normal velocity field on the boundary can be shown to be the adjoint[2] of the operator that maps pressures on the boundary to net force and torque on the solid. It's this property that will end up, after discretization, giving us a symmetric matrix to solve for pressure.

A simpler form of the equations are given by Batty et al. [Batty et al. 07]. We keep the rigid body update Equations (11.4) and (11.5), but avoid the boundary conditions by instead seeking a pressure that minimizes the kinetic energy of the entire system. Recall that the kinetic energy of the rigid body is just $\frac{1}{2}m\|\vec{V}\|^2 + \frac{1}{2}\vec{\Omega}^T I \vec{\Omega}$.

[2]Adjoint simply means transpose when talking about matrices but is also used for operators involving infinite-dimensional spaces such as the space of normal velocity fields here.

It is this variational form of the equations that we choose to discretize. We already have discussed how to approximate the pressure update to the rigid body (i.e., the net force and torque) in the earlier weak-coupling section; we need only make this concrete with a sparse matrix J which, when multiplied with a vector containing the grid pressure values yields the force and torque. Using Equation (11.2), we get the first three rows of J that correspond to the net force. For example, the x-component F_1 (the first row) is determined from

$$F_1 = -\sum_{i,j,k} V_{i+1/2,j,k} \frac{p_{i+1,j,k} - p_{i,j,k}}{\Delta x},$$

where $V_{i+1/2,j,k}$ is the volume of the solid in u-cell $(i+1/2, j, k)$—note that this is the complement of the cell volumes for the fluid! This gives us

$$J_{1,(i,j,k)} = \frac{V_{i+1/2,j,k} - V_{i-1/2,j,k}}{\Delta x}.$$

Similarly, the next two rows of J, corresponding to the y- and z-components of net force, are

$$J_{2,(i,j,k)} = \frac{V_{i,j+1/2,k} - V_{i,j-1/2,k}}{\Delta x},$$

$$J_{3,(i,j,k)} = \frac{V_{i,j,k+1/2} - V_{i,j,k-1/2}}{\Delta x}.$$

Similarly, from Equation (11.3), we can get the other three rows of J that correspond to the net torque. The first component T_1 is, in continuous variables,

$$T_1 = \iiint \frac{\partial}{\partial y} (p(z - Z)) - \frac{\partial}{\partial z} (p(y - Y)),$$

where the center of mass coordinates are $\vec{X} = (X, Y, Z)$. This simplifies to

$$T_1 = \iiint (z - Z)\frac{\partial p}{\partial y} - (y - Y)\frac{\partial p}{\partial z},$$

which we approximate as

$$T_1 \approx \sum_{i,j,k} V_{i,j+1/2,k}(z_k - Z)\frac{p_{i,j+1,k} - p_{i,j,k}}{\Delta x}$$
$$- \sum_{i,j,k} V_{i,j,k+1/2}(y_j - Y)\frac{p_{i,j,k+1} - p_{i,j,k}}{\Delta x},$$

where x_i, y_j and z_k give the coordinates of the center of grid cell (i, j, k). From this we see that the fourth row of J is given by

$$J_{4,(i,j,k)} = -(z_k - Z)\frac{V_{i,j+1/2,k} - V_{i,j-1/2,k}}{\Delta x} + (y_j - Y)\frac{V_{i,j,k+1/2} - V_{i,j,k-1/2}}{\Delta x}.$$

Similarly, the last two rows of J, corresponding to the second and third components of net torque, are

$$J_{5,(i,j,k)} = -(x_i - X)\frac{V_{i,j,k+1/2} - V_{i,j,k-1/2}}{\Delta x}$$
$$+ (z_k - Z)\frac{V_{i+1/2,j,k} - V_{i-1/2,j,k}}{\Delta x},$$
$$J_{6,(i,j,k)} = -(y_j - Y)\frac{V_{i+1/2,j,k} - V_{i-1/2,j,k}}{\Delta x}$$
$$+ (x_i - X)\frac{V_{i,j+1/2,k} - V_{i,j-1/2,k}}{\Delta x}.$$

Note that away from the boundary of the solid, all of these volume differences are just zero, so J is quite sparse: it has non-zero columns only for cells near the boundary of the solid.

To be perfectly consistent, and thus be able to get exact hydrostatic rest for neutrally buoyant bodies fully immersed in fluid, we can also use the same volumes to approximate the rigid body's inertia tensor—however, outside of this particular scenario this is probably unnecessary work and thus we leave it to the reader to derive it if interested.

For notational convenience, we'll put the rigid body's translational velocity $\vec{V}$ and angular velocity Ω together into one six-dimensional vector $\vec{U}$. Similarly we can construct a 6×6 mass matrix M from the mass and inertia tensor:

$$M = \begin{pmatrix} m & 0 & 0 & \vec{0} \\ 0 & m & 0 & \vec{0} \\ 0 & 0 & m & \vec{0} \\ \vec{0} & \vec{0} & \vec{0} & I \end{pmatrix}.$$

Then the kinetic energy of the body is $\frac{1}{2}\vec{U}^T M \vec{U}$ and the pressure update is $\vec{U}^{n+1} = \vec{U} + \Delta t M^{-1} Jp$.

Finally, we are ready for the discrete minimization. Taking the gradient of the new kinetic energy with respect to pressure gives

$$\frac{\partial}{\partial p}\left[\frac{1}{2}\left(\vec{U} + \Delta t M^{-1}Jp\right)^T M \left(\vec{U} + \Delta t M^{-1}Jp\right)\right] =$$
$$\Delta t^2 J^T M^{-1} Jp + \Delta t J^T \vec{U}.$$

Combining this with the derivation of the fluid kinetic energy from the end of Chapter 4, and rescaling as was done there (dividing by Δt and replacing actual volumes by dimensionless volume fractions) we see we just add $\Delta t J^T M^{-1} J$ to the matrix and $-J^T \vec{U}$ to the right-hand side.

This is precisely where we need more general sparse matrices: $\Delta t J^T M^{-1} J$ doesn't correspond to a simple grid structure. In fact, it forms a dense submatrix, connecting up all the cells near the boundary of the object. If you're interested in the linear algebra, it's also simple to see that it is (at most) rank six and must be symmetric positive semi-definite—so PCG still works! The density may, however, cause memory and performance problems: these can mostly be overcome by keeping the extra terms separate in factored form. The matrix-vector multiplies in PCG can be significantly accelerated then by multiplying $J^T M^{-1} J s$ as $J^T (M^{-1}(J^T s))$, and since they are only rank six can be ignored in constructing the preconditioner without too big a penalty.

For large objects, which overlap many grid cells, this is actually a considerable problem: a large amount of memory will be required to store it, and PCG will run slowly due to all the work multiplying with this dense submatrix. One possibility for improvement is to add the new rigid body velocity $\vec{U}^{n+1}$ as an auxiliary variable in the pressure solve, giving the following slightly larger but much sparser system:

$$\begin{pmatrix} A & J^T \\ J & -\frac{1}{\Delta t}M \end{pmatrix} \begin{pmatrix} p \\ \vec{U}^{n+1} \end{pmatrix} = \begin{pmatrix} -d \\ -\frac{1}{\Delta t}M\vec{U} \end{pmatrix}.$$

While this still leads to a symmetric matrix, it is unfortunately now indefinite, which means PCG no longer can work. Nevertheless, this is in a well-studied class of matrices, sometimes termed "saddle-point" matrices (in fact, apart from the constant pressure null-space, it would be a "symmetric quasi-definite" matrix), and it seems promising to solve it as such. For example, it would be worthwhile trying an iterative method such as MINRES in conjunction with an incomplete Cholesky preconditioner in LDL^T form (where L has unit diagonal, and D is a diagonal matrix with positive entries for the pressure unknowns and negative entries for the rigid body unknowns). For more on solving this class of matrix problems, see the review article by Benzi et al. [Benzi et al. 05] for example.

Another interesting direction to consider is to generalize this approach to include strong coupling of articulated rigid bodies: for example, the Lagrange multiplier approach to constraints can also be phrased as a minimization of kinetic energy. Frictional contact forces fall in the same category, albeit with inequality constraints that complicate the minimization considerably.

Turning to deformable objects, the energy minimization framework falters. Strong coupling in this context means combining an implicit time step of the internal dynamics of the deformable object with the pressure solve; however, implicitly advancing elastic forces (involving potential energy) apparently cannot be interpreted as a minimization of energy with respect to forces. At the time of writing, within graphics only the work of Chentanez et al. [Chentanez et al. 06] has tackled this problem, discretizing the fluid on an unstructured tetrahedral mesh that conforms to the boundary mesh of the deformable object; so far the generalization to regular grids with volume fractions hasn't been made. We thus end the chapter here.

- 12 -
Shallow Water

We'll finish off the book with two chapters on special cases of water simulation that allow much faster and simpler algorithms. In both cases, we will use the simplifying assumption that the water surface can be represented as a *height field* $y = h(x, z)$: the water region is all of the points where $y < h(x, z)$, excluding solids. The most important solid is of course the bottom, which we also represent as a height field $y = b(x, z)$, giving a water region defined by

$$b(x, z) < y < h(x, z),$$

and thus the water depth is $d(x, z) = h(x, z) - b(x, z)$. We will actually use depth d as a primary simulation variable, reconstructing the height $h = b+d$ as needed. This geometric simplification rules out many interesting effects such as convincing splashes, breaking waves, droplets or sprays, but still allows many interesting wave motions.[1] For the purposes of the book, we'll also restrict the bottom to be stationary—$b(x, z)$ remains constant—though allowing it to move is a fairly easy generalization if you follow the modeling steps in this chapter.

For the height field assumption to remain a good approximation for the water throughout the simulation, we also need to restrict our attention to height fields that aren't too steep and velocities which aren't too extreme: mainly we will be looking at fairly calm waves. For example, a tall column of water can be represented with a height field in the first frame, but when it starts to collapse it is almost bound to start splashing around in more general ways that will rule it out.

While you can of course use the height field representation to track the water surface in conjunction with a full three-dimensional solver as detailed earlier in the book—see Foster and Metaxas [Foster and Metaxas 96]—we'll make some further approximations to reduce the complexity of the equations. In this chapter we'll look at the case where the water is shallow,

---

[1]Many authors have worked out ways to bring back some of these features, usually by way of adding a particle system for the extra effects. For example, see the articles by O'Brien and Hodgins [O'Brien and Hodgins 95] and Thürey et al. [Thuerey et al. 07].

i.e., the depth $d = h - b$ is very small compared to the horizontal length scale of waves or other flow features, and in the next chapter we'll instead consider the water very deep relative to this scale.

12.1 Deriving the Shallow Water Equations

12.1.1 Assumptions

The shallowness assumption means essentially that we can ignore vertical variations in the velocity field: the fluid doesn't have "room" for vertical features like vortices stacked on top of each other. We'll then just track the *depth-averaged* horizontal velocities, $u(x, z)$ and $w(x, z)$, which are the average of u and w for y varying along the depth of the water. For the inviscid flow we're modeling in this chapter, you can think of u and w as constant along y; for viscous flow a better model would be that u and w vary linearly from zero at the bottom to some maximum velocity at the free surface.

Just as an interjection: the process of depth averaging is used in many more contexts than the one here. For example, avalanches have been modeled this way (the snow layer is thin compared to the extent of the mountainside it flows along) as well as large-scale weather patterns (the atmosphere and oceans are extremely thin compared to the circumference of the Earth). The resulting systems of equations are still commonly called "shallow water equations," even if referring to fluids other than water.

The other fundamental simplification we'll make is assuming hydrostatic pressure. That is, if we look at the vertical component of the momentum equation

$$\frac{\partial v}{\partial t} + u \frac{\partial v}{\partial x} + v \frac{\partial v}{\partial y} + w \frac{\partial v}{\partial z} + \frac{1}{\rho} \frac{\partial p}{\partial y} = -g,$$

(where $g \approx 9.81 \text{m/s}$ is the magnitude of acceleration due to gravity) we will assume that the dominant terms are the pressure gradient and gravity, with the rest much smaller. This is consistent with the requirement that the water is shallow and relatively calm, with accelerations in the fluid much smaller than g. Dropping the small terms gives the equation for hydrostatic pressure:

$$\frac{1}{\rho} \frac{\partial p}{\partial y} = -g.$$

Combining that with the free surface boundary condition $p = 0$ at $y = h$ gives

$$p(x, y, z, t) = \rho g \left(h(x, z, t) - y \right). \tag{12.1}$$

Again, this isn't strictly true if the water is moving, but it's a good approximation. The fact that we can directly write down the pressure in the shallow water case, as opposed to solving a big linear system for pressure as we had to in fully three-dimensional flow, is one of the key speed-ups.

12.1.2 Velocity

Assuming that u and w are constant along y means $\partial u / \partial y = \partial w / \partial y = 0$, which means the horizontal parts of the momentum equation are reduced to

$$\frac{\partial u}{\partial t} + u \frac{\partial u}{\partial x} + w \frac{\partial u}{\partial z} + \frac{1}{\rho} \frac{\partial p}{\partial x} = 0,$$
$$\frac{\partial w}{\partial t} + u \frac{\partial w}{\partial x} + w \frac{\partial w}{\partial z} + \frac{1}{\rho} \frac{\partial p}{\partial z} = 0.$$

This is just two-dimensional advection along with the horizontal parts of the pressure gradient. Note that although pressure varies linearly in y, the horizontal components of its gradient are in fact constant in y; substituting in Equation (12.1) gives

$$\frac{\partial u}{\partial t} + u \frac{\partial u}{\partial x} + w \frac{\partial u}{\partial z} + g \frac{\partial h}{\partial x} = 0,$$
$$\frac{\partial w}{\partial t} + u \frac{\partial w}{\partial x} + w \frac{\partial w}{\partial z} + g \frac{\partial h}{\partial z} = 0. \tag{12.2}$$

That is, the horizontal velocity components are advected in the plane as usual, with an additional acceleration proportional to gravity that pulls water down from higher regions to lower regions.

What about vertical velocity v? It turns out this is fully determined from the "primary" shallow water variables (u, w and d) that we will be simulating. We won't actually need v in the simulation (unless for some reason you need to evaluate it for, say, particle advection in the flow) but it will come in handy to figure out how the surface height evolves in a moment.

First take a look at the incompressibility condition:

$$\frac{\partial u}{\partial x} + \frac{\partial v}{\partial y} + \frac{\partial w}{\partial z} = 0 \tag{12.3}$$

$$\Leftrightarrow \quad \frac{\partial v}{\partial y} = -\frac{\partial u}{\partial x} - \frac{\partial w}{\partial z}. \tag{12.4}$$

The right-hand side of this equation doesn't depend on y, so $\partial v/\partial y$ must be a constant along the y-direction too—which implies v has to be a linear function of y. It's fully determined from its value at the bottom $y = b(x, z)$ and the gradient we just derived.

The bottom velocity comes from the boundary condition $\vec{u} \cdot \hat{n} = 0$, remembering again that we're assuming the bottom is stationary. Recalling some basic calculus, the normal at the bottom is proportional to $(-\partial b/\partial x, 1, -\partial b/\partial z)$, so at the bottom $y = b(x, z)$:

$$-u\frac{\partial b}{\partial x} + v - w\frac{\partial b}{\partial z} = 0$$

$$\Leftrightarrow \quad v = u\frac{\partial b}{\partial x} + w\frac{\partial b}{\partial z}.$$

Note that if the bottom is flat, so the partial derivatives of b are zero, this reduces to $v = 0$ as expected. Combined with Equation (12.3) we get the following vertical velocity at any point in the fluid:

$$v(x, y, z, t) = u\frac{\partial b}{\partial x} + w\frac{\partial b}{\partial z} - \left(\frac{\partial u}{\partial x} + \frac{\partial w}{\partial z}\right)(y - b). \qquad (12.5)$$

In other words, for shallow water we take v to be whatever it requires for the flow to be incompressible and to satisfy the bottom solid boundary condition.

12.1.3   Height

We can also evaluate the vertical velocity at the free surface, in a different way. Note that the function $\phi(x, y, z) = y - h(x, z)$ implicit defines the free surface as its zero isocontour—similar to how we tracked general liquid surfaces back in Chapter 6. We know that the free surface, i.e., the zero isocontour, moves with the velocity of the fluid, and so ϕ should satisfy an advection equation

$$\frac{D\phi}{Dt} = 0$$

$$\Leftrightarrow \quad \frac{\partial \phi}{\partial t} + u\frac{\partial \phi}{\partial x} + v\frac{\partial \phi}{\partial y} + w\frac{\partial \phi}{\partial z} = 0$$

$$\Leftrightarrow \quad -\frac{\partial h}{\partial t} + u\left(-\frac{\partial h}{\partial x}\right) + v(1) + w\left(-\frac{\partial h}{\partial z}\right) = 0$$

at least at the surface $y = h$ itself. Plugging in what we derived for the velocity in Equation (12.5) at $y = h$ gives us an equation for the rate of change of height:

$$-\frac{\partial h}{\partial t} - u\frac{\partial h}{\partial x} + \left[u\frac{\partial b}{\partial x} + w\frac{\partial b}{\partial z} - \left(\frac{\partial u}{\partial x} + \frac{\partial w}{\partial z}\right)(h - b)\right] - w\frac{\partial h}{\partial z} = 0,$$
$$\frac{\partial h}{\partial t} + u\frac{\partial(h - b)}{\partial x} + w\frac{\partial(h - b)}{\partial z} = -(h - b)\left(\frac{\partial u}{\partial x} + \frac{\partial w}{\partial z}\right).$$
(12.6)

Using the depth $d = h - b$, and remembering that b is stationary, this can be simplified to

$$\frac{\partial d}{\partial t} + u\frac{\partial d}{\partial x} + w\frac{\partial d}{\partial z} = -d\left(\frac{\partial u}{\partial x} + \frac{\partial w}{\partial z}\right).$$
(12.7)

That is, the water depth is advected by the horizontal velocity and, in addition, increased or decreased proportional to the depth and the two-dimensional divergence.

We can simplify Equation (12.7) even further, putting it into what's called *conservation law form*:

$$\frac{\partial d}{\partial t} + \frac{\partial}{\partial x}(ud) + \frac{\partial}{\partial z}(wd) = 0.$$
(12.8)

This can in fact be directly derived from conservation of mass, similar to the approach in Appendix B. It's significant here because it leads to numerical methods that exactly conserve the total volume of water in the system— avoiding the mass-loss problems we saw earlier with three-dimensional free surface flow.[2] However, discretizing this accurately enough (to avoid numerical dissipation) is a topic that lies outside the scope of this book.

12.1.4 Boundary Conditions

Equations (12.2) and (12.7) or (12.8) also need boundary conditions, where the water ends (in the x–z horizontal plane) or the simulation domain ends. The case of a solid wall is simplest: if $\hat{n}$ is the two-dimensional normal to the wall in the x–z plane, then we require

$$(u, w) \cdot \hat{n} = 0.$$

---

[2]This conservation law form can also be applied in three dimensions, leading to a *volume-of-fluid* or *VOF* simulation that exactly conserves volume as well. However, in three dimensions, VOF techniques have their own share of problems in terms of accurately localizing the surface of the fluid.

Of course, for a moving solid wall, this should instead be $(u_{\text{solid}}, w_{\text{solid}}) \cdot \hat{n}$. To maintain that velocity in the normal direction, following the velocity equations (12.2), we also need

$$\left(\frac{\partial h}{\partial x}, \frac{\partial h}{\partial z}\right) \cdot \hat{n} = 0.$$

This also applies at an inflow/outflow boundary, where we pump water in or out of the simulation. The utility of such a boundary may be enhanced by adding a source term to the height equation, directly adding (or subtracting) water in some regions; such source terms are also perfect for modeling vertical sinks or sources of water (such as a drop falling from above, perhaps in a particle system, or a drainage hole).

It's much more difficult dealing with the edge of the simulation domain, if it's assumed that the water continues on past the edge. If you expect all the waves in the system to travel parallel to the edge, it's perfectly reasonable to put an invisible solid wall boundary there. If you determine waves should be entering along one edge, perhaps from a simple sinusoid model (see the next section for how to choose such a wave), you can further specify normal velocity and height. However, if you also expect waves to leave through the edge, things are much, much trickier: solid walls, even if invisible or specifying fancy normal velocities and heights, reflect incoming waves. Determining a *non-reflecting* (or *absorbing*) boundary condition is not at all simple and continues as a subject of research in numerical methods. The usual approach taken is to gradually blend away the simulated velocities and heights with a background field (such as a basic sinusoid wave, or flat water at rest), over the course of many grid cells: if the blend is smooth and gradual enough, reflections should be minimal.

Finally one boundary condition of prime importance for many shallow water simulations is at the *moving contact line*: where the depth of the water drops to zero, such as where the water ends on a beach. In fact, no boundary conditions need to be applied in this case: if desired for a numerical method, the velocity can be extrapolated to the dry land as usual, and the depth is zero ($h = b$).

12.2   The Wave Equation

Before jumping to numerical methods for solving the shallow water equations, it's worth taking a quick look at a further simplification. For very calm water we can completely neglect the advection terms, leaving us with

$$\frac{\partial u}{\partial t} + g\frac{\partial h}{\partial x} = 0,$$

$$\frac{\partial w}{\partial t} + g\frac{\partial h}{\partial z} = 0,$$

$$\frac{\partial h}{\partial t} = -d\left(\frac{\partial u}{\partial x} + \frac{\partial w}{\partial z}\right).$$

Divide the height equation through by the depth d and differentiate in time:

$$\frac{\partial}{\partial t}\left(\frac{1}{d}\frac{\partial h}{\partial t}\right) = -\frac{\partial}{\partial x}\frac{\partial u}{\partial t} - \frac{\partial}{\partial z}\frac{\partial w}{\partial t}.$$

Then substitute in the simplified velocity equations to get

$$\frac{\partial}{\partial t}\left(\frac{1}{d}\frac{\partial h}{\partial t}\right) = \frac{\partial}{\partial x}\left(g\frac{\partial h}{\partial x}\right) + \frac{\partial}{\partial z}\left(g\frac{\partial h}{\partial z}\right).$$

Expanding the left-hand side, but further neglecting the quadratic term as being much smaller, gives

$$\frac{\partial^2 h}{\partial t} = gd\nabla \cdot \nabla h,$$

where the Laplacian $\nabla \cdot \nabla$ here is just in two dimensions (x and z). Finally, with the assumption that the depth d in the right-hand side remains near enough constant, this is known as the *wave equation*.

The wave equation also pops up naturally in many other phenomena— elastic waves in solid materials, electromagnetic waves, acoustics (sound waves), and more—and has been well studied. Fourier analysis can provide a full solution, but to keep things simple let's just try a single sinusoid wave.[3] Take a unit-length vector $\hat{k}$ (in two dimensions) which will represent the direction of wave motion; the peaks and troughs of the waves will lie on lines perpendicular to $\hat{k}$. Let λ be the wavelength, A the amplitude, and c the speed of the wave. Putting this all together gives

$$A\sin\left(\frac{2\pi(\hat{k} \cdot (x, z) - ct)}{\lambda}\right).$$

---

[3]In fact, any wave shape will do—we pick sinusoids simply out of convention and to match up with the ocean wave modeling in the next chapter where sinusoids are critical.

If you plug this in as a possible $h(x, z, t)$ in the wave equation, we get the following equation:

$$-A\frac{4\pi^2 c^2}{\lambda^2}\sin\left(\frac{2\pi(\hat{k}\cdot(x,z)-ct)}{\lambda}\right) = -gdA\frac{4\pi^2}{\lambda^2}\sin\left(\frac{2\pi(\hat{k}\cdot(x,z)-ct)}{\lambda}\right).$$

This reduces to

$$c^2 = gd.$$

In other words, the wave equation has solutions corresponding to waves moving at speed $\sqrt{gd}$.

The key insight to glean from all these simplifications and models is that shallow water waves move at a speed related to the depth: the deeper the water, the faster the waves move. For example as a wave approaches the shore, the depth decreases and the wave slows down. In particular, the front of the wave slows down earlier, and so water from the back of the wave starts to pile up as the wave front slows down. Waves near the shore naturally get bigger and steeper, and if conditions are right, they will eventually crest and overturn. The shallow water equations we've developed in this chapter do contain this feature, though of course the height field assumption breaks down at the point of waves breaking: we won't be able to quite capture that look, but we'll be able to come close.

12.3   Discretization

There are many possibilities for discretizing the shallow water equations, each with its own strengths and weaknesses. You might in particular take a look at Kass and Miller's introduction of the equations to animation [Kass and Miller 90], and Layton and van de Panne's unconditionally stable method [Layton and van de Panne 02]. Here we'll provide a small variation on the Layton and van de Panne method that avoids the need for a linear solver at the expense of having a stability restriction on the time step.

We begin with the two-dimensional staggered MAC grid as usual, storing the velocity components u and w at the appropriate edge midpoints and the depth d at the cell centers. Where needed, the height h is reconstructed from the depth as $h = b + d$. We also use the usual time-splitting approach of handling advection in an initial stage, perhaps with the semi-Lagrangian method we've been using so far:

$$u^A = \text{advect}(\vec{u}^n, \Delta t, u^n),$$
$$w^A = \text{advect}(\vec{u}^n, \Delta t, w^n),$$
$$d^A = \text{advect}(\vec{u}^n, \Delta t, d^n).$$

We then compute the intermediate height field $h^A = b + d^A$ and extrapolate it to non-fluid cells, i.e., setting h equal to the value in the nearest fluid cell. Note that it is important to extrapolate height h, not depth d, as we want to make sure water sitting still on a sloped beach, for example, will remain still. We then update the velocities with the pressure acceleration:

$$u_{i+1/2,k}^{n+1} = u_{i+1/2,k}^A - \Delta t\, g\, \frac{h_{i+1,k}^A - h_{i,k}^A}{\Delta x},$$
$$w_{i,k+1/2}^{n+1} = w_{i,k+1/2}^A - \Delta t\, g\, \frac{h_{i,k+1}^A - h_{i,k}^A}{\Delta x}.$$

We extrapolate these velocities to non-fluid cells as usual and finally update the depth with the divergence term:

$$d_{i,k}^{n+1} = d_{i,k}^A - \Delta t d_{i,k}^A \left(\frac{u_{i+1/2,k}^{n+1} - u_{i-1/2,k}^{n+1}}{\Delta x} + \frac{w_{i,k+1/2}^{n+1} - w_{i,k-1/2}^{n+1}}{\Delta x} \right).$$

That's all there is to it!

There is a stability time-step restriction here, however. A simple analysis in the same vein as the approximations made in Section 12.2 to get to the wave equation can be made, showing that for stability we require

$$\Delta t \lesssim \frac{\Delta x}{\sqrt{gD}},$$

where D is the maximum depth value in the simulation. For safety a fraction of this quantity, such as 0.2, should be used.

- 13 -
Ocean Modeling

Simulating the ocean is an ongoing challenge in computer animation. This chapter will demonstrate a series of simplifications that allow relatively calm ocean surfaces to be efficiently simulated; efficiently handling rough oceans, or large-scale interactions between the ocean and solid objects immersed or floating in it, is currently an open research problem. The chief resource in graphics is the work by Tessendorf [Tessendorf 04].

The main difficulty in the ocean setting is scale. Essential to the look of waves are both large-scale swells and small ripples, and as we'll see in a moment, to get the relative speeds of these different sizes of waves correct, a simulation needs to take into account the true depth of the water. (In particular, the shallow water model of the previous chapter is completely wrong.) A naïve brute-force approach of just running a 3D fluid simulator like the ones we've looked at so far would result in an excessively and impractically large grid. Therefore we'll take a look at changing the equations themselves.

13.1   Potential Flow

Recall the vorticity equation (9.1) from Chapter 9, and since we're dealing with large-scale water, drop the small viscosity term:

$$\frac{\partial \vec{\omega}}{\partial t} + \vec{u} \cdot \nabla \vec{\omega} = -\omega \cdot \nabla \vec{u}.$$

It's not hard to see that if vorticity starts at exactly zero in a region, it has to stay zero unless modified by boundary conditions. Since the ocean at rest (with zero velocity) has zero vorticity, it's not too much of a stretch to guess that vorticity should stay nearly zero once calm waves have developed, as long as boundaries don't become too important—i.e., away from the shoreline or large objects, and assuming the free surface waves don't get too violent. That is, we will model the ocean as *irrotational*, meaning the vorticity is zero: $\nabla \times \vec{u} = \vec{\omega} = 0$.

A basic theorem of vector calculus tells us that if a smooth vector field has zero curl in a simply-connected region, it must be the gradient of some scalar potential:

$$\vec{u} = \nabla \phi.$$

Note that the ϕ used here has nothing to do with the signed distance function or any other implicit surface function we looked at earlier. Combining this with the incompressibility condition, $\nabla \cdot \vec{u} = 0$, indicates that the potential ϕ must satisfy Laplace's equation:

$$\nabla \cdot \nabla \phi = 0.$$

This is the basis of *potential flow*: instead of solving the full non-linear Navier-Stokes equations, once we know the fluid is irrotational and the region is simply-connected, we only need solve a single linear PDE.

The boundary conditions for potential flow are where it gets interesting. For solid walls the usual $\vec{u} \cdot \hat{n} = \vec{u}_{\text{solid}} \cdot \hat{n}$ condition becomes a constraint on $\nabla \phi \cdot \hat{n}$. Free surfaces, where before we just said $p = 0$, are a bit trickier: pressure doesn't enter into the potential flow equation directly. However, there is a striking resemblance between the PDE for the potential and the PDE for pressure in the projection step: both involve the Laplacian $\nabla \cdot \nabla$. We'll use this as a clue in a moment.

The equation that pressure does appear in is momentum: let's substitute $\vec{u} = \nabla \phi$ into the inviscid momentum equation and see what happens:

$$\frac{\partial \nabla \phi}{\partial t} + (\nabla \phi) \cdot (\nabla \nabla \phi) + \frac{1}{\rho} \nabla \phi = \vec{g}.$$

Exchanging the order of the space and time derivatives in the first term, and assuming ρ is constant so it can be moved inside the gradient in the pressure term, takes us to

$$\nabla \frac{\partial \phi}{\partial t} + (\nabla \phi) \cdot (\nabla \nabla \phi) + \nabla \frac{p}{\rho} = \vec{g}.$$

Seeing a pattern start to form, we can also write the gravitational acceleration as the gradient of the gravity potential, $\vec{g} \cdot \vec{x} = -gy$ where $g = 9.81 \text{ m/s}^2$ and y is height (for concreteness, let's take $y = 0$ at the average sea level).

$$\nabla \frac{\partial \phi}{\partial t} + (\nabla \phi) \cdot (\nabla \nabla \phi) + \nabla \frac{p}{\rho} + \nabla(gy) = 0.$$

Only the advection term is left. Writing it out in component form

$$(\nabla\phi) \cdot (\nabla\nabla\phi) = \begin{pmatrix} \dfrac{\partial\phi}{\partial x}\dfrac{\partial^2\phi}{\partial x^2} + \dfrac{\partial\phi}{\partial y}\dfrac{\partial^2\phi}{\partial x\partial y} + \dfrac{\partial\phi}{\partial z}\dfrac{\partial^2\phi}{\partial x\partial z} \\[2mm] \dfrac{\partial\phi}{\partial x}\dfrac{\partial^2\phi}{\partial x\partial y} + \dfrac{\partial\phi}{\partial y}\dfrac{\partial^2\phi}{\partial y^2} + \dfrac{\partial\phi}{\partial z}\dfrac{\partial^2\phi}{\partial y\partial z} \\[2mm] \dfrac{\partial\phi}{\partial x}\dfrac{\partial^2\phi}{\partial x\partial z} + \dfrac{\partial\phi}{\partial y}\dfrac{\partial^2\phi}{\partial y\partial z} + \dfrac{\partial\phi}{\partial z}\dfrac{\partial^2\phi}{\partial z^2} \end{pmatrix},$$

and it becomes clear that this is actually the same as

$$(\nabla\phi) \cdot (\nabla\nabla\phi) = \begin{pmatrix} \dfrac{\partial}{\partial x}\dfrac{1}{2}\left(\dfrac{\partial\phi}{\partial x}\right)^2 + \dfrac{\partial}{\partial x}\dfrac{1}{2}\left(\dfrac{\partial\phi}{\partial y}\right)^2 + \dfrac{\partial}{\partial x}\dfrac{1}{2}\left(\dfrac{\partial\phi}{\partial z}\right)^2 \\[2mm] \dfrac{\partial}{\partial y}\dfrac{1}{2}\left(\dfrac{\partial\phi}{\partial x}\right)^2 + \dfrac{\partial}{\partial y}\dfrac{1}{2}\left(\dfrac{\partial\phi}{\partial y}\right)^2 + \dfrac{\partial}{\partial y}\dfrac{1}{2}\left(\dfrac{\partial\phi}{\partial z}\right)^2 \\[2mm] \dfrac{\partial}{\partial z}\dfrac{1}{2}\left(\dfrac{\partial\phi}{\partial x}\right)^2 + \dfrac{\partial}{\partial z}\dfrac{1}{2}\left(\dfrac{\partial\phi}{\partial y}\right)^2 + \dfrac{\partial}{\partial z}\dfrac{1}{2}\left(\dfrac{\partial\phi}{\partial z}\right)^2 \end{pmatrix}$$

$$= \nabla\left(\tfrac{1}{2}\|\nabla\phi\|^2\right).$$

Using this now brings the momentum equation to

$$\nabla\frac{\partial\phi}{\partial t} + \nabla\left(\tfrac{1}{2}\|\nabla\phi\|^2\right) + \nabla\frac{p}{\rho} + \nabla(gy) = 0$$

$$\Rightarrow \quad \nabla\left[\frac{\partial\phi}{\partial t} + \left(\tfrac{1}{2}\|\nabla\phi\|^2\right) + \frac{p}{\rho} + gy\right] = 0.$$

The only function whose gradient is everywhere zero is a constant, and since constants added to ϕ (a theoretical abstraction) have no effect on the velocity field (the real physical thing), we can assume that the constant is just zero for simplicity. This gives *Bernoulli's equation*:

$$\frac{\partial\phi}{\partial t} + \left(\tfrac{1}{2}\|\nabla\phi\|^2\right) + \frac{p}{\rho} + gy = 0.$$

You may have already heard of this. For example, in the steady-state case, where $\partial\phi/\partial t = 0$, and after subtracting out the hydrostatic component of pressure, we end up with the pressure variation $\Delta p = -\tfrac{1}{2}\rho\|\vec{u}\|^2$. Many simple experiments, such as blowing over the top ofa sheet of paper held

along one edge, verify how fast-moving air can induce a pressure drop which
sucks things towards it.[1]

Bernoulli's equation gives us a relationship, admittedly non-linear, between pressure and the potential ϕ. In the interior of the fluid this can be
used to get pressure from our solution for ϕ. At a free surface where $p = 0$
is known, we can instead use it as a boundary condition for ϕ:

$$\frac{\partial \phi}{\partial t} + \left(\tfrac{1}{2}\|\nabla\phi\|^2\right) + gy = 0.$$

Well, almost—this is more of a boundary condition on $\partial\phi/\partial t$, not ϕ itself.
But it's not hard to see that as soon as we discretize in time, this will end
up as a boundary condition on the new value of ϕ that happens to also
depend on old values of ϕ.

13.2 Simplifying Potential Flow for the Ocean

Unfortunately as it stands we still have to solve a three-dimensional PDE
for the potential ϕ, and though it's a much simpler linear problem in the
interior of the water, it now has a fairly nasty non-linear boundary condition
at the free surface. In this section we'll go through a series of simplifications
to make it solvable in an efficient way. The critical assumption underlying
all the simplifications is that we're only going to look at fairly calm oceans.

The first step is to rule out breaking waves so the geometry of the free
surface can be described by a height field, just like the previous chapter:

$$y = h(x, z).$$

Of course h is also a function of time, $h(x, z, t)$, but we'll omit the t to emphasize the dependence on just two of the spatial variables. For a perfectly
calm flat ocean we'll take $h(x, z) = 0$; our chief problem will be to solve
for h as a function of time. In fact, given the velocity field $\vec{u}$ we know that
the free surface should follow it—and in fact viewing the surface as implicit
defined as the zero level set of $h(x, z) - y$, we already know the advection

---

[1]It also unfortunately figures in a bogus explanation of the lift on an airplane wing,
namely that due to the curved shape of the airfoil the air has to go faster over the top
than over the bottom to meet at the other side; hence there is lower pressure on the
top surface, which gives lift. It's not hard to see this is almost completely wrong: angle
of attack is the biggest factor in determining lift, allowing airplanes to fly even when
upside-down, and allowing flat fan blades with no fancy curvature to effectively push air
around.

equation it should satisfy:

$$\frac{D}{Dt}(h(x,z) - y) = 0$$

$$\Rightarrow \quad \frac{\partial h}{\partial t} + u\frac{\partial h}{\partial x} - v + w\frac{\partial h}{\partial z} = 0$$

$$\Leftrightarrow \quad \frac{\partial h}{\partial t} + (u,w) \cdot \left(\frac{\partial h}{\partial x}, \frac{\partial h}{\partial z}\right) = v.$$

Just as with shallow water, this looks like a two-dimensional material derivative of height, with vertical velocity v as an additional term.

We'll also make the assumption that the ocean floor is flat, at depth $y = -H$ for some suitably large H. While this is almost certainly false, the effect of variations in the depth will not be apparent for the depths and the wavelengths we're considering.[2] The solid "wall" boundary condition at the bottom, where the normal is now $(0, 1, 0)$, becomes $\partial\phi/\partial y = 0$.

We can now write down the exact set of differential equations we want to solve:

$$\nabla \cdot \nabla\phi = 0 \qquad\qquad \text{for } -H \leq y \leq h(x, z),$$

$$\frac{\partial\phi}{\partial y} = 0 \qquad\qquad \text{at } y = -H,$$

$$\frac{\partial\phi}{\partial t} + \left(\tfrac{1}{2}\|\nabla\phi\|^2\right) + gh(x,z) = 0 \quad \text{at } y = h(x,z),$$

$$\frac{\partial h}{\partial t} + (u,w) \cdot \left(\frac{\partial h}{\partial x}, \frac{\partial h}{\partial z}\right) = v.$$

This is still hard to deal with, thanks to the non-linear terms at the free surface. We will thus use the clever mathematical trick of ignoring them—in effect, assuming that $\vec{u}$ is small enough and h is smooth enough that all the quadratic terms are negligible compared to the others. This cuts them down to

$$\frac{\partial\phi}{\partial t} = -gh(x,z) \qquad \text{at } y = h(x,z),$$

$$\frac{\partial h}{\partial t} = v.$$

---

[2] Once you get to truly big waves, tsunamis, variation in ocean depth becomes important: for a tsunami the ocean looks shallow, and so the previous chapter actually provides a better model. However, in the deep ocean these waves are practically invisible, since they tend to have wavelengths of tens or hundreds of kilometers but very small heights on the order of a meter.

However, it's still difficult to solve since the location at which we are applying the free surface boundary condition moves according to the solution of h. Assuming that the waves aren't too large, i.e., h is small, we can cheat and instead put the boundary condition at $y = 0$, leading to a new simplified problem:

$$\nabla \cdot \nabla \phi = 0 \qquad \text{for } -H \le y \le 0,$$

$$\frac{\partial \phi}{\partial y} = 0 \qquad \text{at } y = -H,$$

$$\frac{\partial \phi}{\partial t} = -gh(x, z) \qquad \text{at } y = 0,$$

$$\frac{\partial h}{\partial t} = \frac{\partial \phi}{\partial y} \qquad \text{at } y = 0.$$

This now is a perfectly linear PDE on a simple slab $-H \le y \le 0$. (We also swapped in $\partial \phi / \partial y$ for v, to make it clear how h and ϕ are coupled.) One of the great properties we now have is that we can add (superimpose) two solutions to get another solution, which we'll exploit to write the general exact solution as a linear combination of simpler solutions.

We haven't yet touched on boundary conditions along x and z: we've implicitly assumed so far that the ocean is infinite, stretching out forever horizontally. We can actually solve this analytically, using Fourier integrals, but clearly this raises some problems when it comes to implementation on a finite computer. Instead we will assume the ocean is *periodic* in x and z, with some suitably large length L being the period. From a graphics standpoint, L should be large enough that the periodicity is inconspicuous—an $L \times L$ ocean "tile" should probably fill a reasonable fraction of the screen. (We'll later discuss a few other tricks to further obscure periodicity.) Any reasonable periodic function can be represented as a Fourier series, which for computer implementation we'll simply truncate to a finite number of terms.

Before jumping to the full Fourier series, let's take a look at a single Fourier mode. Though it may be a little mind-bending to try and visualize it, we'll actually use a complex exponential for this: ultimately this is more convenient mathematically and corresponds best to what a typical Fast Fourier transform library offers in its API, even though the PDE as we have written it only involves real numbers.

Let's start with a generic Fourier component of the height field:

$$h(x, z, t) = \hat{h}_{ij}(t) e^{\sqrt{-1} 2\pi(ix + jz)/L}.$$

The *Fourier coefficient* is $\hat{h}_{ij}(t)$; the t is included to emphasize that it depends on time, but not on spatial variables. In general $\hat{h}_{ij}(t)$ will be a complex number, even though in the end we'll construct a real-valued height field—more on this in a minute. I use the notation $\sqrt{-1}$ instead of the usual i (for mathematicians) or j (for engineers) since i and j are reserved for integer indices. Speaking of which, the integers i and j are the indices of this Fourier component—they may be negative or zero as well as positive. The vector $(i, j)/L$ gives the spatial frequency, and the vector $\vec{k} = 2\pi(i, j)/L$ is called the *wave vector*. Define the *wave number* k as

$$k = \|\vec{k}\| = \frac{2\pi\sqrt{i^2 + j^2}}{L}.$$

The *wavelength* is $\lambda = 2\pi/k = L/\sqrt{i^2 + j^2}$. As you can probably guess, this corresponds precisely to what we would physically measure as the length of a set of waves that this Fourier mode represents.

We'll now make the guess, which will prove to be correct, that when we plug this in for the height field, the corresponding solution for $\phi(x, y, z, t)$ will be in the following form:

$$\phi(x, y, z, t) = \hat{\phi}_{ij}(t)e^{\sqrt{-1}2\pi(ix+jz)/L}d_{ij}(y).$$

We don't yet know what the depth function $d_{ij}(y)$ should be. Let's first try this guess in the interior of the domain, where $\nabla \cdot \nabla \phi = 0$ should hold:

$$\nabla \cdot \nabla \phi = 0$$

$$\Leftrightarrow \quad \frac{\partial^2 \phi}{\partial x^2} + \frac{\partial^2 \phi}{\partial y^2} + \frac{\partial^2 \phi}{\partial z^2} = 0$$

$$\Leftrightarrow \quad \frac{-4\pi^2 i^2}{L^2}\phi + \frac{d_{ij}''}{d_{ij}}\phi + \frac{-4\pi^2 j^2}{L^2}\phi = 0$$

$$\Leftrightarrow \quad \frac{d_{ij}''}{d_{ij}}\phi = k^2\phi$$

$$\Leftrightarrow \quad d_{ij}'' = k^2 d_{ij}.$$

We now have an ordinary differential equation for d_{ij}, with the general solution being a linear combination of e^{ky} and e^{-ky}. Note that the bottom boundary condition, $\partial\phi/\partial y = 0$ at $y = -H$, reduces to $d_{ij}'(-H) = 0$. Since our guess at ϕ already has a yet-to-be-determined factor $\hat{\phi}_{ij}(t)$ built in, we take

$$d_{ij}(y) = e^{ky} + e^{-2kH}e^{-ky}.$$

With this choice, ϕ now satisfies the Laplace equation in the interior of the fluid and the bottom boundary condition. Let's write out what we have for this Fourier mode so far:

$$\phi(x,y,z,t) = \hat{\phi}_{ij}(t)e^{\sqrt{-1}2\pi(ix+jz)/L}\left(e^{ky} + e^{-2kH}e^{-ky}\right). \qquad (13.1)$$

All that's left to determine is the time dependence of the potential $\hat{\phi}_{ij}(t)$ and the height field $\hat{h}_{ij}(t)$, and the only equations we have left are the boundary conditions at $y = 0$: $\partial\phi/\partial t = -gh$ and $\partial h/\partial t = \partial\phi/\partial y$. These two boundary equations at the free surface become (after cancelling out the common $e^{\sqrt{-1}2\pi(ix+jz)/L}$ factor):

$$\begin{aligned}
\frac{\partial\hat{\phi}_{ij}}{\partial t}(1 + e^{-2kH}) &= -g\hat{h}_{ij}, \\
\frac{\partial\hat{h}_{ij}}{\partial t} &= \hat{\phi}_{ij}(k - ke^{-2kH}).
\end{aligned} \qquad (13.2)$$

Now, differentiate the second equation with respect to time, and replace the $\partial\hat{\phi}_{ij}/\partial t$ term with the first equation, to get

$$\frac{\partial^2\hat{h}_{ij}}{\partial t^2} = -kg\frac{1 - e^{-2kH}}{1 + e^{-2kH}}\hat{h}_{ij}. \qquad (13.3)$$

This is another simple ordinary differential equation, with general solution consisting of yet more Fourier sinusoids, $e^{\sqrt{-1}\omega_k t}$ and $e^{-\sqrt{-1}\omega_k t}$ where the wave frequency ω_k (how fast the wave is going up and down, no relation at all to vorticity) is given by

$$\omega_k = \sqrt{kg\frac{1 - e^{-2kH}}{1 + e^{-2kH}}}. \qquad (13.4)$$

Before going on to the full solution, and accompanying numerical method, it's instructive to pause a moment and reinterpret this height field solution.

Writing out the one of the components of the height field gives

$$\begin{aligned}
h(x,z,t) &= e^{-\sqrt{-1}\omega_k t}e^{\sqrt{-1}2\pi(ix+jz)/L} \\
&= e^{\sqrt{-1}(\vec{k}\cdot(x,z) - \omega_k t)} \\
&= e^{\sqrt{-1}\vec{k}\cdot[(x,z) - c_k t\hat{k}]},
\end{aligned} \qquad (13.5)$$

where $\hat{k} = \vec{k}/k$ is the unit-length direction of the wave (normal to the crests and troughs) and c_k is the wave speed, defined as

$$\begin{aligned}
c_k &= \frac{\omega_k}{k} \\
&= \sqrt{\frac{g(1 - e^{-2kH})}{k(1 + e^{-2kH})}}.
\end{aligned} \qquad (13.6)$$

Equation (13.5) tells us that the value at a horizontal position (x, z) and time t is the same as the initial wave form at time t and position $(x, z) - c_k t \hat{k}$. It's a lot like the advection equations we have seen over and over again, only this time it's just the wave moving at that speed, not the individual molecules of water. Equation (13.6) is called the *dispersion relation*, giving the speed of a wave as a function of its wave number k. Remembering that wavelength is inversely proportional to k, the dispersion relation shows that waves of different sizes will travel at different speeds—in particular if they all start off in the same patch of ocean, as time progresses they will disperse, hence the name. This fact is probably the most crucial visual element in a convincing ocean: it's what communicates to the audience that there is significant depth below the water, whether or not they know the physics underlying it.

In fact, what we have derived so far is just as valid for shallow water (H small) as deep water (H big). If the waves are shallow, i.e., H is small compared to the wavelength so that kH is small, then asymptotically $c \sim \sqrt{gH}$. That is, the speed depends on gravity and depth but not wavelength, which is exactly what we saw for shallow water in Chapter 12. On the other hand, for deep water and moderate-sized waves, i.e., where kH is very large, to a very good approximation we have

$$c_k \approx \sqrt{\frac{g}{k}}, \qquad \omega_k \approx \sqrt{gk}, \tag{13.7}$$

which is in fact the simplified formula normally used in the ocean—beyond a certain depth the dependence on H doesn't really matter. This form makes it clear that longer waves (k small) move faster than short waves (k large) in the ocean, which again is a very characteristic look: big swells rushing past underneath slow moving ripples.[3]

13.3 Evaluating the Height Field Solution

We derived the wave speed using only one component of the general solution in time for the height field. You can double check that the other component gives a wave moving at the same speed, but in the opposite direction $-\hat{k}$. This leads to some redundancy with the Fourier mode associated with wave vector $-\vec{k}$, which has the same wave number k, the same wave speed, and

---

[3]Incidentally, the full spectrum of dispersion is also very easily seen in boat wakes: if you look far enough away from the boat, the wake will have separated into big wavelengths at the leading edge and smaller scale stuff behind.

the same directions. We'll sort this out now and also clean up the issue of how to make sure the height field is only real-valued despite all the complex numbers flying around. We now build the general real-valued solution from a collection of real cosine waves:

$$h(x, z, t) = \sum_{i,j} A_{ij} \cos(\vec{k} \cdot (x, z) - \omega_k t + \theta_{ij}). \qquad (13.8)$$

Here A_{ij} is the real-valued constant amplitude of the wave, $\vec{k} = 2\pi(i, j)/L$ is the wave vector as before and now points in the direction of the wave's motion, ω_k is the time frequency of the wave from Equation (13.7), and θ_{ij} is a constant phase shift. We'll get to picking A_{ij} and θ_{ij} later on in the chapter.

Equation (13.8) can be used directly to evaluate the height field at any point in space and time, but if a lot of waves are involved the summation becomes expensive. However a cheaper alternative exists by way of the Fast Fourier Transform (FFT). Let $n = 2^m$ be a power of two—this isn't essential as FFT algorithms exist for any n, but typically the transform is fastest for powers of two—and restrict the wave indices to

$$-n/2 + 1 \le i, j \le n/2. \qquad (13.9)$$

We thus have an $n \times n$ grid of wave parameters. We'll additionally specify that the constant term is zero, $A_{00} = 0$, as this is not a wave but the average sea level, and to simplify life also zero out the highest positive frequency (which doesn't have a matching negative frequency): $A_{n/2,j} = A_{i,n/2} = 0$. The sum will then actually only be up to $i = n/2 - 1$ and $j = n/2 - 1$.

We'll now show how to evaluate $h(x, z, t)$ for any fixed time t on the $n \times n$ regular grid of locations $0 \le x, z < L$, i.e., where $x_p = pL/n$ and $z_q = qL/n$ for integer indices p and q. This grid of h values can then be fed directly into a renderer. Note that this in fact gives an $L \times L$ tile that can be periodically continued in any direction: we'll talk more about that at the end of the chapter.

The problem is to determine, for a fixed time t and all integer indices $0 \le p, q < n$, the height values as specified by

$$h_{pq} = \sum_{i=-n/2+1}^{n/2-1} \sum_{j=-n/2+1}^{n/2-1} A_{ij} \cos(\vec{k} \cdot (x_p, z_q) - \omega_k t + \theta_{ij}). \qquad (13.10)$$

This is not quite in the form that an FFT code can handle, so we will need to manipulate it a little, first by substituting in the wave vector $\vec{k} = 2\pi(i, j)/L$

and the coordinates of the grid $x_p = pL/n$, $z_q = qL/n$:

$$h_{pq} = \sum_{i=-n/2+1}^{n/2-1} \sum_{j=-n/2+1}^{n/2-1} A_{ij} \cos(2\pi(ip+jq)/n - \omega_k t + \theta_{ij}). \qquad (13.11)$$

Next we write the cosine in terms of complex exponentials:

$$h_{pq} = \sum_{i=-n/2+1}^{n/2-1} \sum_{j=-n/2+1}^{n/2-1} A_{ij} \frac{1}{2} e^{\sqrt{-1}(2\pi(ip+jq)/n - \omega_k t + \theta_{ij})}$$

$$+ \frac{1}{2} e^{-\sqrt{-1}(2\pi(ip+jq)/n - \omega_k t + \theta_{ij})}$$

$$= \sum_{i=-n/2+1}^{n/2-1} \sum_{j=-n/2+1}^{n/2-1} \frac{1}{2} e^{\sqrt{-1}(\theta_{ij} - \omega_k t)} A_{ij} e^{\sqrt{-1}(2\pi(ip+jq)/n)}$$

$$+ \frac{1}{2} e^{-\sqrt{-1}(\theta_{ij} - \omega_k t)} A_{ij} e^{\sqrt{-1}(2\pi(-ip-jq)/n)}$$

$$(13.12)$$

Finally we shuffle terms around in the sum to get

$$h_{pq} = \sum_{i=-n/2+1}^{n/2-1} \sum_{j=-n/2+1}^{n/2-1} \left[\frac{1}{2} e^{\sqrt{-1}(\theta_{ij} - \omega_k t)} A_{ij} + \frac{1}{2} e^{-\sqrt{-1}(\theta_{-i,-j} - \omega_k t)} A_{-i,-j} \right]$$

$$\times e^{\sqrt{-1}(2\pi(ip+jq)/n)}$$

$$= \sum_{i=-n/2+1}^{n/2-1} \sum_{j=-n/2+1}^{n/2-1} Y_{ij}(t) e^{\sqrt{-1}(2\pi(ip+jq)/n)},$$

$$(13.13)$$

where the complex Fourier coefficients $Y_{ij}(t)$ are defined as

$$Y_{ij}(t) = \frac{1}{2} e^{\sqrt{-1}(\theta_{ij} - \omega_k t)} A_{ij} + \frac{1}{2} e^{-\sqrt{-1}(\theta_{-i,-j} - \omega_k t)} A_{-i,-j}$$

$$= \frac{1}{2} \left[\cos(\theta_{ij} - \omega_k t) + \sqrt{-1} \sin(\theta_{ij} - \omega_k t) \right] A_{ij}$$

$$+ \frac{1}{2} \left[\cos(\theta_{-i,-j} - \omega_k t) - \sqrt{-1} \sin(\theta_{ij} - \omega_k t) \right] A_{-i,-j}$$

$$= \left[\frac{1}{2} \cos(\theta_{ij} - \omega_k t) A_{ij} + \frac{1}{2} \cos(\theta_{-i,-j} - \omega_k t) A_{-i,-j} \right]$$

$$+ \sqrt{-1} \left[\frac{1}{2} \sin(\theta_{ij} - \omega_k t) A_{ij} - \frac{1}{2} \sin(\theta_{-i,-j} - \omega_k t) A_{-i,-j} \right]$$

$$(13.14)$$

In the last two line it's spelled out in real and imaginary parts. Evaluating Equation (13.13) is exactly what FFT software is designed to do: all you need to do is evaluate $Y_{ij}(t)$ for each i and j and pass in that 2D array of Y values, getting back the heights. The results should be real, up to round-off errors—you can safely ignore the imaginary parts, though a good bug check is to make sure they all are zero or very close to zero. Some FFT libraries allow you to specify that the result should be real-valued and then allow you to define and pass in only half the Y coefficients: this can certainly be a worthwhile optimization, but the specifics of how to do it vary from library to library.

13.4   Unsimplifying the Model

We made a lot of simplifying assumptions to get to an easily solved fully linear PDE. Unfortunately, the resulting height field solution isn't terribly convincing beyond very small amplitudes. In this section we'll try to boost our solution to look better even at larger amplitudes, by compensating for some of the terms we dropped earlier.

The first order of business is looking at the solution for the potential ϕ that accompanies our height field solution in Equation (13.8). We left this hanging before, rushing on to the height field instead, but ϕ offers some extremely useful information: in particular, $\nabla\phi$ gives us the implied velocity field. As we'll see in a moment, the plain height field solution is what you get when you ignore horizontal motion, letting the water bob up and down but not side to side; the characteristic look of larger waves, with wide flat troughs and sharper peaks, is largely due to this horizontal motion so we will bring it back.

It's not hard to verify that the potential ϕ which matches the height field in Equation (13.8) is as follows, building on our earlier incomplete form and taking the limit as $H \to \infty$ as we did for the wave speed c_k and time frequency ω_k:

$$\phi(x, y, z, t) = \sum_{i,j} \frac{A_{ij}\omega_k}{k} \sin(\vec{k} \cdot (x, z) - \omega_k t + \theta_{ij})e^{ky}. \qquad (13.15)$$

Taking the gradient gives us the complete velocity field, both at the surface ($y \approx 0$) and even far below:

$$u(x, y, z, t) = \frac{\partial \phi}{\partial x} = \sum_{i,j} \frac{A_{ij}\omega_k 2\pi i}{kL} \cos(\vec{k} \cdot (x, z) - \omega_k t + \theta_{ij})e^{ky},$$

$$v(x, y, z, t) = \frac{\partial \phi}{\partial y} = \sum_{i,j} A_{ij}\omega_k \sin(\vec{k} \cdot (x, z) - \omega_k t + \theta_{ij})e^{ky}, \qquad (13.16)$$

$$w(x, y, z, t) = \frac{\partial \phi}{\partial z} = \sum_{i,j} \frac{A_{ij}\omega_k 2\pi j}{kL} \cos(\vec{k} \cdot (x, z) - \omega_k t + \theta_{ij})e^{ky}.$$

These formulas are in of themselves fairly useful if you want velocity vectors at arbitrary points, say to aid in simulating the motion of a small solid in the water.

However we'll go one step further. Imagine tracking a blob of water starting at some initial position. The velocity field implied by a single wave, evaluated at that fixed point in space, is just a periodic sinusoid in time. As long as these velocities are small enough, the particle can't stray too far, so to a good approximation the velocity of the particle itself will be that periodic sinusoid. This means its position, the integral of velocity, will also be a periodic sinusoid: the particle will follow an elliptic orbit round and round as waves pass by. Experimental observation confirms this is a fairly accurate description of the motion; it's not perfect—there is a very small net movement in the direction of the wave propagation, termed *Stokes drift*—but it's pretty good.

Solving for the motion of a blob of water starting at position $\vec{x}_0$, from the simplified equation $d\vec{x}/dt = \vec{u}(\vec{x}_0, t)$, gives this general solution for the displacement from $\vec{x}_0$:

$$\Delta x = \sum_{i,j} \frac{-2\pi A_{ij} i}{kL} \sin(\vec{k} \cdot (x_0, z_0) - \omega_k t + \theta_{ij}) e^{ky_0},$$

$$\Delta y = \sum_{i,j} A_{ij} \cos(\vec{k} \cdot (x_0, z_0) - \omega_k t + \theta_{ij}) e^{ky_0}, \qquad (13.17)$$

$$\Delta z = \sum_{i,j} \frac{-2\pi A_{ij} j}{kL} \sin(\vec{k} \cdot (x_0, z_0) - \omega_k t + \theta_{ij}) e^{ky_0}.$$

This displacement field can be evaluated anywhere for $y_0 \leq 0$ to give the location where a particle that's moving with the water should be displaced to at any given time. For example, for a solid floating on the surface of the water you can get its position at any time by plugging in $y_0 = 0$ and its "resting" horizontal x_0 and z_0 coordinates. Objects suspended underneath the surface are the same, just with an exponential reduction of the motion by e^{ky_0} for each component. (Note that the components with large k will be nearly zero deep enough down, so they can be dropped for more efficient evaluation—as you go deeper, only the large wavelength, small wave number k, waves have an effect.)

In fact this displacement field also tells us how to get a more accurate free surface: we use it to deform the $y = 0$ plane. The technical term for this, when applied to enrich a single Fourier component, is a *Gerstner wave*, first introduced to graphics by Fournier and Reeves [Fournier and Reeves 86]. Our earlier height field solution only included the vertical

displacement (notice $h(x, z, t)$ and Δy at $y = 0$ are identical), and now we
will add in the matching horizontal displacement. Just as with the height
field vertical displacement, we can evaluate this horizontal displacement on
a regular grid efficiently with the FFT. Using the same process as we did
before with the height field to reduce it to the desired complex exponential
form, we get

$$
\Delta x_{pq} = \sum_{i=-n/2+1}^{n/2-1} \sum_{j=-n/2+1}^{n/2-1} X_{ij}(t) e^{\sqrt{-1}(2\pi(ip+jq)/n)},
$$

$$
\Delta z_{pq} = \sum_{i=-n/2+1}^{n/2-1} \sum_{j=-n/2+1}^{n/2-1} Z_{ij}(t) e^{\sqrt{-1}(2\pi(ip+jq)/n)},
$$

(13.18)

where the Fourier coefficients are defined from

$$
X_{ij}(t) = \left[-\frac{\pi A_{ij} i}{kL} \sin(\theta_{ij} - \omega_k t) + \frac{\pi A_{-i,-j} i}{kL} \sin(\theta_{-i,-j} - \omega_k t) \right]
$$
$$
+ \sqrt{-1} \left[\frac{\pi A_{ij} i}{kL} \cos(\theta_{ij} - \omega_k t) + \frac{\pi A_{-i,-j} i}{kL} \cos(\theta_{-i,-j} - \omega_k t) \right],
$$
$$
Z_{ij}(t) = \left[-\frac{\pi A_{ij} j}{kL} \sin(\theta_{ij} - \omega_k t) + \frac{\pi A_{-i,-j} j}{kL} \sin(\theta_{-i,-j} - \omega_k t) \right]
$$
$$
+ \sqrt{-1} \left[\frac{\pi A_{ij} j}{kL} \cos(\theta_{ij} - \omega_k t) + \frac{\pi A_{-i,-j} j}{kL} \cos(\theta_{-i,-j} - \omega_k t) \right],
$$

(13.19)

or more simply,

$$
(X_{ij}(t), Z_{ij}(t)) = \sqrt{-1} \frac{\vec{k}}{k} Y_{ij}(t).
$$

(13.20)

These can be evaluated just like the vertical component Fourier coefficients
$Y_{ij}(t)$, and for each component a call to the FFT library will then return
that component of the displacement evaluated on a regular grid. Adding
this fully 3D displacement to the coordinates of a regular grid at $y = 0$ gives
a much more convincing ocean surface. Tessendorf recommends including
a tunable choppiness parameter $\lambda \in [0, 1]$ to scale down the horizontal
displacement, allowing more range in the look: $\lambda = 0$ gives the soft look
of the pure height field solution, and $\lambda = 1$ the choppy full displacement
solution. We can go even further, in fact, getting a bit of a wind-blown look
by displacing in the horizontal direction of the wind, by a small amount
proportional to the height—more tunable parameters.

However, all the approximations we've taken to get to this point aren't
entirely self-consistent. If the amplitudes A_{ij} are too large the full dis-

placement field might actually cause self-intersections, giving strange loopy inside-out artifacts. This is fairly easy to detect—if a surface normal is pointing downwards (has a negative y component) anywhere, it's a self-intersection. These spots could be interpreted as points where the waves got so steep and pointed that this solution breaks down, i.e., the wave is breaking; the problem can then be plausible covered up with a procedural foam shader, or used as an emitter for a spray and mist particle system.

13.5 Wave Parameters

We turn now to the selection of the wave parameters, the amplitudes A_{ij} and phase shifts θ_{ij}, which so far have been left as unspecified constants. The phase shifts are straightforward: they have no special significance, and so each θ_{ij} may be chosen as an independent uniform random number from $[0, 2\pi]$. The amplitudes, however, are a little more interesting.

The first point to make follows from the nature of the solution method itself: if the ratio of amplitude to wavelength is too large, the approximations we made are unjustifiable and the result looks unconvincing—real waves simply don't get that steep, and simulating very rough violent oceans is a continuing research problem beyond this method. Therefore it makes sense to put a limit of, say, $A_{ij} \lesssim O(1/k)$. However, beyond this our physical model doesn't give us much guidance for automatically picking a convincing set of amplitudes; ultimately waves are driven by the wind or by ocean currents, which we are not even considering. Tessendorf recommends instead turning to phenomological models garnered from observations, such as the *Phillips spectrum*, which biases waves to align with some chosen wind direction, but there is a lot of freedom to experiment. The FFTs can run fast enough to give interactive feedback even on half-decent grids (say 128^2), allowing you to tune the amplitudes effectively.

13.6 Eliminating Periodicity

The ocean model we've defined so far often works just fine for ocean shots. However, it is periodic: if the perspective of a shot allows the audience to see many of these tiles, there is a chance that the periodicity will be visible and distracting. One way of overcoming this, which in fact is a simple trick to turn any unstructured periodic texture into a nonperiodic pattern, is to superimpose two repeating tiles of different sizes. That is, add to our $L \times L$ repeating ocean tile another one of dimension $\alpha L \times \alpha L$. (In practice, this means evaluating both tiles, then interpolating values from both onto one master grid.) If α is an irrational number, the sum of the two is nonperiodic. You can see if α is rational, it's not hard to prove the sum *is* periodic, in fact if $\alpha = r/s$ for integers r and s then the period is L times the least common multiple of r and s, divided by s. If α is irrational but very close to a rational number r/s with small integers r and s, the sum will not be exactly periodic but look very close to it, which still might appear objectionable. One of the best choices then is the golden ratio $(\sqrt{5}+1)/2 = 1.61803\ldots$ which (in a sense we will not cover in this book) is as far as possible from small integer fractions.

Other possible techniques involve layering in further effects based on nonperiodic noise. For example, combinations of upwelling currents in the sea and wind gusts above often give the ocean a patchy look, where in some regions there are lots of small ripples to reflect light but in others the surface is much smoother. This can be modeled procedurally, but here we stop as it lies outside the realm of simulation.

– A –
Background

A.1 Vector Calculus

The following three differential operators are fundamental to vector calculus: the gradient ∇, the divergence $\nabla\cdot$, and the curl $\nabla\times$. They occasionally are written in equations as grad, div, and curl instead.

A.1.1 Gradient

The gradient simply takes all the spatial partial derivatives of the function, returning a vector. In two dimensions,

$$\nabla f(x, y) = \left(\frac{\partial f}{\partial x}, \quad \frac{\partial f}{\partial y}\right),$$

and in three dimensions,

$$\nabla f(x, y, z) = \left(\frac{\partial f}{\partial x}, \quad \frac{\partial f}{\partial y}, \quad \frac{\partial f}{\partial z}\right).$$

It can sometimes be helpful to think of the gradient operator as a symbolic vector, e.g., in three dimensions:

$$\nabla = \left(\frac{\partial}{\partial x}, \quad \frac{\partial}{\partial y}, \quad \frac{\partial}{\partial z}\right).$$

The gradient is often used to approximate a function locally:

$$f(\vec{x} + \Delta\vec{x}) \approx f(\vec{x}) + \nabla f(\vec{x}) \cdot \Delta\vec{x}.$$

In a related vein we can evaluate the *directional derivative* of the function; that is how fast the function is changing when looking along a particular vector direction, using the gradient. For example, if the direction is $\hat{n}$,

$$\frac{\partial f}{\partial n} = \nabla f \cdot \hat{n}.$$

Occasionally we will take the gradient of a vector-valued function, which results in a matrix (sometimes called the *Jacobian*). For example, in three dimensions,

$$\nabla \vec{f} = \nabla(f, g, h) = \begin{pmatrix} \dfrac{\partial f}{\partial x} & \dfrac{\partial f}{\partial y} & \dfrac{\partial f}{\partial z} \\ \dfrac{\partial g}{\partial x} & \dfrac{\partial g}{\partial y} & \dfrac{\partial g}{\partial z} \\ \dfrac{\partial h}{\partial x} & \dfrac{\partial h}{\partial y} & \dfrac{\partial h}{\partial z} \end{pmatrix}.$$

Note that each *row* is the gradient of one component of the function. One way to remember that it's the rows and not the columns is that it should work with the approximation

$$\vec{f}(\vec{x} + \Delta \vec{x}) \approx \vec{f}(\vec{x}) + \nabla \vec{f}(\vec{x})\Delta \vec{x}.$$

The matrix-vector product is just computing the dot-product of each row of the matrix with the vector, and so each row should be a gradient of the function:

$$\nabla(f, g, h) = \begin{pmatrix} \nabla f \\ \nabla g \\ \nabla h \end{pmatrix}.$$

An alternative notation for the gradient that is sometimes used is

$$\nabla f = \frac{\partial f}{\partial \vec{x}}.$$

Using a vector in the denominator of the partial derivative indicates we're taking derivatives with respect to each component of $\vec{x}$.

A.1.2 Divergence

The divergence operator only is applied to vector fields and measures how much the vectors are converging or diverging at any point. In two dimensions it is

$$\nabla \cdot \vec{u} = \nabla \cdot (u, v) = \frac{\partial u}{\partial x} + \frac{\partial v}{\partial y},$$

and in three dimensions,

$$\nabla \cdot \vec{u} = \nabla \cdot (u, v, w) = \frac{\partial u}{\partial x} + \frac{\partial v}{\partial y} + \frac{\partial w}{\partial z}.$$

Note that the input is a vector and the output is a scalar.

The notation $\nabla\cdot$ is explained by thinking of it as symbolically taking a dot-product between the gradient operator and the vector field, e.g., in three dimensions,

$$\nabla\cdot\vec{u} = \left(\frac{\partial}{\partial x},\ \frac{\partial}{\partial y},\ \frac{\partial}{\partial z}\right)\cdot(u,v,w)$$

$$= \frac{\partial}{\partial x}u + \frac{\partial}{\partial y}v + \frac{\partial}{\partial z}w.$$

A.1.3 Curl

The curl operator measures how much a vector field is rotating around any point. In three dimensions this is a vector:

$$\nabla\times\vec{u} = \nabla\times(u,v,w) = \left(\frac{\partial w}{\partial y}-\frac{\partial v}{\partial z},\ \frac{\partial u}{\partial z}-\frac{\partial w}{\partial x},\ \frac{\partial v}{\partial x}-\frac{\partial u}{\partial y}\right).$$

We can reduce this formula to two dimensions in two ways. The curl of a two-dimensional vector field results in a scalar, the third component of the expression above, as if we were looking at the three-dimensional vector field $(u,v,0)$:

$$\nabla\times\vec{u} = \nabla\times(u,v) = \frac{\partial v}{\partial x}-\frac{\partial u}{\partial y}.$$

The curl of a two-dimensional scalar field results in a vector field, as if we were looking at the three-dimensional field $(0,0,w)$:

$$\nabla\times w = \left(\frac{\partial w}{\partial y},\ -\frac{\partial w}{\partial x}\right).$$

The simple way to remember these formulas is that the curl is taking a symbolic cross-product between the gradient operator and the function. For example, in three dimensions,

$$\nabla\times\vec{u} = \left(\frac{\partial}{\partial x},\ \frac{\partial}{\partial y},\ \frac{\partial}{\partial z}\right)\times(u,v,w)$$

$$= \left(\frac{\partial}{\partial y}w - \frac{\partial}{\partial z}v,\ pdzu - \frac{\partial}{\partial x}w,\ pdxv - \frac{\partial}{\partial y}u\right).$$

The curl is a way of measuring how fast (and in three dimensions along what axis) a vector field is rotating locally. If you imagine putting a little paddle wheel in the flow and letting it be spun, then the curl is twice the angular velocity of the wheel. You can check this by taking the curl of the velocity field representing a rigid rotation.

A vector field whose curl is zero is called curl-free, or *irrotational* for obvious reasons.

A.1.4 Laplacian

The Laplacian is usually formed as the divergence of the gradient (as it repeatedly appears in fluid dynamics). Sometimes it is written as ∇^2 or Δ, but since these symbols are occasionally used for other purposes, I will stick to writing it as $\nabla \cdot \nabla$. In two dimensions,

$$\nabla \cdot \nabla f = \frac{\partial^2 f}{\partial x^2} + \frac{\partial^2 f}{\partial y^2}$$

and in three dimensions,

$$\nabla \cdot \nabla f = \frac{\partial^2 f}{\partial x^2} + \frac{\partial^2 f}{\partial y^2} + \frac{\partial^2 f}{\partial z^2}.$$

The Laplacian can also be applied to vector or even matrix fields, and the result is simply the Laplacian of each component.

Incidentally, the partial differential equation $\nabla \cdot \nabla f = 0$ is called Laplace's equation, and if the right-hand side is replaced by something non-zero, $\nabla \cdot \nabla f = q$ we call it the Poisson equation. More generally, you can multiply the gradient by a scalar field a (such as $1/\rho$), like $\nabla \cdot (a \nabla f) = q$ and still call it a Poisson problem.

A.1.5 Differential Identities

There are several identities based on the fact that changing the order of mixed partial derivatives doesn't change the result (assuming reasonable smoothness), e.g.,

$$\frac{\partial}{\partial x} \frac{\partial}{\partial y} f = \frac{\partial}{\partial y} \frac{\partial}{\partial x} f.$$

Armed with this, it's simple to show that for any smooth function,

$$\nabla \cdot (\nabla \times \vec{u}) \equiv 0,$$
$$\nabla \times (\nabla f) \equiv 0.$$

Another identity that shows up in vorticity calculations is

$$\nabla \times (\nabla \times \vec{u}) \equiv \nabla (\nabla \cdot \vec{u}) - \nabla \cdot \nabla \vec{u}.$$

The Helmholtz or Hodge decomposition is the result that any smooth vector field $\vec{u}$ can be written as the sum of a divergence-free part and a curl-free part. In fact, referring back to the first two identities above, the divergence-free part can be written as the curl of something and the curl-free part can be written as the gradient of something else. In three dimensions,

$$\vec{u} = \nabla \times \vec{\psi} - \nabla \phi,$$

where $\vec{\psi}$ is a vector-valued potential function and ϕ is a scalar potential function. In two dimensions this reduces to ψ being a scalar potential function as well:

$$\vec{u} = \nabla \times \psi - \nabla \phi.$$

This decomposition is highly relevant to incompressible fluid flow, since we can interpret the pressure projection step as decomposing the intermediate velocity field $\vec{u}^{n+1}$ into a divergence-free part and something else which we throw away, just keeping the divergence-free part. When we express a divergence-free velocity field as the curl of a potential ψ, we call ψ the *streamfunction*.

Some more useful identities are generalizations of the product rule:

$$\nabla(fg) = (\nabla f)g + f\nabla g,$$
$$\nabla \cdot (f\vec{u}) = (\nabla f) \cdot \vec{u} + f\nabla \cdot \vec{u}.$$

A.1.6   Integral Identities

The Fundamental Theorem of Calculus (that the integral of a derivative is the original function evaluated at the limits) can be generalized to multiple dimensions in a variety of ways.

The most common generalization is the divergence theorem discovered by Gauss:

$$\iiint_\Omega \nabla \cdot \vec{u} = \iint_{\partial\Omega} \vec{u} \cdot \hat{n}.$$

That is, the volume integral of the divergence of a vector field $\vec{u}$ is the boundary integral of $\vec{u}$ dotted with the unit outward normal $\hat{n}$. This actually is true in any dimension (replacing volume with area or length or hypervolume as appropriate). This provides our intuition of the divergence measuring how fast a velocity field is expanding or compressing: the boundary integral above measures the net speed of fluid entering or exiting the volume.

Stokes' Theorem applies to the integral of a curl. Suppose we have a bounded surface S with normal $\hat{n}$ and with boundary curve Γ whose tangent vector is τ. Then,

$$\iint_S (\nabla \times \vec{u}) \cdot \hat{n} = \int_\Gamma \vec{u} \cdot \tau.$$

This can obviously be restricted to two dimensions with $\hat{n} = (0,0,1)$. The curve integral is called the *circulation* in the context of a fluid velocity field.

We can also integrate a gradient:

$$\iiint_\Omega \nabla f = \iint_{\partial\Omega} f\hat{n}.$$

Some of the most useful identities of all are ones called *integration by parts*, which is what we get when we combine integration identities based on the Fundamental Theorem of Calculus with the product rule for derivatives. They essentially let us move a differential operator from one factor in a product to the other. Here are some of the most useful:

$$\iiint_\Omega (\nabla f)g = \iint_{\partial\Omega} fg\hat{n} - \iiint_\Omega f(\nabla g),$$

$$\iiint_\Omega f\nabla \cdot \vec{u} = \iint_{\partial\Omega} f\vec{u} \cdot \hat{n} - \iiint_\Omega (\nabla f) \cdot \vec{u},$$

$$\iiint_\Omega (\nabla f) \cdot \vec{u} = \iint_{\partial\Omega} f\vec{u} \cdot \hat{n} - \iiint_\Omega f\nabla \cdot \vec{u}.$$

Replacing $\vec{u}$ by ∇g in the last equation gives us one of Green's identities:

$$\iiint_\Omega (\nabla f) \cdot (\nabla g) = \iint_{\partial\Omega} f\nabla g \cdot \hat{n} - \iiint_\Omega f\nabla \cdot \nabla g$$

$$= \iint_{\partial\Omega} g\nabla f \cdot \hat{n} - \iiint_\Omega g\nabla \cdot \nabla f.$$

A.1.7 Basic Tensor Notation

When you get into two or three derivatives in multiple dimensions, it can get very confusing if you stick to using the ∇ symbols. An alternative is to use tensor notation, which looks a little less friendly but makes it trivial to keep everything straight. Advanced differential geometry is almost impossible to do without this notation. We'll present a simplified version that is adequate for most of fluid dynamics.

The basic idea is to label the separate components of a vector with subscript indices 1, 2, and in three dimensions, 3. Usually we'll use variables i, j, k, etc., for these indices. Note that this can get very confusing if you also are thinking of discretizing on a grid—if you want to avoid that confusion, it's often a good idea to only use Greek letters for your tensor indices, e.g., α, β, γ instead.

The gradient of a function is $(\partial f/\partial x_1, \partial f/\partial x_2, \partial f/\partial x_3)$. This is still a bit longwinded, so we instead use the generic $\partial f/\partial x_i$ without specifying what i is: it's a "free" index.

We could then write the divergence, for example, as

$$\sum_i \frac{\partial u_i}{\partial x_i}.$$

This brings us to the *Einstein summation convention*. It's tedious to have to write the sum symbol Σ again and again. Thus we just won't bother writing it: instead, we will assume that in any expression that contains the index i twice, there is an implicit sum over i in front of it. If we don't want a sum, we use different indices, like i and j. For example, the dot-product of two vectors $\vec{u}$ and $\hat{n}$ can be written very succinctly as

$$u_i n_i.$$

Note that by expression I mean a single term or a product—it does not include addition. So this

$$u_i + r_i$$

is a vector, $\vec{u} + \vec{r}$, not a scalar sum.

Einstein notation makes it very simple to write a matrix-vector product, such as $A\vec{x}$:

$$A_{ij} x_j.$$

Note that the free index in this expression is j: this is telling us the jth component of the result. This is also an introduction to second-order tensors, which really are a fancy name for matrices: they have two indices instead of the one for a vector (which can be called a first-order tensor). We can write matrix multiplication just as easily: the product AB is

$$A_{ij} B_{jk}$$

with free indices i and k: this is the i, k entry of the result. Similarly, the outer-product matrix of vectors $\vec{u}$ and $\hat{n}$ is

$$u_i n_j.$$

Other useful symbols for tensor expressions are the Kronecker delta δ_{ij} and the Levi-Civita symbol ϵ_{ijk}. The Kronecker delta is δ_{ij}, which is actually just the identity matrix in disguise: $\delta_{ij}x_j = x_i$. The Levi-Civita symbol has three indices, making it a third-order tensor (kind of like a three-dimensional version of a matrix!). It is zero if any of the indices are repeated, $+1$ if (i, j, k) is just a rotation of $(1, 2, 3)$, and -1 if (i, j, k) is a rotation of $(3, 2, 1)$. What this boils down to is that we can write a cross-product using it: $\vec{r} \times \vec{u}$ is just

$$\epsilon_{ijk} r_j u_k,$$

which is a vector with free index i.

Putting all this together, we can translate the definitions, identities and theorems from before into very compact notation. Furthermore, just by keeping our indices straight, we won't have to puzzle over what an expression like $\nabla\nabla\vec{u} \cdot \hat{n} \times \nabla f$ might actually mean. Here are some of the translations that you can check:

$$(\nabla f)_i = \frac{\partial f}{\partial x_i},$$

$$\nabla = \frac{\partial}{\partial x_i},$$

$$f(x_i + \Delta x_i) \approx f(x_i) + \frac{\partial f}{\partial x_i}\Delta x_i,$$

$$\frac{\partial f}{\partial n} = \frac{\partial f}{\partial x_i}n_i,$$

$$(\nabla\vec{f})_{ij} = \frac{\partial f_i}{\partial x_j},$$

$$\nabla \cdot \vec{u} = \frac{\partial u_i}{\partial x_i},$$

$$(\nabla \times \vec{u})_i = \epsilon_{ijk}\frac{\partial u_k}{\partial x_j},$$

$$\nabla \cdot \nabla f = \frac{\partial^2 f}{\partial x_i \partial x_i},$$

$$\frac{\partial}{\partial x_i}\epsilon_{ijk}\frac{\partial u_k}{\partial x_j} = 0,$$

$$\epsilon_{ijk}\frac{\partial}{\partial x_j}\frac{\partial f}{\partial x_k} = 0.$$

The different versions of the product rule for differentiation, in tensor notation, all just fall out of the regular single-variable calculus rule. For example,

$$\frac{\partial}{\partial x_i}(fg) = \frac{\partial f}{\partial x_i}g + f\frac{\partial g}{\partial x_i},$$

$$\frac{\partial}{\partial x_i}(fu_i) = \frac{\partial f}{\partial x_i}u_i + f\frac{\partial u_i}{\partial x_i}.$$

The integral identities also simplify. For example,

$$\iiint_\Omega \frac{\partial u_i}{\partial x_i} = \iint_{\partial\Omega} u_i n_i,$$

$$\iiint_\Omega \frac{\partial f}{\partial x_i} = \iint_{\partial\Omega} f n_i,$$

$$\iiint_\Omega \frac{\partial f}{\partial x_i}g = \iint_{\partial\Omega} f g n_i - \iiint_\Omega f\frac{\partial g}{\partial x_i}.$$

A.2 Numerical Methods

This book concentrate on methods based on finite differences, which themselves boil down simply to applications of Taylor series.

Assuming a function f has at least k smooth derivatives, then

$$f(x + \Delta x) = f(x) + \frac{\partial f}{\partial x}(x)\Delta x + \frac{1}{2}\frac{\partial^2 f}{\partial x^2}(x)\Delta x^2 + \frac{1}{6}\frac{\partial^3 f}{\partial x^3}(x)\Delta x^3 + \cdots$$

$$+ \frac{1}{(k-1)!}\frac{\partial^{k-1} f}{\partial x^{k-1}}(x)\Delta x^{k-1} + R_k.$$

The remainder term R_k can be expressed in several ways, for example,

$$R_k = \int_x^{x+\Delta x} \frac{1}{k!}\frac{\partial^k f}{\partial x^k}(s)s^{k-1}ds,$$

$$R_k = \frac{1}{k!}\frac{\partial^k f}{\partial x^k}(s)\Delta x^k \quad \text{for some } s \in [x, x + \Delta x],$$

$$R_k = O(\Delta x^k).$$

Note that Δx could be negative, in which case the second form of the remainder uses the interval $[x + \Delta x, x]$. We'll generally stick with the last form, using the simple $O()$ notation, but do remember that the hidden constant is related to the kth derivative of f—and if f isn't particularly smooth, that could be huge and the Taylor series (taken up to that term) isn't particularly useful.

A.2.1   Finite Differences in Space

Partial derivatives of smooth functions sampled on a grid can be estimated using Taylor's theorem. For example, for a function $q(x)$ sampled at grid points spaced Δx apart, i.e., $q_i = q(x_i) = q(i\Delta x)$, Taylor's theorem gives

$$q_{i+1} = q_i + \Delta x \frac{\partial q}{\partial x}(x_i) + O(\Delta x^2).$$

We can rearrange this to get an estimate of $\partial q/\partial x$ at x_i:

$$\frac{\partial q}{\partial x}(x_i) = \frac{q_{i+1} - q_i}{\Delta x} + O(\Delta x).$$

Note that after dividing through by Δx, the error term was reduced to *first order*, i.e., the exponent of Δx in the $O()$ notation is one.

Of course, you can also estimate the same derivative from q_{i-1}, using Taylor's theorem for $q_{i-1} = q(x_{i-1})$:

$$\frac{\partial q}{\partial x}(x_i) = \frac{q_i - q_{i-1}}{\Delta x} + O(\Delta x).$$

This is also only first-order accurate. Both this and the previous finite difference are *one-sided*, since values of q only to one side of the approximation point are used.

We can get second-order accuracy by using both q_{i+1} and q_{i-1}, for a *centered* or *central* finite difference: the value we're approximating lies in the center of the points we use. Write down the Taylor series for both these points:

$$q_{i+1} = q_i + \Delta x \frac{\partial q}{\partial x}(x_i) + \frac{\Delta x^2}{2} \frac{\partial^2 q}{\partial x^2}(x_i) + O(\Delta x^3),$$

$$q_{i-1} = q_i - \Delta x \frac{\partial q}{\partial x}(x_i) + \frac{\Delta x^2}{2} \frac{\partial^2 q}{\partial x^2}(x_i) + O(\Delta x^3).$$

Now subtract them to get, after cancellation,

$$q_{i+1} - q_{i-1} = 2\Delta x \frac{\partial q}{\partial x}(x_i) + O(\Delta x^3).$$

Dividing through gives the second-order accurate central finite difference:

$$\frac{\partial q}{\partial x}(x_i) = \frac{q_{i+1} - q_{i-1}}{2\Delta x} + O(\Delta x^2).$$

Similar reasoning also shows that the first formula we saw is a second-order accurate central finite difference for the point $x_{i+1/2} = (i + 1/2)\Delta x$:

$$\frac{\partial q}{\partial x}(x_{i+1/2}) = \frac{q_{i+1} - q_i}{\Delta x} + O(\Delta x^2).$$

Throughout this book we also deal with functions sampled at midpoints, $q_{i+1/2} = q(x_{i+1/2})$, for which we can similarly write down

$$\frac{\partial q}{\partial x}(x_i) = \frac{q_{i+1/2} - q_{i-1/2}}{\Delta x} + O(\Delta x^2).$$

Higher derivatives can also be estimated. In particular, we can get a second-order accurate central finite difference for the second derivative $\partial^2 q/\partial x^2$ by writing down the Taylor series yet again:

$$q_{i+1} = q_i + \Delta x \frac{\partial q}{\partial x}(x_i) + \frac{\Delta x^2}{2}\frac{\partial^2 q}{\partial x^2}(x_i) + \frac{\Delta x^3}{6}\frac{\partial^3 q}{\partial x^3}(x_i) + O(\Delta x^4),$$

$$q_{i-1} = q_i - \Delta x \frac{\partial q}{\partial x}(x_i) + \frac{\Delta x^2}{2}\frac{\partial^2 q}{\partial x^2}(x_i) + \frac{\Delta x^3}{6}\frac{\partial^3 q}{\partial x^3}(x_i) + O(\Delta x^4).$$

The following combination cancels out most of the terms:

$$q_{i+1} - 2q_i + q_{i-1} = \Delta x^2 \frac{\partial^2 q}{\partial x^2}(x_i) + O(\Delta x^4).$$

Dividing through by Δx^2 gives the finite difference formula,

$$\frac{\partial^2 q}{\partial x^2}(x_i) = \frac{q_{i+1} - 2q_i + q_{i-1}}{\Delta x^2} + O(\Delta x^2).$$

A.2.2 Time Integration

Solving differential equations in time generally revolves around the same finite difference approach. For example, to solve the differential equation

$$\frac{\partial q}{\partial t} = f(q)$$

with initial conditions $q(0) = q^0$, we can approximate q at discrete times t^n, with $q^n = q(t^n)$. The time step Δt is simply the length of time between these discrete times: $\Delta t = t^{n+1} - t^n$. This time-step size may or may not stay fixed from one step to the next. The process of time integration is determining the approximate values $q^1, q^2, \dots$ in sequence; it's called integration since we are approximating the solution

$$q(t) = \int_0^t f(q(\tau))\,d\tau,$$

which has an integral in it.

The simplest time integration method is *forward Euler*, based on the first one-sided finite difference formula we saw:

$$\frac{q^{n+1} - q^n}{\Delta t} = \frac{\partial q}{\partial t}(t^n) + O(\Delta t).$$

Plugging in the differential equation and rearranging gives the formula for the new value q^{n+1} based on the previous value q^n:

$$q^{n+1} = q^n + \Delta t f(q^n)$$

This is only first-order accurate, however.

This book makes use of a few more advanced time integration schemes, such as Runge-Kutta methods. The Runge-Kutta family gets higher-order accuracy and other numerical advantages by evaluating f at several points during a time step. For example, one of the classic second-order accurate Runge-Kutta methods can be written as

$$q^{n+1/2} = q^n + \tfrac{1}{2}\Delta t f(q^n),$$
$$q^{n+1} = q^n + \Delta t f(q^{n+1/2}).$$

One of the better third-order accurate Runge-Kutta formulas is

$$k_1 = f(q^n),$$
$$k_2 = f(q^n + \tfrac{1}{2}\Delta t k_1),$$
$$k_3 = f(q^n + \tfrac{3}{4}\Delta t k_2),$$
$$q^{n+1} = q^n + \tfrac{2}{9}\Delta t k_1 + \tfrac{3}{9}\Delta t k_2 + \tfrac{4}{9}\Delta t k_3.$$

Note that these are not easy to derive in general!

Many time integration schemes come with a caveat that unless Δt is chosen small enough, the computed solution exponentially blows up despite the exact solution staying bounded. This is termed a *stability time-step restriction*. For some problems, a time integration scheme may even be unstable no matter how small Δt is: both forward Euler and the second-order accurate Runge-Kutta scheme above suffer from this flaw in some cases. The third-order accurate Runge-Kutta scheme may be considered the simplest general-purpose method as a result.

– B –
Derivations

B.1 The Incompressible Euler Equations

The classic derivation of the incompressible Euler equations is based on conservation of mass and momentum. Consider an arbitrary but fixed region of space Ω, in the fluid. The mass of the fluid in Ω is

$$M = \iiint_\Omega \rho,$$

and the total momentum of the fluid in Ω is

$$\vec{P} = \iiint_\Omega \rho \vec{u}.$$

The rate of change of M, as fluid flows in or out of Ω, is given by the integral around the boundary of the speed at which mass is entering or exiting, since mass cannot be created or destroyed inside Ω:

$$\frac{\partial M}{\partial t} = -\iint_{\partial\Omega} \rho \vec{u} \cdot \hat{n}.$$

Here $\hat{n}$ is the outward-pointing normal. We can transform this into a volume integral with the divergence theorem:

$$\frac{\partial M}{\partial t} = -\iiint_\Omega \nabla \cdot (\rho \vec{u}).$$

Expanding M and differentiating with respect to time (recalling that Ω is fixed) gives

$$\iiint_\Omega \frac{\partial \rho}{\partial t} = -\iiint_\Omega \nabla \cdot (\rho \vec{u}).$$

Since this is true for any region Ω, the integrands must match:

$$\frac{\partial \rho}{\partial t} + \nabla \cdot (\rho \vec{u}) = 0.$$

This is called the *continuity equation*. For an incompressible fluid the material derivative of density $D\rho/Dt$ is zero, i.e.,

$$\frac{\partial \rho}{\partial t} + \vec{u} \cdot \nabla \rho = 0.$$

Subtracting this from the continuity equation gives $\rho \nabla \cdot \vec{u} = 0$, or more simply

$$\nabla \cdot \vec{u} = 0,$$

which is termed the *incompressibility condition*. Note that this is independent of density, even for problems where fluids of different densities mix together.

We can apply the same process to the rate of change of momentum:

$$\frac{\partial \vec{P}}{\partial t} = \iiint_\Omega \frac{\partial (\rho \vec{u})}{\partial t}.$$

Momentum can change in two ways: the transport of fluid across the boundary and a net force $\vec{F}$ applied to region. The transport of momentum with the fluid is the boundary integral of momentum $\rho \vec{u}$ times the speed of the fluid through the boundary:

$$-\iint_{\partial \Omega} (\rho \vec{u}) \vec{u} \cdot \hat{n}.$$

(The negative sign comes from the fact that the normal is outward-pointing.) There are two forces in play for an inviscid fluid: pressure p on the boundary and gravity ρg throughout the region:

$$\vec{F} = -\iint_{\partial \Omega} p\hat{n} + \iiint_\Omega \rho g.$$

(Again, we get a negative sign in front of the pressure integral since the normal is outward-pointing.) Combining all these terms we get

$$\iiint_\Omega \frac{\partial (\rho \vec{u})}{\partial t} = -\iint_{\partial \Omega} (\rho \vec{u}) \vec{u} \cdot \hat{n} - \iint_{\partial \Omega} p\hat{n} + \iiint_\Omega \rho g.$$

Transforming the boundary integrals into volume integrals with the Fundamental Theorem of Calculus and rearranging gives

$$\iiint_\Omega \frac{\partial (\rho \vec{u})}{\partial t} + \iiint_\Omega \nabla \cdot (\rho \vec{u} \otimes \vec{u}) + \iiint_\Omega \nabla p = \iiint_\Omega \rho g.$$

Here $\vec{u} \otimes \vec{u}$ is the 3×3 outer-product matrix. Again, since this is true for any arbitrary region Ω, the integrands must be equal:

$$\frac{\partial(\rho\vec{u})}{\partial t} + \nabla \cdot (\rho\vec{u} \times \vec{u}) + \nabla p = \rho g.$$

This is the *conservation law* form of the *momentum equation*. Using the product rule of differentiation, exploiting $D\rho/Dt = 0$ for an incompressible fluid, and dividing through by ρ, this can readily be reduced to the form of the momentum equation used in the rest of this book.

B.2   The Pressure Problem as a Minimization

Here we go through a *calculus of variations* argument illustrated by Batty et al. [Batty et al. 07] that the pressure problem,

$$\nabla \cdot \frac{\Delta t}{\rho}\nabla p = \nabla \cdot \vec{u} \qquad \text{inside } \Omega,$$

$$p = 0 \qquad \text{on } F, \qquad (\text{B.1})$$

$$\frac{\Delta t}{\rho}\nabla p \cdot \hat{n} = \vec{u} \cdot \hat{n} - \vec{u}_{\text{solid}} \cdot \hat{n} \qquad \text{on } S,$$

is equivalent to the following energy minimization problem introduced in Chapter 4:

$$\min_{\substack{p \\ p = 0 \text{ on } F}} \iiint_\Omega \frac{1}{2}\rho \left\| \vec{u} - \frac{\Delta t}{\rho}\nabla p \right\|^2 - \iiint_\Omega \frac{1}{2}\rho \|\vec{u}\|^2 + \iint_S p\hat{n} \cdot \Delta t\vec{u}_{\text{solid}}$$

$$(\text{B.2})$$

Here Ω is the fluid region, and its boundary is partitioned into S, the part in contact with solids, and F, the free surface. The functional being minimized is the total work done by pressure, measured as the change in kinetic energy of the fluid plus the work done on the solid by the fluid pressure over the next time step, which accounts for all work done by the pressure. As we said, in incompressible flow there is no "elastic" potential energy, thus the pressure is fully inelastic and dissipates as much energy as possible, hence the minimization. Also as we said before, the kinetic energy of the intermediate velocity field is a constant, hence we can just drop it in the minimization.

The calculus of variations is a way to solve problems such as this, minimizing an integral with respect to a *function*, as opposed to just a finite set of variables. We'll walk through the standard method of reducing the minimization to a PDE.

Suppose that p is the minimum of (B.2). Let q be an arbitrary non-zero function in Ω that is zero on the free surface too. Then for any scalar ϵ, the function $p + \epsilon q$ is also zero on the free surface. We can define a regular single-variable function $g(\epsilon)$ as

$$g(\epsilon) = \iiint_\Omega \tfrac{1}{2}\rho \left\| \vec{u} - \frac{\Delta t}{\rho}\nabla(p + \epsilon q) \right\|^2 + \iint_S (p + \epsilon q)\hat{n} \cdot \Delta t \vec{u}_{\text{solid}}.$$

Let's expand this out to see that it's just a quadratic in ϵ:

$$g(\epsilon) = \iiint_\Omega \tfrac{1}{2}\rho \left(\frac{\Delta t}{\rho}\nabla(p + \epsilon q) - \vec{u} \right) \cdot \left(\frac{\Delta t}{\rho}\nabla(p + \epsilon q) - \vec{u} \right)$$

$$+ \iint_S (p + \epsilon q)\hat{n} \cdot \Delta t \vec{u}_{\text{solid}}$$

$$= \iiint_\Omega \tfrac{1}{2}\rho \left(\frac{\Delta t}{\rho}\nabla p - \vec{u} \right) \cdot \left(\frac{\Delta t}{\rho}\nabla p - \vec{u} \right)$$

$$+ \epsilon \rho \left(\frac{\Delta t}{\rho}\nabla q \right) \cdot \left(\frac{\Delta t}{\rho}\nabla p - \vec{u} \right)$$

$$+ \tfrac{1}{2}\epsilon^2 \rho \left(\frac{\Delta t}{\rho}\nabla q \right) \cdot \left(\frac{\Delta t}{\rho}\nabla q \right)$$

$$+ \iint_S p\hat{n} \cdot \Delta t \vec{u}_{\text{solid}} + \epsilon \iint_S q\hat{n} \cdot \Delta t \vec{u}_{\text{solid}}$$

$$= \left[\iiint_\Omega \tfrac{1}{2}\rho \left\| \frac{\Delta t}{\rho}\nabla p - \vec{u} \right\|^2 + \iint_S p\hat{n} \cdot \Delta t \vec{u}_{\text{solid}} \right]$$

$$+ \epsilon \left[\iiint_\Omega \tfrac{1}{2}\rho \left(\frac{\Delta t}{\rho}\nabla q \right) \cdot \left(\frac{\Delta t}{\rho}\nabla p - \vec{u} \right) + \iint_S q\hat{n} \cdot \Delta t \vec{u}_{\text{solid}} \right]$$

$$+ \epsilon^2 \left[\iiint_\Omega \tfrac{1}{2}\rho \left\| \frac{\Delta t}{\rho}\nabla q \right\|^2 \right].$$

Since we assumed p was the minimum, $\epsilon = 0$ is the minimum of $g(\epsilon)$, thus $g'(0) = 0$. In other words, the coefficient of the linear term in the quadratic must be zero:

$$\iiint_\Omega \rho \left(\frac{\Delta t}{\rho}\nabla q \right) \cdot \left(\frac{\Delta t}{\rho}\nabla p - \vec{u} \right) + \iint_S q\hat{n} \cdot \Delta t \vec{u}_{\text{solid}} = 0$$

$$\Rightarrow \quad \iiint_\Omega \nabla q \cdot \left(\frac{\Delta t}{\rho}\nabla p - \vec{u} \right) + \iint_S q\hat{n} \cdot \vec{u}_{\text{solid}} = 0.$$

Integrating by parts transforms this into

$$-\iiint_\Omega q\nabla \cdot \left(\frac{\Delta t}{\rho}\nabla p - \vec{u} \right) + \iint_{F \cup S} q \left(\frac{\Delta t}{\rho}\nabla p - \vec{u} \right) \cdot \hat{n} + \iint_S q\hat{n} \cdot \vec{u}_{\text{solid}} = 0.$$

Now, q is zero on the F part of the boundary, so we're left with

$$-\iiint_\Omega q\nabla \cdot \left(\frac{\Delta t}{\rho}\nabla p - \vec{u}\right) + \iint_S q\left(\frac{\Delta t}{\rho}\nabla p - \vec{u} + \vec{u}_{\text{solid}}\right) \cdot \hat{n}.$$

And finally we observe that we showed this to be true for an arbitrary function q. Since these integrals always evaluate to zero no matter what q we stick in, then whatever is multiplying q must actually be zero. And that's precisely the original PDE (B.1)!

Bibliography

[Adams et al. 07] B. Adams, M. Pauly, R. Keiser, and L. Guibas. "Adaptively Sampled Particle Fluids." *ACM Trans. Graph. (SIGGRAPH Proc.)* 26:3 (2007), Article 48.

[Angelidis and Neyret 05] A. Angelidis and F. Neyret. "Simulation of Smoke Based on Vortex Filament Primitives." In *SCA '05: Proceedings of the 2005 ACM SIGGRAPH/Eurographics Symposium on Computer Animation*, pp. 87–96. Aire-la-Ville, Switzerland: Eurographics Association, 2005.

[Angelidis et al. 06] A. Angelidis, F. Neyret, K. Singh, and D. Nowrouzezahrai. "A Controllable, Fast and Stable Basis for Vortex Based Smoke Simulation." In *SCA '06: Proceedings of the 2006 ACM SIGGRAPH/Eurographics symposium on Computer Animation*, pp. 25–32. Aire-la-Ville, Switzerland: Eurographics Association, 2006.

[Aslam 04] T. D. Aslam. "A Partial Differential Equation Approach to Multidimensional Extrapolation." *J. Comp. Phys.* 193 (2004), 349–355.

[Batty et al. 07] C. Batty, F. Bertails, and R. Bridson. "A Fast Variational Framework for Accurate Solid-Fluid Coupling." *ACM Trans. Graph. (Proc. SIGGRAPH)* 26:3 (2007), Article 100.

[Benzi et al. 05] M. Benzi, G. H. Golub, and J. Liesen. "Numerical Solution of Saddle Point Problems." *Acta Numerica* 14 (2005), 1–137.

[Blinn 82] J. Blinn. "A Generalization of Algebraic Surface Drawing." *ACM Trans. Graph.* 1:3 (1982), 235–256.

[Bonner 07] M. Bonner. "Compressible Subsonic Flow on a Staggered Grid." Master's thesis, UBC Dept. Computer Science, 2007.

[Brackbill and Ruppel 86] J. U. Brackbill and H. M. Ruppel. "FLIP: A Method for Adaptively Zoned, Particle-in-Cell Calculuations of Fluid Flows in Two Dimensions." *J. Comp. Phys.* 65 (1986), 314–343.

[Bridson et al. 07] R. Bridson, J. Hourihan, and M. Nordenstam. "Curl-Noise for Procedural Fluid Flow." *ACM Trans. Graph. (Proc. SIGGRAPH)* 26:3 (2007), Article 46.

[Brochu and Bridson 06] T. Brochu and R. Bridson. "Fluid Animation with Explicit Surface Meshes." In *Proc. ACM SIGGRAPH/Eurographics Symp. Comp. Anim. (posters)*. Aire-la-ville, Switzerland: Eurographics Association, 2006.

[Carlson et al. 02] M. Carlson, P. Mucha, R. Van Horn III, and G. Turk. "Melting and Flowing." In *Proc. ACM SIGGRAPH/Eurographics Symp. Comp. Anim.*, pp. 167–174. Aire-la-Ville, Switzerland: Eurographics Association, 2002.

[Carlson et al. 04] M. Carlson, P. J. Mucha, and G. Turk. "Rigid Fluid: Animating the Interplay Between Rigid Bodies and Fluid." *ACM Trans. Graph. (Proc. SIGGRAPH)* 23:3 (2004), 377–384.

[Chentanez et al. 06] N. Chentanez, T. G. Goktekin, B. E. Feldman, and J. F. O'Brien. "Simultaneous Coupling of Fluids and Deformable Bodies." In *Proc. ACM SIGGRAPH/Eurographics Symp. Comp. Anim.*, pp. 83–89. Aire-la-Ville, Switzerland: Eurographics Association, 2006.

[Chorin 73] A. J. Chorin. "Numerical Study of Slightly Viscous Flow." *J. Fluid Mechanics* 57:4 (1973), 785–796.

[Corbett 05] R. Corbett. "Point-Based Level Sets and Progress Towards Unorganised Particle Based Fluids." Master's thesis, UBC Dept. Computer Science, 2005.

[Courant et al. 28] R. Courant, K. Friedrichs, and H. Lewy. "Über die partiellen Differenzengleichungen der mathematischen Physik." *Mathematische Annalen* 100:1 (1928), 32–74.

[Desbrun and Cani 96] M. Desbrun and M.-P. Cani. "Smoothed Particles: A New Paradigm for Animating Highly Deformable Bodies." In *Comput. Anim. and Sim. '96 (Proc. of EG Workshop on Anim. and Sim.)*, pp. 61–76. Aire-la-Ville, Switzerland: Eurographics Association, 1996.

[DeWolf 05] I. DeWolf. "Divergence-Free Noise." Technical report, Martian Labs., 2005. Available online (http://martian-labs.com/martiantoolz/files/DFnoiseR.pdf).

[Elcott et al.] S. Elcott, Y. Tong, E. Kanso, P. Schröder, and M. Desbrun. "Stable, Circulation-Preserving, Simplicial Fluids." *ACM Trans. Graph.* 26:1 , Article 4.

[Enright et al. 02a] D. Enright, R. Fedkiw, J. Ferziger, and I. Mitchell. "A Hybrid Particle Level Set Method for Improved Interface Capturing." *J. Comp. Phys.* 183 (2002), 83–116.

[Enright et al. 02b] D. Enright, S. Marschner, and R. Fedkiw. "Animation and Rendering of Complex Water Surfaces." *ACM Trans. Graph. (Proc. SIGGRAPH)* 21:3 (2002), 736–744.

[Fattal and Lischinski 04] R. Fattal and D. Lischinski. "Target-Driven Smoke Animation." *ACM Trans. Graph. (SIGGRAPH Proc.)* 23:3 (2004), 441–448.

[Fedkiw et al. 01] R. Fedkiw, J. Stam, and H. W. Jensen. "Visual Simulation of Smoke." In *SIGGRAPH '01: Proceedings of the 28th Annual Conference on Computer Graphics and Interactive Techniques*, pp. 15–22. New York: ACM, 2001.

[Feldman et al. 03] B. E. Feldman, J. F. O'Brien, and O. Arikan. "Animating Suspended Particle Explosions." *ACM Trans. Graph. (Proc. SIGGRAPH)* 22 (2003), 708–715.

[Feldman et al. 05] B. E. Feldman, J. F. O'Brien, B. M. Klingner, and T. G. Goktekin. "Fluids in Deforming Meshes." In *Proc. ACM SIGGRAPH/Eurographics Symp. Comp. Anim.*, pp. 255–259. Aire-la-Ville, Switzerland: Eurographics Association, 2005.

[Foster and Fedkiw 01] N. Foster and R. Fedkiw. "Practical Animation of Liquids." In *SIGGRAPH '01: Proceedings of the 28th Annual Conference on Computer Graphics and Interactive Techniques*, pp. 23–30. New York: ACM, 2001.

[Foster and Metaxas 96] N. Foster and D. Metaxas. "Realistic Animation of Liquids." *Graph. Models and Image Processing* 58 (1996), 471–483.

[Foster and Metaxas 97] N. Foster and D. Metaxas. "Modeling the Motion of a Hot, Turbulent Gas." In *SIGGRAPH '97: Proceedings of the 24th Annual Conference on Computer Graphics and Interactive Techniques*, pp. 181–188. Reading, MA: Addison Wesley, 1997.

[Fournier and Reeves 86] A. Fournier and W. T. Reeves. "A Simple Model of Ocean Waves." *ACM Computer Graphics (Proc. SIGGRAPH)* 20:4 (1986), 75–84.

[Gamito et al. 95] M. N. Gamito, P. F. Lopes, and M. R. Gomes. "Two-Dimensional Simulation of Gaseous Phenomena Using Vortex Particles." In *Computer Animation and Simulation '95*, edited by Dimitri Terzopoulos and Daniel Thalmann, pp. 2–15. Berlin: Springer-Verlag, 1995.

[Gamito 95] M. N. Gamito. "Two Dimensional Simulation of Gaseous Phenomena Using Vortex Particles." In *Proc. of the 6th Eurographics Workshop on Comput. Anim. and Sim.*, pp. 3–15. Berlin: Springer-Verlag, 1995.

[Gibou et al. 02] F. Gibou, R. Fedkiw, L.-T. Cheng, and M. Kang. "A Second-Order-Accurate Symmetric Discretization of the Poisson Equation on Irregular Domains." *J. Comp. Phys.* 176 (2002), 205–227.

[Goktekin et al. 04] T. G. Goktekin, A. W. Bargteil, and J. F. O'Brien. "A Method for Animating Viscoelastic Fluids." *ACM Trans. Graph. (Proc. SIGGRAPH)* 23 (2004), 463–468.

[Guendelman et al. 05] E. Guendelman, A. Selle, F. Losasso, and R. Fedkiw. "Coupling Water and Smoke to Thin Deformable and Rigid Shells." *ACM Trans. Graph. (Proc. SIGGRAPH)* 24:3 (2005), 973–981.

[Harlow and Welch 65] F. Harlow and J. Welch. "Numerical Calculation of Time-Dependent Viscous Incompressible Flow of Fluid with Free Surface." *Phys. Fluids* 8 (1965), 2182–2189.

[Harlow 63] F. H. Harlow. "The Particle-in-Cell Method for Numerical Solution of Problems in Fluid Dynamics." In *Experimental Arithmetic, High-Speed Computations and Mathematics*, pp. 269–269. Providence, RI: American Math. Society, 1963.

[Harlow 04] F. H. Harlow. "Fluid Dynamics in Group T-3 Los Alamos National Laboratory." *J. Comput. Phys.* 195:2 (2004), 414–433.

[Hong and Kim 05] J.-M. Hong and C.-H. Kim. "Discontinuous Fluids." *ACM Trans. Graph. (Proc. SIGGRAPH)* 24 (2005), 915–920.

[Hong et al. 07] J.-M. Hong, T. Shinar, and R. Fedkiw. "Wrinkled Flames and Cellular Patterns." *ACM Trans. Graph. (Proc. SIGGRAPH)* 26:3 (2007), Article 47.

[Houston et al. 03] B. Houston, C. Bond, and M. Wiebe. "A Unified Approach for Modeling Complex Occlusions in Fluid Simulations." In *ACM SIG-GRAPH Technical Sketches*, pp. 1–1. New York: ACM, 2003.

[Houston et al. 06] B. Houston, M. B. Nielsen, C. Batty, O. Nilsson, and K. Museth. "Hierarchical RLE Level Set: A Compact and Versatile Deformable Surface Representation." *ACM Trans. Graph.* 25:3 (2006), 151–175.

[Irving 07] G. Irving. "Methods for the Physically Based Simulation of Solids and Fluids." Ph.D. thesis, Stanford University Dept. Computer Science, 2007.

[Jones et al. 06] M. Jones, A. Bærentzen, and M. Sramek. "3D Distance Fields: A Survey of Techniques and Applications." *IEEE Transactions on Visualization and Computer Graphics* 12:4 (2006), 581–599.

[Kang et al. 00] M. Kang, R. Fedkiw, and X.-D. Liu. "A Boundary Condition Capturing Method for Multiphase Incompressible Flow." *J. Sci. Comput.* 15 (2000), 323–360.

[Kass and Miller 90] Michael Kass and Gavin Miller. "Rapid, Stable Fluid Dynamics for Computer Graphics." In *SIGGRAPH '90: Proceedings of the 17th Annual Conference on Computer Graphics and Interactive Techniques*, pp. 49–57. New York: ACM, 1990.

[Kim et al. 07] B. Kim, Y. Liu, I. Llamas, X. Jiao, and J. Rossignac. "Simulation of Bubbles in Foam with the Volume Control Method." *ACM Trans. Graph. (Proc. SIGGRAPH)* 28:3 (2007), Article 98.

[Kniss and Hart 04] J. Kniss and D. Hart. *Volume Effects: Modeling Smoke, Fire, and Clouds.* New York: ACM, 2004. Available online (http://www.cs.unm.edu/~jmk/sig04_modeling.ppt)".

[Layton and van de Panne 02] A. T. Layton and M. van de Panne. "A Numerically Efficient and Stable Algorithm for Animating Water Waves." *The Visual Computer* 18:1 (2002), 41–53.

[Losasso et al. 04] F. Losasso, F. Gibou, and R. Fedkiw. "Simulating Water and Smoke with an Octree Data Structure." *ACM Trans. Graph. (Proc. SIGGRAPH)* 23 (2004), 457–462.

[Losasso et al. 06] F. Losasso, G. Irving, E. Guendelman, and R. Fedkiw. "Melting and Burning Solids into Liquids and Gases." *IEEE Trans. Vis. Graph.* 12 (2006), 343–352.

[Melek and Keyser 02] Z. Melek and J. Keyser. "Interactive Simulation of Fire."
In *PG '02: Proceedings of the 10th Pacific Conference on Computer Graphics
and Applications*, pp. 431–432. Washington, DC: IEEE Computer Society,
2002.

[Melek and Keyser 03] Z. Melek and J. Keyser. "Interactive Simulation of Burn-
ing Objects." In *PG '03: Proceedings of the 10th Pacific Conference on
Computer Graphics and Applications*, pp. 462–466. Washington, DC: IEEE
Computer Society, 2003.

[Miller and Pearce 89] G. Miller and A. Pearce. "Globular Dynamics: A Connected Particle System for Animating Viscous Fluids." 13:3 (1989), 305–309.

[Müller et al. 03] M. Müller, D. Charypar, and M. Gross. "Particle-based
Fluid Simulation for Interactive Applications." In *Proc. ACM SIG-
GRAPH/Eurographics Symp. Comp. Anim.*, pp. 154–159. Aire-la-Ville,
Switzerland: Eurographics Association, 2003.

[Nguyen et al. 02] D. Q. Nguyen, R. Fedkiw, and H. W. Jensen. "Physically
Based Modeling and Animation of Fire." In *SIGGRAPH '02: Proceedings
of the 29th Annual Conference on Computer Graphics and Interactive Techniques*, pp. 721–728. New York: ACM, 2002.

[O'Brien and Hodgins 95] J. F. O'Brien and J. K. Hodgins. "Dynamic Simulation of Splashing Fluids." In *CA '95: Proc. Computer Animation*, p. 198.
Washington, DC: IEEE Computer Society, 1995.

[Osher and Fedkiw 02] S. Osher and R. Fedkiw. *Level Set Methods and Dynamic
Implicit Surfaces*. New York: Springer-Verlag, 2002.

[Park and Kim 05] S. I. Park and M. J. Kim. "Vortex Fluid for Gaseous Phenomena." In *Proc. ACM SIGGRAPH/Eurographics Symp. Comp. Anim.*,
pp. 261–270. Aire-la-Ville, Switzerland: Eurographics Association, 2005.

[Perlin and Neyret 01] K. Perlin and F. Neyret. "Flow Noise." In *ACM SIG-
GRAPH Technical Sketches and Applications*, p. 187. New York: ACM,
2001. Available online (http://www-evasion.imag.fr/Publications/2001/
PN01/).

[Peskin 02] C. S. Peskin. "The Immersed Boundary Method." *Acta Numerica*
11 (2002), 479–517.

[Premoze et al. 03] S. Premoze, T. Tasdizen, J. Bigler, A. Lefohn, and
R. Whitaker. "Particle–Based Simulation of Fluids." *Comp. Graph. Forum (Eurographics Proc.)* 22:3 (2003), 401–410.

[Ralston 62] A. Ralston. "Runge-Kutta Methods with Minimum Error Bounds."
Mathematics of Computation 16:80 (1962), 431–437.

[Rasmussen et al. 03] N. Rasmussen, D. Nguyen, W. Geiger, and R. Fedkiw.
"Smoke Simulation for Large Scale Phenomena." *ACM Trans. Graph. (Proc.
SIGGRAPH)* 22:3 (2003), 703–707.

[Rasmussen et al. 04] N. Rasmussen, D. Enright, D. Nguyen, S. Marino, N. Sum-
ner, W. Geiger, S. Hoon, and R. Fedkiw. "Directable Photorealistic Liquids."
In *Proc. ACM SIGGRAPH/Eurographics Symp. Comp. Anim.*, pp. 193–202.
Aire-la-Ville, Switzerland: Eurographics Association, 2004.

[Selle et al. 05] A. Selle, N. Rasmussen, and R. Fedkiw. "A Vortex Particle Method for Smoke, Water and Explosions." *ACM Trans. Graph. (Proc. SIGGRAPH)* 24:3 (2005), 910–914.

[Sethian 96] J. Sethian. "A Fast Marching Level Set Method for Monotonically Advancing Fronts." *Proc. Natl. Acad. Sci.* 93 (1996), 1591–1595.

[Shinya and Fournier 92] M. Shinya and A. Fournier. "Stochastic Motion: Motion under the Influence of Wind." *Computer Graphics Forum* 11:3 (1992), 119–128.

[Stam and Fiume 93] J. Stam and E. Fiume. "Turbulent Wind Fields for Gaseous Phenomena." In *SIGGRAPH '93: Proceedings of the 20th Annual Conference on Computer Graphics and Interactive Techniques*, pp. 369–376. New York: ACM, 1993.

[Stam 99] J. Stam. "Stable Fluids." In *SIGGRAPH 99 Conference Proceedings, Annual Conference Series*, pp. 121–128. New York: ACM, 1999.

[Steinhoff and Underhill 94] J. Steinhoff and D. Underhill. "Modification of the Euler Equations for "Vorticity Confinement": Application to the Computation of Interacting Vortex Rings." *Phys. of Fluids* 6:8 (1994), 2738–2744.

[Takahashi et al. 02] T. Takahashi, U. Heihachi, and A. Kunimatsu. "The Simulation of Fluid-Rigid Body Interaction." In *SIGGRAPH '02: ACM SIGGRAPH 2002 Conference Abstracts and Applications*, pp. 266–266. New York: ACM, 2002.

[Tessendorf 04] J. Tessendorf. "Simulating Ocean Water." In *SIGGRAPH Course Notes*. New York: ACM, 1999–2004.

[Thuerey et al. 07] N. Thuerey, M. Müller, S. Schirm, and M. Gross. "Real-Time Breaking Waves for Shallow Water Simulations." In *PG '07: Proceedings of the 15th Pacific Conference on Computer Graphics and Applications*, pp. 39–46. Washington, DC: IEEE Computer Society, 2007.

[Tsai 02] Y.-H. R. Tsai. "Rapid and Accurate Computation of the Distance Function Using Grids." *J. Comput. Phys.* 178:1 (2002), 175–195.

[Tsitsiklis 95] J. Tsitsiklis. "Efficient Algorithms for Globally Optimal Trajectories." *IEEE Trans. on Automatic Control* 40 (1995), 1528–1538.

[von Funck et al. 06] W. von Funck, H. Theisel, and H.-P. Seidel. "Vector Field Based Shape Deformations." *ACM Trans. Graph. (Proc. SIGGRAPH)* 25:3 (2006), 1118–1125.

[Wang et al. 05] H. Wang, P. J. Mucha, and G. Turk. "Water Drops on Surfaces." *ACM Trans. Graph. (Proc. SIGGRAPH)* 24:3 (2005), 921–929.

[Wendt et al. 07] J. D. Wendt, W. Baxter, I. Oguz, and M. C. Lin. "Finite Volume Flow Simulations on Arbitrary Domains." *Graph. Models* 69:1 (2007), 19–32.

[Yaeger et al. 86] L. Yaeger, C. Upson, and R. Myers. "Combining Physical and Visual Simulation—Creation of the Planet Jupiter for the Film 2010." *Computer Graphiucs (Proc.SIGGRAPH)* 20:4 (1986), 85–93.

[Zhao 05] H. Zhao. "A Fast Sweeping Method for Eikonal Equations." *Math. Comp.* 74 (2005), 603–627.

[Zhu and Bridson 05] Y. Zhu and R. Bridson. "Animating Sand as a Fluid." *ACM Trans. Graph. (Proc. SIGGRAPH)* 24:3 (2005), 965–972.

Index

5/3-law, 134

absorbing boundary condition, 174
acceleration, 4, 15, 32, 78, 103, 107,
    110, 146, 147, 159, 170, 171,
    177, 180
acceleration structure, 139
accuracy
    boundary conditions, 62–71, 93,
        95–99
    cell volumes, 67
    distance, 90–92
    Eulerian methods, 150
    finite difference, 23, 204
    FLIP, 150
    interpolation, 38
    level sets, 150
    PIC, 148
    regular grids, 138
    time integration, 19, 30, 32, 120,
        140, 158, 206
acoustics, 11, 175
adaptive meshes, 86, 138
adjoint, 164
advection, 8, 10, 19–21, 27–39, 71,
    75–77, 83, 84, 87, 92–94, 97,
    102–106, 116–117, 119, 120,
    129–131, 135, 137–141,
    144–152, 158, 171, 172, 175,
    176, 181, 182, 187
affine, 61
air, 3, 7–9, 11, 15, 16, 31, 112, 151
air pockets, 93
airfoil, 182
airplane, 182
allocation, 161
alpha channel, 71

ambient, 76, 78, 79, 105
amplitude, 136, 175, 188, 190, 192, 193
angular momentum, 109, 113, 164
angular velocity, 127, 128, 155–157,
    160, 164, 166, 197
animation, 3, 4, 11, 13, 46, 54, 71, 87,
    107, 135, 136, 139, 141
anisotropic, 84
architecture, software, 159
articulated rigid bodies, 167
artifacts, 27, 33, 62, 84–87, 93, 95,
    103, 137, 138, 153, 160, 193
atmosphere, 15, 133, 170
auxiliary variable, 167
auxiliary vector, 55
avalanche, 170
axis, 4, 84, 91, 131, 137, 197

backward Euler, 120, 121
ballistic motion, 153
balloon, 7
band, 151
band-limiting, 138
beach, 174, 177
Bernoulli's equation, 181, 182
binary weights, 67
black box functions, 18
black-body radiation, 105, 106
BLAS (Basic linear algebra
    subroutines), 55
blast waves, 11
blending, 71, 149, 174
blob of fluid, 4–6, 64, 119, 191
blobbies, 84–87
blue core, 105
blur, 35, 71, 77, 86, 112, 142